ADOPTING

AFTER·INFERTILITY

ADOPTING

AFTER · INFERTILITY

Patricia Irwin Johnston

Perspectives Press
Indianapolis, Indiana

Perspectives Press
P.O. Box 90318
Indianapolis, Indiana 46290
U.S.A.

Manufactured in the United States of America

ISBN #0-944934-06-4 Hardcover
ISBN #0-944934-10-2 Paperback

Library of Congress Cataloging-in-Publication Data:
Johnston, Patricia Irwin.
    Adopting after infertility / Patricia Irwin Johnston.
        p.   cm.
    Includes bibliographical references and index.
    ISBN #0-944934-06-4 : $21.95   ISBN 0-944934-10-2 : $14.00
    1. Adoption--United States.   2. Adoption--United States--Psychological aspects.   3. Infertility--United States--Psychological aspects.
I. Title
HV875.55.J63   1992
362.7'34'0973--dc20   92-21825
                                               CIP

To Dave
without whose love and support
the choice to make this field my
work could not have been
an option.

Acknowledgments

A book like this comes to print much as does a play—after it has been sketched and tested, practiced and performed, revised and tried again—over and over. *Adopting after Infertility* comes to print after many years of practice and performance. First there was the twenty-years-ago experience of living infertility among a very small group of couples who were infertile, too, but who had no professional or written resources from whom to have their emotional experiences validated. Then there was the fourteen-years-past epiphany of finding RESOLVE and discovering to my surprise how really common infertility was and how really normal my own reactions to it had been. I then became an infertility and adoption advocate and educator, and moved out into the international world of infertility and adoption where I learned from thousands more.

To all of the couples and professionals from Ontario to California, from Washington to Georgia, and over 100 places in between who have helped me to learn more as I shared with you what little I already I knew and then taught me what I needed to know, thank you. To good friends and wonderful teachers met through my work with the national RESOLVE network and the Adoptive Families of America system—thank you so much. Carol Hallenbeck, Bud Keye, Judy Calica, Aline Zoldbrod, Gary Gross, Jean Carter, Joan Jack, Susan Freivalds, Nancy Ng, Roanne Elliott, Ann Freeman, Ruth McRoy were especially good at helping me to stretch and grow! To the trainers I have been privileged to hear, to the authors I have been honored to read—and sometimes to publish—I give you thanks. To the callers and the letter writers who have been both hummers and bummers in their insistence that I get it right, thank you for keeping me on track.

Thanks especially to an eclectic mix of advocates and professionals whom (though in most cases they could not have known it and in some cases barely know me) I have considered to have served as milestone mentors in unique ways through the years—Barbara Eck Menning, Jerry Smith, David Kirk, Vera Fahlberg, Bill Pierce, Claudia Jewett-Jarratt, David Brodzinsky, Sharon Kaplan Roszia, Kay Donley, Betsy Cole, Mary Anne Cohen, Susan Freivalds.

Two very special supporters, Julie Berry and Wendy Williams, spent hours pouring over this manuscript, talking to me on the phone, refusing to let me make something only "good enough," and so nudged and cajoled, argued and convinced, corrected and improved this work, thank goodness! Graphic designer Wade Smola went above and beyond his role as cover and book designer to show me just how some key sections of the book were not going to work for the "uninitiated." Meanwhile, Charles Berry gave a great deal of careful thought to "the title problem."

Through it all, my husband and my children have been supportive of the fact that I share great chunks of their time and of our lives with you, my readers and listeners. If this book is of value to you, please join me in thanking them for being so generous!

PIJ
Indianapolis, May, 1992

Table of Contents

Introduction

"You can always adopt." That's how they tried to comfort you. If the testing and the treatment didn't work, you could always adopt.

Yet somehow you knew that your birth control generation peers meant it—but not really. With their carefully planned conceptions, their glowing storybook pregnancies, their perfect childbirth experiences, their bouncing Gerber babies who looked just like their parents, they thought of adoption as second best. Those fertile others who offered the series of platitudes which began with, "Just relax, you're probably trying too hard," and months later included, "My college roommate's second cousin finally got pregnant when they changed their diets, learned to meditate correctly, saw an acupuncturist, and then did it at high noon in Jakarta," and ultimately culminated with, "Well, you know, I saw on Donahue that there are hundreds of babies abandoned at birth in hospitals in New York City every month. You can always adopt," wouldn't have wanted to form their own families by adoption. And somehow, you fear now that if you do adopt, the comments from those same well meaning others will include, "Do you know anything about his real mother?" and "Too bad there are none of your own," or ...

And so here you are, having struggled long enough with the infertility dragons and demons to have decided that you need at least to examine lifestyle alternatives beyond treatment. Adoption is one such alternative—the one which seems to trip off most tongues as a logical next step. Perhaps looking at this step was your own idea, perhaps it was your partner's. It may even have been that neither of you really wanted to look at this book and that a friend or a family member has given you a push. However you came to be reading this, the question right now is clear: **Is adoption an option for you?**

Whether or not it is is what this book is all about. Whether it is good for you today. Whether it will be good for you tomorrow. Whether this choice that will affect not just you and your spouse, but the lines that have been your family for generations and will become your legacy to the future, is for you.

The decision is a momentous one, and because it affects not just you and your partner and your families, but the future of an innocent child and of that child's birthfamily, this choice is far more consequential than any decision you have ever made in the past—even the choice of a life's partner. It is perhaps the most important choice you will ever make.

In this book we'll be taking a look at the lifelong impact of the choice to adopt by couples who have experienced infertility. We'll need to look back again at the experience of being infertile and being in treatment, acknowledging that the initial choice to become pregnant carried with it the assumption that doing so would be a relatively simple, straightforward process. When becoming pregnant turned out to be more complicated than we had expected, we were playing a whole new game, with different rules, different expectations, different possible outcomes, so that in the midst of infertility we are called upon to make the decision to become parents all over again.

We'll work through the process of examining differing styles of adoption and considering the placement of children of various ages and abilities and ethnicities as family building options. We'll talk about adoption and its impact on you and on your children over your lifetimes. There are many questions to ask of yourself and of your spouse. There are many hard realities left to face.

Let me be honest with you. In every one of the chapters which follow I'm going to be telling you like I know it is—no soft peddling, no pulling of punches. I believe that not to do so would be doing my readers a serious disservice. There are enough syrupy treatments of adoption of the love-conquers-all variety out there, enough adopters who've never read a thing and who will deny that adoption is different to the end. As a result, there are some families in trouble. Because you and I belong to the baby-boom (and later) generations of people who demand immediate answers and immediate gratifications, we belong to a group of people who often make decisions poorly. I hope to be able to help readers of this book make good, well thought out decisions.

I belong to a family which has experienced over 60 years worth of hard-as-it-gets, permanent infertility. This branch of the Johnston family still exists only because two generations of infertile people have

chosen adoption. My husband's parents began fighting infertility in the
1930's and finally came to be parents over 50 years ago with the first of
three adoptions. Dave and I began trying to form the family we expected
to consist of three children two years apart within two years of our
marriage, but we celebrated our tenth anniversary three months after our
first child's arrival, and our third child arrived nine years after that. In these
two generations, we've learned a lot from our own experience, and, as a
family of omnivorous learners, we've made it our business to read and
listen and question and educate ourselves even more.

We've been where you are now, so I know pefectly well that many
readers (and especially men) don't want to hear any more about infertility
and will be tempted to skip the early chapters of this book. Others of you
who make it through the first two sections on deciding first to adopt at all
and then deciding how and who to adopt will be tempted to forego the
third section, which, while not meant to be a guide to parenting in adoption,
provides a brief examination of a number of important issues which are
likely to arise throughout a lifetime of being part of a family expanded by
adoption.

The issues raised in this book are hard ones. I doubt that most
readers will be likely to put *Adopting after Infertility* on a list of their all
time favorite easy reads. But, I'm asking you to stick with me. If you stay
with it, if you follow the process, if you agree to be honest with yourself
and with your partner, I am confident that you will finish this book having
made the precisely right decision for your family—whether that means
that adoption is for you or that it is not.

I

The
Challenge
of
Infertility

1

Behold the Dragon

Once upon a time lived a princess so beautiful both inside and out that every man in her parents' realm longed to marry her. After many months of grueling challenges, a noble, kind, and handsome prince won her hand, and they were married.

As they left the palace of her parents to make their own way in the world, the young people were given the blessings of the monarchs, who presented them with a carefully drawn map. On it were plotted the roads and the rivers, the mountains and the mansions, the forests and the fields, the towns and the trading posts of their known world. It was a beautiful map, complete in every way—for as far as it went, that is.

For, all around the edge of the map, beyond the blue of the wide sea and the purple of the impenetrable mountains, were printed warnings in bold red ink, "DANGER. Here there be dragons!"

Most of us spent many childhood days curled in warm laps reading even more sexist versions of stories much like this one. Surrounding us was the firm shape of a parent who would keep us safe and secure. The fairy tales gave way to more realistic stories, but the themes remained substantially the same: for those who are good and noble and true, for those who try their best, the dangerous unknown is only a fairy tale. Those who try hard will succeed.

And so, like the fairy tale princes and princesses of our childhood, our expectations about love and family building were idealistic and simplistic. Two people fall in love. They commit to one another. They establish a firm foundation on which to build a secure home. They have children.

In biology class, in family living, in health and sex education there were drawings and diagrams and a lot of warnings about the danger of premarital sex. The message was that our maturing bodies were time bombs set to go off. Growing up in the pre-AIDS era, we heard a great deal about certain demons related to our emerging sexuality: about damaging our reputations, about getting sexually transmitted diseases, and most of all about unplanned pregnancy. But in all of those classes in all of those years nobody ever told us about the dragon—infertility.

When this dragon rears its head, we tend first to play ostrich, burying our heads in the sand and pretending not to see. For months we may deny the possibility of a problem. We're under a lot of stress at work. Our timing is off. The travel schedule has gotten in the way. Looking back on those early months now and remembering your own denial, you may wonder why it took so long for you to realize that you needed help, why you wasted so much time at the wrong doctor, why you refused to acknowledge the fact of infertility.

The answer is not so difficult. You were afraid. Somewhere, in the back of your mind you sensed that a dragon was there, and you hoped to avoid the crisis of facing the dragon by ignoring it.

The Chinese—an ancient and philosophically sophisticated culture—write not with an alphabet, but with complex word pictures. Interestingly, in Chinese the written expression of the concept of crisis is drawn by putting together the characters for two other words: danger and opportunity.

危機

Because we sense danger in the face of any crisis, we often seek to deny the reality of what we are facing. And so it was with infertility. To acknowledge a fertility impairment was to face imminent danger. Though at first we might not have been able to clearly identify precisely what we feared, our subconscious sensed the possibility of loss ahead.

Remember that childhood friend who moved away when you were four? The special toy lost irretrievably on the plane to Grandma's? The cat that ran away? The math test you failed? The first love who dumped you unceremoniously? The college which turned you down? Getting fired from that great job? Every day we experience losses. Some of them are painful and etch themselves on our memory and our being. Some pass by nearly unnoticed because we have become so accustomed to dealing with them. But every loss—the large and the small—is one of the lessons which contribute to the development of a unique pattern of coping with loss, a pattern which becomes so familiar, so automatic, that one rarely even realizes it has begun and is going on again.

Do you recall, for instance, having found yourself in a situation like the following . . .

After having spent a day shopping, you arrive at home with your house key in your pocket and your arms loaded with packages only to hear the insistent ringing of your telephone on the other side of the door. Twentieth century North Americans have a terrible time allowing a phone to go unanswered, so as a typical member of your generation you struggle with the packages you are juggling in order to fish out the key and rush inside to answer the phone.

As you put the phone to your ear you hear yourself saying, "Hello? Hello?" to a dial tone (*denial.*) You're *surprised* to hear that dial tone. How could they have hung up? You begin a litany of "if only's" (*bargaining*) ("If only I had had my key out and ready."... "If only they'd let it ring one more time.") Feeling frustrated and disappointed and maybe even a little *angry* at somebody ("Doggone it, they should have let it ring"... "Darn it, won't I ever learn to make more than one trip") because of the loss of this call, you look at the packages strewn in your foyer and subconsciously begin the familiar process of coping with (*accepting/resolving*) the loss.

Perhaps you shrug it off with an "Oh, well, if it was important, they'll call back" and go about your business of picking up the packages and putting away the groceries. Or perhaps you allow the ice cream to melt on the floor while you pick up the phone and call a friend. "Hi. did you just call?... No?... Yeah, well, I missed a call just as I got in from shopping... So, what're ya doin'?..." Perhaps your reaction to the frustration of an accumulation of lost phone calls would inspire you to rush right back out to the electronics store to buy an answering machine.[1]

There are many ways of coping with loss. Some people are more comfortable than others in accepting loss as normal and natural—as a part of their fate. Some people cope with loss by seeking substitutions for the lost item or issue. Some people aggressively seek to avoid loss by assuming as much control as possible over every situation.

Because infertility is an experience which involves multiple losses, each with its own degree of significance, taking the time right now to determine how it is that you and your partner each cope with loss is an important step toward deciding what alternative is right for you. But first you must acknowledge the series of losses built into the infertility experience. Over many years of thinking about it, reading about it, talking with hundreds of couples about it, I have come to see six distinct areas of significant loss, many of which encompass several other related losses.[2]

Losses Perceived to Be a Consequence of Permanent Infertility

1   Control over many aspects of life

2   Individual genetic continuity linking past and future

3   The joint conception of a child with one's life partner

4   The physical satisfactions of pregnancy and birth

5   The emotional gratifications of pregnancy and birth

6   The opportunity to parent

Perhaps most clearly and immediately felt by those who experience infertility is the loss of **control** over numerous aspects of our lives. Today's couple, who came to sexual maturity and selected a partner after the birth control revolution precipitated by the wide availability of the birth control pill in the mid sixties, have always had the distinct expectation that they would be able to control their fertility. Unfortunately, because infertility was not discussed as they grew up, this expectation included not just the expectation that they would be able to avoid pregnancy when they so desired, but that they would be able to achieve pregnancy when they so desired. Losing control of a part of life which their peers take so completely for granted is devastating and, for many people, precipitates a humiliating blow to self esteem.

Treating infertility demands that couples give up even more control. Control of their sexual privacy and spontaneity, for example, is forfeited to a medical team which asks them to chart their intercourse, supply semen samples, appear within hours after intercourse for a post-coital test, etc. Control of their calendars is given over to treatment.

Couples often comment that with infertility they feel that they have lost control of every aspect of their lives. What type or size car to buy depends on whether or not it will be carrying children. Accepting a new job or a promotion can become dependent on how travel impacts on the treatment program, whether or not the new company has excellent health care benefits which cover infertility treatments, as well as whether or not the new employee's coverage for infertility treatment would be excluded because it was defined by the insurance company as a pre-existing condition. Continuing education may be put on hold when a woman expects that any day she will become pregnant, so that finishing a term might be difficult or impossible. Whether to buy a house in the suburbs with sidewalks for Big Wheels or a condo in the city close to work and cultural events is controlled by infertility. Social calendars may be driven by the menstrual cycle. Even the most private of decisions—how much time to spend in a hot tub, how much coffee to drink, how many miles to run each week, whether to buy briefs or boxer shorts—can be controlled by the infertility experience.

To many individuals for whom being in control is an important part of their ability to feel confident and competent, infertility represents a devastating loss, but this is not infertility's only loss.

Potentially, infertility means the loss of our **individual genetic continuity**—our expectation that we will continue the genes of our families in an unbroken blood line from some distant past into a promising future. For those raised in blood-is-thicker-than-water cultures, this loss is significant enough to be avoided at all costs. While some families are entirely comfortable with the idea of adopting in order to carry a family into the future, others believe strongly that the family blood line cannot be grafted onto. Why we feel this way is not so important as is the fact that we do. Further, as we'll discuss later, for infertile individuals for whom this loss is central and powerful, pursuing family building alternatives which allow the other partner to retain genetic continuity can be devastating to the relationship.

Our dreams about parenting included the expectation of our parenting a **jointly conceived child**. In choosing a life's partner all of us do at least a little fantasizing about what our children might be like. Will he have her intellect and his sense of humor? Grandpa's red hair and Aunt Wilma's athletic prowess? Gosh, think of the medical expenses if she inherits both her mother's crossed eye and her father's terrible overbite! This child who represents the blending of both the best and the worst of our most intimate selves also represents for many a kind of ultimate bonding of partner to partner. In giving our genes to one another for blending, we offer our most vulnerable and intimate and valuable sense of ourselves—a gift that is perhaps the most precious we can offer. Losing that dream and so feeling forced to consider alternatives such as donor insemination, hiring a surrogate mother, adopting, etc. can be painful indeed for those for whom this expectation was particularly important.

There is also the loss of the **physical satisfaction of the pregnancy and birth experiences.** Though many people see the loss of a pregnancy as belonging entirely to women, this is not true. Though the physical changes and challenges of pregnancy and birth are experienced by women alone, producing a child, as any counselor of pregnant teens will verify, is the ultimate rite of passage for both men and women—the final mark of having reached adulthood. You're grown up now, man, and your parents aren't in charge anymore. Beyond that, the physical ability to impregnate a woman or to carry and birth a child represents the ultimate expression of maleness or femaleness—our bodies at work doing what they were built to do. For many people, losing such capacities challenges their feelings about their maturity or their sexuality or both—about their competence as adult men and women. It is their own discomfort with and fear of this loss which generates from outsiders the tasteless humor which relates infertility to sexuality in comments such as, "Do you need a little help there? Happy to offer my services!" or "Let me show you how it's done." or "Hey, all Steve has to do is look at me and I'm pregnant—must be in the water!"

Over the last two decades, a substantial element of our society, fearful of the impact of massive changes in family structure, has mysticized the experience of birth to an exaggerated extent. In search of the perfect "bonding" experience (a kind of magical superglue without which many fear that families will disintegrate) couples carefully choose specific kinds of childbirth preparation, attend classes together, read books, practice breathing, etc. They expect to experience a magical closeness in spousal relationships, an irreplaceable wonder in sharing the birth experience, an expected instant eye-to-eye bonding between parents and child. Hospitals marketing to the expectations of these couples compete with one another to provide birthing rooms with the perfect equipment (birthing beds, chairs, tanks) the perfect atmosphere (music, guests allowed, etc.)

This set of expectations about the **emotional gratifications of a** shared pregnancy, prepared childbirth, breast-feeding experience, though far too often unrealistic, is widely held. To risk losing such an experience is much more significant to today's couple than it would have been to their parents and grandparents—whose mothers gave birth anesthetized in sterile operating rooms while fathers paced in waiting rooms outside, who often didn't see and hold their children until hours after their births, who bottle fed formula to their infants.

And finally, to be permanently infertile threatens the **opportunity to parent**, which is a major developmental goal for most adults. The psychologist Eric Erickson has identified a series of developmental milestones humans work toward throughout the life span. In adulthood, the major goals are regenerativity and parenting. To be infertile, on the surface, threatens our ability to achieve that goal, so that for many this represents a devastating blow.

Erickson and others have clearly demonstrated that it is possible for individuals to achieve the developmental goal and to satisfy the need for parenting without becoming parents. Many adults find other ways of redirecting or rechanneling their need to nurture—through interaction with nieces and nephews and family friends; by choosing work which brings them in frequent contact with children; by volunteering as religious class teachers, scout leaders, or for a group such as Big Brothers/Big Sisters; by becoming active in non-child centered volunteer work; by nurturing the earth through nature hobbies such as gardening, etc. This is not to imply that lists of possible redirections like these are seen as equivalent substitutions or as realistic direct replacements for the lifelong experience of parenting a child jointly conceived and birthed with a much loved partner. While some adults can and do actively choose to meet their developmental needs to nurture without becoming parents, for couples who have once made the choice to become parents and have then been thwarted by infertility, the choice to redirect that energy is much more difficult.

For couples reading this book, couples who are considering adopting, reactions about this particular loss (parenting) are the most important of all. Adoption provides the opportunity to avoid this loss and this one alone. Couples who adopt *will* become parents, but in doing so they will give up even more control, they will forfeit their genetic continuity, lose the jointly conceived child of their dreams, be deprived of the emotional and physical expectations of pregnancy. So unless the loss of the opportunity to parent strikes you as the one loss you would most like to prevent—the one you would find most devastating—adoption may not be for you.

It is these potential and realized losses which tore at your gut during those days or weeks or months when you tried to deny the infertility.

These losses were the danger lurking in the crisis, and they were difficult to face. Now you are asking yourself to examine adoption—one of the potential opportunities which is a part of the crisis. Facing your feelings about infertility's losses can help you to decide if adoption is right for you.

There are several ways that people deal with crisis. Many people spend significant amounts of time allowing themselves to become the victims of the crisis, floundering in a sea of despair as they are overwhelmed by waves of decisions that must be made. This tendency to see oneself as a victim is undergirded by a sense of damaged self esteem. Some fertility-impaired people react by feeling that they are somehow less competent than they were before their infertility was discovered. If their reproductive systems aren't working, they somehow illogically reason, then maybe they shouldn't trust their judgment, either. (Maybe Uncle Charlie was right, we're just trying too hard. Perhaps Mom's manicurist's cousin's doctor in Podunk *is* better than the reproductive endocrinologist at the medical center. Maybe my neighbor who thinks adoption is a sad substitute for *real* parenting because nobody could ever *really* love somebody else's reject isn't so far off base!)

Feeling neither confident nor competent, such people become unwilling and unable to make decisions. They begin to abdicate more and more control to others.

When I was a child we had a toy—a child-sized plastic figure with a clownish face filled with air and weighted on the bottom with beans or sand. It's purpose was to be punched, and to rise from the blow grinning, waiting to be punched again.

It has often seemed to me that as my husband and I experienced infertility we were like a pair of those punching bag toys placed on a conveyor belt moving through a system punctuated by swing arm gates. As we moved along that conveyor belt from doctor to lab to bed, to doctor to hospital to bed, to doctor to pharmacy to bed, to doctor to counselor to agency to attorney, and on and on, we found that the belt began to speed out of control (rather like the conveyor belt in the candy factory where Lucy and Ethel scrambled to fill boxes that rushed by).

Grinning madly (stiff upper lip, and all that) we were knocked askew by alternating swing arm gates— the doctor, the lab, the hospital, etc.—and sent separately reeling to cope with new information, new alternatives. Occasionally in swinging upright again from a blow we would bump against each other and provide one another with a momentary steadiness. But each time we were hit again, we went our own separate ways—alone.

———————————

These are the people who will drift from treatment to treatment, who will drift into a childless future they do not want because they haven't been able to make the decisions that might have helped them consider choices available to them, who will fall into a dropped-into-their laps adoption because someone they saw as competent told them it was the next logical step, and, unprepared for the challenging differences in adoptive parenting, will struggle for years with a feeling that things aren't quite right, that this didn't work either.

Caught up in the panic of the situation, such people tend to make decisions only when they must be made, struggling forward from crisis to crisis. I worry because when one operates by crisis management—deciding only when one is forced to decide—there is little opportunity for reflection. We stumble forward on that conveyor belt carried by a panicky momentum much like that we felt as out-of-control young runners about to skin our knees again.

I worry because fertility-impaired people operating in such a mode tend to act out of desperation. With self conscious laughter, they tell you that they would do *anything* to have a baby—even drink poison! Sadly, many really would. They beg for one more cycle of a drug their doctor has decided isn't working. They borrow money for yet another in a long string of unsuccessful GIFT or IVF attempts. They risk it all on a not-quite-legal adoption. They juggle two or more potential adoptions or an adoption and a high risk pregnancy at the same time. Obsessively driven toward the goal of bringing a baby home to a waiting nursery, they have thought very little beyond arrival day.

I worry about these couples, because by allowing themselves to become victims of infertility, by allowing themselves to avoid thinking about the ramifications of their crisis management style, they almost guarantee that they won't effectively deal with their losses, and that years later those losses will reappear as reopened wounds when new and different losses set a grief reaction in motion, for example losses of jobs, divorce, death of a parent or close friend or spouse.

I worry because the self-absorption of people operating as victims won't allow them to feel compassion for others—for birthparents, for people dealing with secondary infertility, for the confused and panicked parents of quads or quints conceived on fertility drugs or in IVF cycles, for couples dealing with an untimely pregnancy, for pregnant infertiles who can't find a place to "fit in" anymore. For one who has experienced a reproductive loss to have lost compassion for those experiencing other types of reproductive loss is particularly ironic.

I worry because for victims there is no joy in living.

There comes a time to stop—to recognize that one has not been in charge and to step off the treadmill, regain balance, and look around for a better way. My hope is that the process for decision making offered in the next chapters of this book can become a tool to help couples make that pause for reexamination happen, offering them practical ways to regain control of their lives again, helping them to look far enough beyond the danger represented by the dragon to see the opportunity lying just ahead.

Many significant beginnings and endings in our lives are marked by rituals that publicly mark the transition and invite the support—either in celebration or in mourning—of others. Weddings, funerals, christenings, baby showers, bar mitzvahs, graduations, going-away parties are examples of transitional rituals. Psychologists and sociologists are increasingly noting that transitions which are not accompanied by ritual—divorce, loss of a job, miscarriage, private changes of direction— are often harder to make, since they lack support.

Many infertile couples are finding it important to create and participate in private or public rituals which acknowledge the progress of their lives. Several RESOLVE chapters have put together periodically repeated mourning ceremonies for miscarried or unborn children. Such ceremonies offer the opportunity for couples and their supportive family and friends to experience a release similar to that in a traditional funeral service. Bonnie and Lawrence Baron of San Diego have written about (though not yet published) their personally composed ceremony in which they formally ended treatment and moved on. Their ceremony was firmly rooted in their Judaic tradition and included elements of several ceremonies and prayers as well as including some nonreligious readings and music. Mike and Jean Carter of North Carolina, authors of *Sweet Grapes: How to Stop Being Infertile and Start Living Again*, note in their book and in their presentations the formal way in which they marked their choice to live a childfree lifestyle. Wendy and Rob Williams of Ontario, Canada, created a poignant and very personal ceremony for saying goodbye to the child whose adoption was not completed because his birthmother changed her mind several weeks after placement.

In many ways the structure of the decision making format which will follow encourages the opportunity for using or developing rituals whether formal or informal. You may wish to explore with your partner the idea of participating in appropriate transitional rituals yourselves as you mark your journey.

━━━━━━━━━━━━━━

In "The Picnic," one of the wonderful short stories in her collection *The Miracle Seekers: An Anthology of Infertility*,[3] Mary Martin Mason tells the story of Jill and Dan, frozen in time and unable to move beyond the miscarriage of Gerald, the baby they had waited for so long. In an awkward attempt to help, Dan takes Jill on a picnic along the raw Rhode Island shore. With her sketch pads and charcoal in hand, Jill makes her way to an ancient cemetery to do some rubbings. Dan finds her later, weeping over a one hundred year old tombstone that bears the names of a couple and their five sons—each of whom was named Josephus, each of whom died in infancy.

Here Jill comes to see that what is preventing her from moving on is the fact that no one—not her mother-in-law, not her friends, not her husband—has allowed her to experience her grief openly, to mourn the loss of her son, to say goodbye in a formal way to the baby who was not to be. And so, together, Dan and Jill say goodbye to Gerald by burying a baby rattle which Jill has brought with them in the earth above the babies Josephus.

━━━━━━━━━━━━━━

All significant endings and beginnings are indeed crises, fraught with the fear that is a part of facing the unknown. The Chinese concept of crisis consisting of both danger and opportunity is an important one for us to keep in mind we do the hard work of making good decisions. Several years ago I clipped a wonderful quote attributed to Merle Shain from a church bulletin

" There are only two ways to approach life—as a victim or as a gallant fighter—and you must decide if you want to act or react... a lot of people forget that."

But not you, the reader of this book! You'll remember and decide!

2

Confronting the Dragon .

With the map in hand, the prince and the princess set off into the world. On the first day they traveled through a deep forest. The prince, intent upon reaching the other side as quickly as possible, hacked away at the underbrush with his sword. Meanwhile, the princess, following behind, examined the lovely flowers and moss beneath the trees and frequently noted a bird fluttering by or a small animal scurrying across the path. The prince became impatient with her dawdling. She, on the other hand, found it difficult to understand why he was in so big a hurry on this honeymoon trip.

On the second day the couple faced a mountain range. Each assessed the situation and offered an opinion for dealing with the obstacle. The prince saw the quickest route as straight over the top and suggested that they abandon unneccessary gear and climb the rocks. The princess, on the other hand, was intensely curious about what they would find in the valley created by the stream that skirted the mountain. She suggested that they take the time to go around the mountain rather than risk injury by going over it.

They entered a small cave to rest and reflect and make a decision. As they sat on the stones at the entrance to the cave, each suddenly sensed that they were not alone.

The prince felt a looming, ominous presence, the princess the warm glow of a fire. They turned together to face... a dragon. Oh boy, now what?

Forgive the fact that our anecdotes about the prince and the princess drip with sexist stereotypes! The decision to allow them to do so was deliberate. After all, those stereotypes were a part of the fairy tales of our generation's childhoods, and in many ways contributed to our expectations about adulthood, no matter how hard we are working to eliminate them.

Communicating with One Another

One of the most confusing and frustrating parts of battling infertility is coming to recognize and deal with the fact that partners do not see the struggle in exactly the same way. An important part of who we are and how adaptable or flexible we are able to be is simply inborn. Some people are just inherently more adaptable than others. The issues of adaptability will become even more important for you to consider when we begin to discuss issues of parenting in adoption, but adaptability is part of why we react to challenges, changes, losses as we do.

But our environment and experiences contribute greatly to who we are too. Because each of us is an individual, brought up in separate homes, different families, our backgrounds have taught us different ways of reacting. We probably attended different schools and houses of worship. Most often we lived at least part of our lives in disparate geographic locations. Growing up, our experiences of place in the family, of friendship, with the people who taught and guided us, with the material we read and the television we viewed—the combination of our experiences—made us unique individuals, with separate needs and expectations.

Most of us understand the impact of such differences only after they are called to our attention, preferring instead to assume that surely two people who have chosen one another to spend their lives with and to form a family with would agree on the most primal of issues and needs.

Though as a society we are acknowledging that there is no one "male" way to look at things and one "female" way to react to things, it remains true that in general the experiences of men and women have caused them to view challenges differently. Men tend to look for logical answers, women to feel things from the heart. Men tend to be less inclined to share their innermost fears, women spill it all for many to see and hear.

Deborah Tannen is a linguist who has spent many years focusing on how people communicate in diverse cultures. Recently her work has focused on the differences in communication between men and women—who experience, even when raised in the same location, different cultures. In her excellent book *You Just Don't Understand: Women and Men in Conversation* Tannen points out that in our closest relationships we look for confirmation and reassurance. "When those closest to us respond to events differently than we do, when they seem to see the same scene as part of a different play, when they say things that we could not imagine saying in the same circumstances, the ground on which we stand seems to tremble and our footing is suddenly unsure. Being able to understand why this happens—*why* and *how* our partners and friends, though like us in many ways are not us, and different in other ways—is a crucial step toward feeling that our feet are planted firmly on the ground."[1]

Tannen observes that men tend to operate in a world they view as having a hierarchical social order in which they are either one-up or one-down. Through a lens where life is viewed as a contest—a struggle to avoid failure and preserve independence, men tend to see conversations as negotiations, where the goal is to retain the upper hand and protect oneself from another's attempt to push one around. Women, on the other hand, view life as a community, and struggle to preserve intimacy and connectedness and to avoid isolation.[2]

When sharing their problems with one another, observes Tannen, women tend to look for and offer reassurance and understanding—intimacy. Men in conversations with other men, on the other hand, jockey for position by a competitive kind of problem solving. As a result, when men and women communicate with one another about problems, often women complain that men just "order them around, tell them what to do" which they often interpret as dismissing their problems as unimportant. Men, on the other hand, assume that when a woman shares a problem she's looking for an answer to it, so they are confused when their advice is not welcome.

If the observations of Tannen and others regarding the differences between women and men both in their style of communicating and in their expectations from communication are correct, they offer some interesting applications to communicating about infertility and about choosing the option of adoption. Consider, for example, the physical and emotional losses of the pregnancy experience. Tannen's theory would suggest that men who feel this loss strongly do so because they experience humiliation in being "one down" from other men—and therefore less a man—through this loss, while women for whom this loss is particularly painful react more strongly to the pain of losing the intimacy of the connection to partner and to child. Certainly many couples have observed retrospectively that they felt out of sync with one another during phases of the infertility experience when, faced with sudden bad news, husbands began to problem solve and look beyond the loss to a next step while their wives were wishing for the comfort of mutual mourning of the disappointment.

Couples often complain that one or the other partner (usually the woman) seems obsessed with the infertility to the exclusion of everything else in life while the other partner (most often the husband) is able to compartmentalize it. Merle Bombardieri, a Massachusetts-based therapist who served for a time as clinical director at RESOLVE and has devoted a significant percentage of her private practice to infertility, has offered a helpful prescription for such couples.

The Twenty Minute Rule is a compromise tactic that acknowledges the diverging needs for talking about infertility. Using it, couples adopt a routine that requires that only twenty minutes a day be spent discussing infertility-related issues. The twenty minutes are mutually agreed upon and preset. They don't get dropped into the middle of one partner's Monday night football game or the other partner's absorption in a good book. The timing chosen takes into account when during the day each partner is likely to be the least stressed, the most relaxed and thus receptive to what the other partner has to say.

During this twenty minutes, both partners agree that each will give undivided attention to listening to and reacting to what the other partner is feeling a need to communicate. The Twenty Minutes should not be spent with one partner listening from behind a newspaper to a monologue from the other, but instead should involve a willingness to engage one another in conversation and dialogue, with the goal being to communicate and work together to make decisions.

The Twenty Minute Rule creates a win-win situation, by offering the partner who most needs communicative interchange the guarantee of a particular time each day during which s/he won't be ignored, rebuffed or rejected but instead will be attentively listened and responded to, and by offering the less verbal partner protection from a sense of being "ambushed" and the opportunity to prepare carefully for what otherwise might be a painful and resented intrusion.

Most of us have not been taught good communication skills. In confronting the dragon, good communication is imperative. Now may be an ideal time to commit to enhancing communication skills. There are many ways to accomplish this. You should begin with a promise to one another to be honest, direct and clear and to be respectful of one another's pain, fears and need for privacy. Adopting Bombardieri's Twenty Minute Rule and using it to deal with infertility in bite-sized pieces may be another useful step. Then you may choose to read some books on communication. Two which I highly recommend as worth the time and effort are Deborah Tannen, Ph.D.'s *You Just Don't Understand: Women and Men in Conversation* and Harville Hendrix, Ph.D.'s *Getting the Love You Want: A Guide for Couples*. Both Dr. Tannen's and Dr. Hendrix' material is also available on tape, and the Hendrix group offers weekend workshops on communication skills.

To this list of recommended reading, please add a third book— Mike and Jean Carter's *Sweet Grapes: How to Stop Being Infertile and Start Living Again* (Perspectives Press, 1989). Yes, I know. You'd decided not to read it because you thought it was about childfree living, and you'd already dismissed that option. Well, it is about childfree living, in that Mike and Jean have chosen a childfree lifestyle and joyfully put their infertility behind them. But more than that, the Carters offer the only organized material on communicating and decision making in infertility that has been written not by a woman, but by a man and a woman, together. Their insights will be helpful to anyone making any decision which is colored by infertility. Mike writes about his early approaches to their infertility: silence and problem solving.

> " It took me a long time to learn that I really wasn't helping.
> Both of my strategies—silence and problem solving—
> were actually ways of keeping problems at arm's length.
> At that distance, I didn't have to feel them. I didn't have
> to be a part of the hurt and confusion that come with
> tough issues.
>   Infertility changed all that...[3] "

No, you haven't been trying too hard. With rare exceptions, stress does not produce infertility. Infertility, however does produce stress. Though it is medically defined as a disease, and though it often produces an emotional reaction very similar to that expressed by sufferers of chronic illness, infertility creates none of the outward signs of illness which would prompt outsiders to offer support or sympathy. Furthermore, infertility involves a couple, not an individual.

Leaping into adoption will not circumvent or solve the stress which is a part of infertility. Infertility's issues are too significant to bypass. Over a lifetime, addressing these issues head on will prove to have been a valuable part of the process of moving on.

Clear and direct communication are vital to healthy relationships. The stress of any kind of crisis makes this communication much more difficult. Searching for ways to reduce stress for oneself and for one another can be an important part of reinforcing the relationship.

Begin by treating your bodies more kindly. They are being poked and prodded and medicated and forced to perform under the glare of spotlights. Try some of the following:

1   Keep regular hours and have regular sit down meals. This is a particular challenge for people who do not have children, since they tend to have developed habits which include eating on the run and sleeping whenever they get around to it.

2   Cut down on caffeine, salt, alcohol, and sweets, since they tend to make your already overworked nervous system work even harder.

3   Become aware of your breathing. Learn to control it with deep breathing exercises in order to manage stress.

4   Begin some form of regular exercise that will relieve tension in order to keep your body and mind tuned.

Other stress relievers are psychological. For example:

1   Reduce the minor irritations in your life that tend to accumulate and cause stress. Oil that squeaky door, clean that dirty window next to your desk, straighten your messy underwear drawer. Even better, rather than work on your own minor irritants, surprise your partner by working on his or hers!

2   Give yourself a few minutes absolutely alone each day during which you allow yourself to regroup.

3   Go easy on yourself. Accept your feelings as legitimate and refuse to allow others to make you feel guilty for feeling the pain and the disappointment of your fertility impairment.

4   Know your limitations and work to avoid people and tasks that irritate you.

5   Treat yourself to something special—a manicure or a massage, a new book you've wanted to read, a weekend away with your spouse.

6   Share with your spouse as much as possible (though remembering the Twenty Minute Rule!) Work at keeping the two of you a family with your own traditions. This is especially important during the holidays, when stress can be magnified by the tendency of others to ignore your pain.

7   Prod your sense of humor. Try to be silly about some things, and, wherever possible, try to find silliness in the things that irk you most. Laugh as often as you can find a good reason to, and create some of those reasons. Avoid melodrama in your T.V. or movie viewing and watch some sitcoms you might usually avoid.

8   Tell people that things are bothering you rather than gunnysacking them until you explode. Let them know how they can help you rather than expect them to read your mind.

Who's Infertile Here?—The Couples Factor

Often it is difficult for couples themselves—let alone outsiders—to understand the significance of the fact that infertility is a couples issue. While in about 30% of cases both partners are subfertile (infertile when paired with an equally infertile partner, but fertile when paired with a normally fertile or super fertile partner), in the majority of cases of infertility one partner's reproductive system is flawed and the other partner is fertile enough to reproduce given a more fertile partner. This dilemma is the root of much angst on the part of less fertile partners—particularly for

36 those who personally feel a strong reaction to the idea of losing their genetic continuity or the pregnancy/birth experience. Such people, while grieving, may test their spouse's commitment to them by suggesting divorce, by insisting on plunging into the use of donor gametes, and so on—suggesting these not necessarily because they sincerely want them, but instead creating challenges which dare the spouse to bail out.

In truth, fertile partners of infertile people most often see themselves as infertile as well. Having made the commitment to a person they chose as a life and parenting partner, fertile partners, too, grieve the loss of their dreams and expectations. Even when they recognize immediately that they retain the option of expressing their fertility with a different reproductive partner (surrogate, semen donor, egg donor), fertile partners of infertile people must seriously address all of infertility's losses, recognizing that in choosing an option which will prevent themselves from losing genetic continuity, the emotional and physical gratifications of a pregnancy experience and the parenting experience, they will still give up a dreamed for, jointly conceived child.

Concerned about their spouses' battered self esteem, the majority of fertile partners indeed choose to render themselves infertile, too, electing to become childfree or to adopt when they come to understand how important this loss of fertility is to their partner. And the majority of infertile people fail to recognize the significance of such a decision and such a sacrifice, which, when acknowledged, might be the greatest self esteem restorer of all.

___

That year was the worst of Jeanine's life. After many years of encouraging infertility testing and treatments, she and Alan were hit with a bombshell: the most recent surgery had not only failed, but her tubes were ruined forever. IVF was not an option. In those years it was still very experimental and rare. Adoption was an option they had already talked about and agreed to pursue, but it would be a long time, they knew, before they became parents that way. Though Jeanine really wanted to be a parent, she also wanted to be able to give her husband a child—not so much for the pregnancy experience, but because they had dreamed so long about their funny blended baby.

Jeanine descended into a dark depression that lasted months and months. As she slowly emerged, the sky was brightened by encouraging news about

adoption. They threw themselves into that and were
thrilled beyond belief when their child arrived a couple
of years after that final diagnosis.

As engrossed as they were in parenting, as
delighted as Jeanine was to mother this particular child
and not another, a piece of her continued to mourn. She
mourned for her body, which didn't work the way it was
supposed to. She felt ugly, unattractive, defective. She
felt guilty that her husband felt he had to stick with her.
Nothing Alan could say seemed to make it any better.

Until one day over five years after the end of
treatment when Jeanine and Alan were thinking about
a second child she attended a RESOLVE conference and
heard a male therapist talk about how men grieve
differently from women—often silently. She went home
and talked at length with Alan, a man who finds it hard
to share his feelings.

That conversation was startling. No message
could ever have been more self esteem enhancing or
more important to their marriage. Alan told Jeanine how
carefully he had thought through all those offers and
threats of divorce from years before and how frightening
they had been for him. What he wanted, he told her (once
again, and for the thousandth time—but this time she
heard) was not fertility, but Jeanine. For him the thought
of losing Jeanine as his wife had been more terrifying
than the thought of losing his fertility.

"I've wondered many times," says Jeanine,
"why I couldn't have understood that earlier. We both
wanted our fertility, and we wanted it together, but
beneath it all what we each wanted most was the other,
and in our badly communicated grief we almost lost it
all."

What is most important here? Sometimes we forget that it was
the marriage that came first and the love we felt for each other that led us
to decide to try to add children to our family of two. Vision tends to blur
when you're bobbling along on that out of control conveyor belt. Get off!
Recommit to one another before deciding how to proceed.

You and I know that it isn't easy to be infertile. In fact, that may be the understatement of the century. Infertility is very hard work—work from which there seem to be no evenings and weekends off, no vacation, not even a real end to the job in sight much of the time. I well remember the period of time when nearly anything and everything could remind me of the loss I was feeling and move me in the span of an instant to fury, to terror or to tears.

But, then, it isn't easy to be the friend or relative of a couple dealing with impaired fertility either, and, having come out the other side of this long dark tunnel, I feel a responsibiity to play devil's advocate on behalf of the people whose lives touch yours. Infertile people tend to be moody, swinging in two week cycles of anticipatory hope followed by crashing despair. They tend to find events that make other people feel excited and celebratory—events like baby showers, a christening or a bris, Mother's Day and Father's Day, little kids' birthday parties, culturally child centered holidays—Christmas, Chanukah, Easter, Halloween—uncomfortable and even unpleasant.

The couple who is absorbed in a course of testing and treatment can often be pretty inwardly focused. Calendars which record a daily basal body temperature and are punctuated with doctor's appointments, days to begin and end medication, a schedule for intercourse, lab dates, etc., don't leave much room for social engagements and just plain fun.

Sometimes it seems as if the infertile couple is the rain on everybody else's parade, the sore spot that must be nursed and treated gingerly by the family at the expense of their own ability to be spontaneously joyful.

But let's face facts. How much did you know about infertility or about adoption before you faced it yourself? Not much, I'll bet. Your friends and family are at that point now. Unless you educate them you can't expect them to understand your frustrations. They have, after all, been exposed to the very same cultural expectations as have you, and, if you'll remember, you were somewhat surprised by your infertility at first.

You probably tended to deny it for a while because the idea was frightening. Well, it frightens your mom, too. She had been expecting to be a grandma. So she says the first thing that comes to her mind, "Relax, honey, you're probably trying too hard."

You may have been a little embarrassed by the infertility at first when you didn't understand how common it was. You might yourself have felt that it was somewhat sexual in nature and expressed a little nervous humor about it. Is that what your brother is feeling when he cracks, "Hey, Bub, ya need a little advice on how it's done?"

Before you were educated, you, too, were likely to believe some of those old myths that have now come to be oh so much more than annoying:

> Take a vacation.
> Have a glass of wine before bedtime.
> Try my doctor.
> Adopt—then you'll get pregnant!
> It's probably all part of God's plan.
> If you *really* wanted a child you'd...

Come on, admit it, you've been guilty of insensitivity, too—back then, before you knew that infertility has emotional consequences rather than emotional causes, before you knew that it wasn't primarily a female condition, before you realized that one in five couples experiences it.

What changed you? Learning about it. That's the answer for your friends and family, too, and since you've probably learned from experience that the information they are likely to stumble across in the daily newspaper (that important medical journal) or in an interview on *Geraldo* (that famous infertile) or on *A Current Affair* (first rate consumer advocates) isn't what you want them to believe, you'll have to educate them yourselves.

There are many ways. Subscribe to RESOLVE's newsletter for them. Give them a copy of my booklet *Understanding: A Guide to Impaired Fertility for Family and Friends* or RESOLVE's brochure for friends and family, or *How Can I Help?* from Merle Bombardieri and Diane Clapp. Take these significant others with you to a RESOLVE meeting or a symposium.

If you decide to pursue adoption, send them Pat Holmes' *Supporting an Adoption* or Linda Bothun's *When Friends Ask about Adoption.* Definitely include a subscription to A.F.A.'s *OURS: The Magazine for Adoptive Families* on your holiday shopping list, and consider *FACE Facts* or *News of FAIR* or *Adopted Child* or *Adoptnet* or *Roots and Wings*—subscribe to several and pass them along to different friends and relatives.

In the back of the booklet *Understanding,* I provide a list of twelve suggestions for caring others to follow in order to provide support for an infertile couple. I'd like to suggest that there are things that your family should expect from you, too:

1   Information. People can't be sensitive toward something they don't understand. Each time that you diplomatically point out a painful error that a friend, a family member, a medical person, a member of the clergy has made in referring to you or to infertility, you increase the likelihood that this person's sensitivity level will be raised to the point of her being unlikely to repeat such errors.

2   Sensitivity. Just as you expect that your family members should be sensitive to your pain, you must realize that your infertility may be painful to them, too. Parents, in particular, often tend to feel guilty that they may have done something to contribute to your medical problem. As well, they shared your assumptions that grand-children would be born who shared the family genes. Just as you mourn the potential loss of your genetic children, so do they. They will, however, feel guilty about publicly mourning such a loss, realizing that you may interpret their mourning to mean that you have failed them. Mourners need one another. Be sensitive and open to each other's pain. Understand, too, how very difficult it will be for your friends and family to enjoy their own pregnancies if you have not given them permission to do so.

3   Patience. Your friends and family are at least one step behind you and your spouse in resolving infertility's impact on your lives together. You will have spent a great deal of private time making decisions before you announce them publicly. Be prepared for the fact that when you announce your decisions, particularly controversial ones, your family has not yet had the time to adjust to them as you have. They may react with shock, with fear, even with revulsion. They must be given time to adjust, and you must support them in this adjustment, just as you wish them to support you in your decision. Beyond this, it is important to accept that fertile people cannot ever be expected to fully understand such a profound experience as is infertility.

4   Openness. Quietly gathering in to yourself each mistake each carelessly hurtful remark, each uncomfortable reaction from family members and friends and socking them away in the gunnysack to be dumped into the middle of Thanksgiving dinner is not fair. No one can be expected to change his behavior if is not made aware that his behavior is causing pain. Use private moments to sensitize your loved ones.

5   Clarity. As you work to sensitize and inform, keep your discussions simple, brief, and factual whenever possible. Most listeners, not absorbed in the daily pain of infertility as are you, are unable to absorb or deal with the heaviness of your situation all at once.

Responsiveness. Sometimes the people who love you can be a bit more objective about your situation than can you. Once you have educated a friend about infertility you should be able to assume that she will no longer offer advice unless she has thought it over carefully and is prepared to accept a negative reaction to it. Consider that sometimes educated friends offering opinions may in fact be right. Blinded by your own obsession with a fertility impairment, you may need to take a step away in order to see clearly. Give some thought, at least, to the opinions of the infertility-educated people who love you.

Having played devil's advocate here on behalf of those insensitive others I must come back and re-advocate for you, too. It's *perfectly fine* to avoid baby showers and child-centered holiday celebrations. In fact, that is often the healthiest thing you can do in finding ways to regain a measure of control.

The challenge is in avoiding the painful situation in a way that does not cause you additional pain or embarrassment and which produces as little discomfort as possible for the friends and family members involved. There are some ways to do this:

1   Create a conflict in your schedule. Miss Manners reminds us that you are under no obligation to explain what it is, just offer your regrets and don't allow yourself to be sucked into explanations. This works particularly well for showers and christenings, etc., but is more difficult to do for holidays. Consider allowing yourself the privilege of leaving town altogether for the holidays, offering your family the exciting news that you've arranged a special get away weekend for yourselves without mentioning your infertility-related holiday discomfort at all.

2   Enlist the help of a sensitive friend or family member who will serve as your advocate with persistently snoopy and insensitive others. Ask this person to have a quiet heart-to-heart with the potentially offended or offensive host or the guest of honor, enlisting them to become part of your sensitivity team as well.

Finally, understand that some people will never respond well. No matter how carefully you try to educate them, no matter how many copies of *Understanding* you pass out, a few people in your sphere of intimacy are likely to remain insensitive. Don't continue to beat yourself up about this by trying over and over again. The best method for coping with these few, no matter how closely they are related to you, is by avoiding them.

———————————————

This chapter has offered suggestions for dealing with issues of communication, but it has not been exhaustive. At the end of Part One of this book you will find a carefully annotated resource section which will direct you to some additional sources of information and support about this issue.

3

The Battle Plan

Faced with the dragon and the need to get around him, our prince and princess knew that they would need a plan of action. It appeared that it would be just the two of them against that enormous obstacle. They retreated to give it some thought.

There were options, of course. Of course, they could always give up—throwing themselves on the dragon's mercy and hoping that they wouldn't become his dinner. They could go back and get reinforcements. They could marshall their courage and risk going straight through. They could look for a way around the dragon.

The prince and the princess were not without resources. They were bright and talented individuals, each with valuable strengths. In order to develop their plan of action, they thought carefully about those strengths and weaknesses, they talked about how to use them to their best advantage, and, after considerable time, they had developed a plan.

The process of decision making involves gathering information, examining long term implications, prioritizing desires, choosing among alternatives, allocating resources, and committing to a course of action. No matter what decision needs to be made, the process is the same.

Having learned to communicate effectively you can now put what you've learned to practical use. In order to conquer a dragon you would develop a battle plan. To manage a business one would develop a business plan. Dealing with infertility lends itself well to similar strategic planning. The planning process outlined in this book has been designed so that it could be used by people who will use it to examine the infertility experience in a series of stages.

1   Beginning to deal with the testing and treatment process and deciding what courses of action to pursue from a list that includes a variety of standard treatment alternatives.

2   Re-evaluating treatment after basic testing has been done, medical issues identified, and standard treatment has not been successful in order to decide whether or not to pursue more costly, invasive or experimental procedures.

3   Re-evaluating the success of treatment, acknowledging the possibility that it may not result in the conception and birth of a child genetically related to both partners and beginning to explore facts and feelings about options beyond treatment: gamete adoption (donor insemination, egg donation, surrogacy), traditional adoption in all of its variations, or embracing the option of child free living.

4   Deciding to end traditional treatment and to aggressively pursue an alternative choice: gamete adoption (will require more medical assistance), adoption, or child free living.

What this means is that couples who are introduced to this planning process early in their infertility experience will probably use this planning format once in its most complicated and time consuming form, and, having spent the time to have evaluated your feelings and shared them with a partner, assessed and inventoried personal resources, and set a general plan for themselves, they would be in a position to come back to the process again and again in order to make other decisions. Most couples find that subsequent opportunities to use the system take significantly less time and energy than does the first complicated round— a set up round.

Of course I do understand that most of the readers of this particular book, *Adopting after Infertility*, have already spent significant time and energy in the treatment process and thus are probably at stage three (beginning to explore options beyond evidently unsuccessful treatment) or stage four (deciding to end treatment and commit to an option which does not involve parenting a child conceived and birthed together.) But I outline the entire process here for the benefit of those couples and those group leaders and those professionals who will find it useful for infertile people still working at stage one or two.

No matter where you *think* you are in the series of four stages when you pick up this book, please consider taking the time to go back to the first step and review the decison making process at each stage so that you can be confident in the future that you have fully explored and made decisions about all of the options that are open to you. Despite the fact that doing so will be time consuming and may be emotionally difficult, you will be glad, later, that you disciplined yourself in this way.

One of the reasons that I believe that it is well worth the significant expenditure of time and energy that initiating this process will take is that humans have a tendency to reflect back on decisions made earlier and to wonder if they made the right ones. "If only's" are a common part of our looking backward with 20/20 hindsight. But decisions properly made can last us a life time. We can look back on them confidently, knowing that *at that time* and *under those circumstances* we made the very best possible decisions. Because infertility will always be a significant part of the people each of you are and become, it is important that you feel comfortable and confident about the decisions you make along the way.

The facts are these: once upon a time you decided to have a baby, and you expected that to be a relatively simple feat. But then you met the dragon, and that earlier decision to have a baby was complicated by an entirely new set of facts. In light of those facts, you have been placed in the position of needing to make that decision to have a baby all over again—perhaps several times. Do you still want to become parents if it means exposing your bodies to potent drug therapies and invasive surgical procedures? Do you still want to become parents if it means borrowing money or risking savings put aside for the future in order to pursue treatments with odds of less than 50% success? Do you still want to be parents if in order to do so you need to be prepared to parent several children born at once? Do you still want to be parents if the route to doing so involves borrowing the reproductive powers of an anonymous donor? Do you still want to be parents if it means that the child you parent will not be genetically connected to you? Do you still want to be parents if it will take years more to accomplish? Do you still want to be parents if it means having others determine whether you are fit to be? Do you still want to be parents???

The process described here can help you decide, but first, a word of caution. This process is a skeletal format for decision-making rather than a road map. Because infertility testing and treatment changes rapidly, it would be impossible to formulate all of the questions to deal with all of the contingencies that will likely arise during the course of your family planning process. Instead, what I hope to do is show you how to go about predicting the questions you need to have answered, gathering the data you need, following a process for evaluating that data, communicating directly with your partner about these issues, and then deciding together on a course of action.

My plan involves several separate steps:

1   Personal *reflection.*

2   *Sharing* your discoveries about yourself with your partner.

3   Discussing ways to blend your separate needs and wishes in order to select a *consensus or compromise* course of action.

4   *Gathering information* about the options you find of interest.

5   *Inventorying personal resources*—time, money, emotional energy and physical capacity.

6   *Building a detailed plan* for pursuing that course of action—developing strategies, assigning tasks,

allocating resources, setting a time for evaluation.

7   *Pursuit of the course of action.*

8   *Evaluating and adjusting* the plan as needed.

The process cannot be done in a few hours. Ideally, in fact, it will take a number of weeks. Each of you will spend several hours separately doing some personal homework (reflection) and then following that with some sharing with the goal of joining your partner for a long retreat weekend where you will use the data gathering you have already done to create a personal plan (step six).

Some couples who are reading this book may well find it helpful to stop with this chapter and spend several days or weeks or even months using the process described here to make the decisions they need to make before or in lieu of reading beyond this third chapter. If, having worked through your feelings, you find that you wish to seriously explore adoption, the following chapters will be waiting for you as a resource.

Before we even begin the process of decision making, let's directly address what I know to be your greatest fear: What if you can't agree? What if it feels as if your needs and desires are in such direct conflict that there is no route to compromise and consensus?

For many couples it is this very fear that prevents them from communicating directly with one another and leads them to drift aimlessly through too many years of treatment, too many years of just waiting. The underlying fear is that without clear agreement the marriage itself is in jeopardy, and for some people this fear tends to lead them to acquiesce to options with which they are not really comfortable.

If at any point during the decision making process you find yourselves stalemated, pause to catch your breaths and recall some of the important things we've already covered. You are each unique individuals with different backgrounds and influences. You cannot feel identically. Your very maleness and femaleness has contributed to those differences in needs and feelings. You chose one another to be life partners both because you shared values and dreams and because there were things about each of you that complemented the other's strengths and weaknesses. You are committed to one another and to finding a solution to the problem you face *together*.

If at any point in the process you find that you are at an impasse— that your needs are in direct conflict and that together you are unable to see a route to compromise, there are at least two important things to try. First, give yourselves some time and space. The issues you are dealing with are profound, emotional, and life changing. One or the other of you may find that you are experiencing a visceral and wrenching reaction which is, purely and simply, grief. Working through a grief reaction cannot be rushed. The most important thing the two of you can do if either or both of you feels temporarily overcome by the confusion or negativism of grief is to agree to postpone further discussion and planning for an agreed upon length of time—usually several months. During that time try to give yourselves a total time out, feeling confident that on some future date that you have mutually agreed upon, you will examine once again whether it is time to pursue the need to make clear decisions about the future.

Second, but no less important than allowing one another time, you may find that several sessions with a mediator or counselor will be valuable. Choosing such a counselor is not always easy. Many human service professionals are not well informed about infertility issues. You may wish to start with someone known to you already—a counselor you have seen or heard good things about, your clergyperson. If you do not know of such a resource or if you find those known to you to be unfamiliar with or insensitive to the unique characteristics of the infertility experience, ask your doctor or the closest infertility support group for a referral.

And so, let us begin...

Reflecting

The process begins with several days or weeks of self reflection and information gathering. Step one is to be done independently of one another. Find a quiet spot away from your partner where you can spend a significant amount of time privately examining the six losses which accompany the infertility experience and your feelings about them.

Infertility's Potential Losses

1   Loss of control

2   Loss of individual genetic continuity

3   Loss of a jointly conceived child

4   Loss of the physical expectations of the pregnancy experience itself and of feeling the power to impregnate

5   Loss of the emotional expectations about a shared pregnancy, birth, breastfeeding experience

6   Loss of the opportunity to parent

Where and when to do this is a matter of personal choice. While some couples prefer to do this separately but at the same time as a first step during the retreat weekend which will be fully discussed later in this chapter and then to share the results immediately with one another, most couples have found it more useful for each partner to accomplish this step days or weeks before their retreat, at a time personally chosen and unknown to their partner, and then to give themselves at least a few days afterwards to ruminate further upon their self discoveries before sharing them with their spouse. Consider these options and decide together which you feel would be most useful for the two of you.

During reflection the task at hand is yours and yours alone. Without trying to predict how your partner might personally react to these losses, and being especially careful to try to avoid worrying about how and their alternatives, think seriously about infertility's six potential losses and try hard to determine how you might rank them as to their importance to you and to you alone.

Without considering at all the physical realities of your personal infertility diagnosis, ask yourself, "If I had the power to avoid personally experiencing one or more of these losses, which would I choose to avoid?"

Try ranking the losses from one to six (the first is the most significant loss, the sixth is the least significant loss). After carefully ranking the losses in order of their importance to you, assign a weight to each loss on a scale of zero to three such as:

Weight	Meaning of the Weight as Applied to Infertility's Losses
0	Experiencing the finality of this loss would mean little or nothing to me
1	This loss, if final, would bother me somewhat, but other losses are more important to avoid
2	This loss is relatively important for me to avoid
3	Experiencing this loss would be very painful for me

You may be wondering why, if you've already ranked the losses from most important to least important, you would need also to give a weighting to each of those losses. This step is an important part of fully understanding the depth of feeling you and your partner each experience about each of these loss issues so that you can creatively work on compromise and consensus plans for your family. Let me share an example of how this ranking and weighting system might work outside infertility. Below is a table which shows how my husband Dave and I might **rank** the appeal of certain vegetables against one another on a scale of one to five, with one being our favorite and five being least favorite.

Vegetable List	Pat's Ranking	Dave's Ranking
Broccoli	2	3
Corn	4	1
Peas	3	2
Potatoes	1	4
Beets	5	5

Now, looking at this list which has only been ranked, only one thing is entirely clear: Dave and I both like beets the least of the five vegetables, and we don't appear to feel similarly about any others! How on earth will we plan our menus?? Oh my!

But, when Dave and I assign **weights** to our feelings about each of these individual vegetables on a scale of 0 to 3 (0 means we can't stand the vegetable, 3 means we love it), we have a great deal more information.

Combined Lists—Ranked and Weighted

Vegetable List	Pat's Rank	Weight	Dave's Rank	Weight
Broccoli	2	3	3	2
Corn	4	1	1	3
Peas	3	2	2	2
Potatoes	1	3	4	1
Beets	5	0	5	0

This **ranked** *and* **weighted** list gives us significantly more information with which to work. What we find is that Dave and I will eliminate beets from our household menu (actually, each of us would have liked to have been able to give beets a -3). Because corn is his favorite vegetable, I eat it fairly frequently, and because potatoes are mine, he eats them more often than he would on his own. But the broccoli and the peas are more in the middle for each of us. We each like them, and so at home we eat them fairly often—more often than either of us gets to eat our favorite vegetable from this list. When we go out to eat, each of us tends to choose that favorite vegetable that we don't get enough of at home.

Ranking and weighting the losses accompanying infertility is significantly more important to planning your future together than is ranking and weighting your feelings about vegetables! As you are asked to weight your reactions to the losses you ranked, do you find yourself feeling equally or almost equally strongly about more than one loss? Or do you find yourself ranking only one loss high on the scale in terms of both its impact on you and its importance to you? As you think about your growing up expectations about family building and being a parent, about the messages you received from your own family about connectedness and parenting, you may be surprised to discover how deeply you feel about some of these losses.

It is imperative that you be honest with yourself in completing this step. Don't try to guess how you think your partner will rank and weigh each loss. Don't consider at this point how what you already know about your own relative fertility or your partner's will impact on your choices and rankings. Simply be gut honest here in ranking and weighing how you feel about these potential losses.

Having completed this step and feeling clearer about your own needs, your own values, your own dreams and how they have been challenged by infertility, you will be able to think more clearly about the four general groups of choices open to couples who are dealing with a fertility impairment.

The Range of Choices for Planning about Infertility

1   Continuing treatment to the point of having tried every possible option.

2   Using donated eggs or sperm to allow one of you to maintain a genetic connection.

3   Adopting.

4   Embracing a childfree lifestyle.

Choosing an option for you and your spouse is a task to be be accomplished together, but it will be helpful if, before you discuss them together, each of you has given some careful thought to your personal reactions to each option so that you will have a clear idea of *why* you feel strongly positively or negatively about any of them. Ask yourself these questions:

In light of what you've learned about yourself and your reactions to the potential losses of infertility, how important do you feel it is to you to learn more about further treatment options which would help you to conceive and birth a child genetically related to both you and your partner?

Now, while you are still alone, think about the options available through assisted reproduction—using the donated gametes of another man or woman, or hiring a surrogate to carry a child conceived with the husband's sperm and the wife's egg, the husband's sperm and the surrogate's egg, the husband's sperm and donated egg, donated sperm and the wife's egg, donated sperm and donated egg? Do these seem worth exploring given what you've identified about your needs?

What about traditional adoption—independent or agency, infant or older child, domestic or international? Is it possible to love, nurture, parent a child not genetically related to you? Do you feel that you might want to explore any of these options further as an alternative to not becoming a parent at all?

And finally, what about the option of not parenting at all in a permanent way. Given what you now know about yourself, are you willing to learn more about and discuss with your partner the idea of electing to follow a childfree lifestyle?

Sharing

After you have had the amount of time you personally need to think through and evaluate your reactions to infertility's losses (and allowing for time to recover, should either of you find that the process of self discovery has heightened your feelings of grief and loss), you will be ready to share your results with one another. Choose a time and place where you can be uninterrupted for at least two hours. Hand your partner a sheet of paper on which you have listed only your own ranking and weighting of infertility's losses. Examine one another's lists and then compare them.

Of course it would be ideal if you found that your lists were identical. How much easier making your next choices would be! But, as you will understand from our having discussed the many factors which make individuals so different when responding to the same crisis, you will likely find that your lists differ.

Discuss the differences. If your lists are ranked similarly, you will move quickly from this step to examining specific treatment options or family planning alternatives. If your lists are quite different, your goal will be to search for areas of agreement as you seek to compromise and build consensus about where you will be going together. Expect this discussion to produce deep feelings in each of you.

Often couples discover that what seems like a clear solution to one partner in reality enhances the other's pain. Let's consider some quick examples of situations like this.

Miguel's low sperm count makes his impregnating Sondra unlikely. Sondra, however, seems to be normally fertile. To Sondra a clear, quick, cheap, private solution to the problem is donor insemination—she even suggests that perhaps Miguel's brother would be willing to be the donor so that at least the baby would share Miguel's genes. She is shocked and even angry to hear that Miguel doesn't immediately agree to this solution which even respects Miguel's genetic pool. Sondra has not taken into consideration how important his own ability to impregnate his wife is to Miguel. If Miguel is to seriously consider this option for building their family, Sondra will need to give him time and space to mourn this significant loss and will need to be respectful of his ultimate decision—which may be that this option is rejected and another compromise route to parenthood is selected.

Bill and Sharon want a family, but Sharon's endometriosis has not responded to treatment. Bill has had it with trying. He's ready to adopt and doesn't understand why Sharon is resisting. But Sharon's endometriosis is incredibly painful. Besides being a reproductive problem, it is taking over other aspects of her life as well. While Bill is focused on putting the infertility behind them, Sharon can't yet see beyond solving the medical problem which would continue to consume her. It's too early for Sharon to consider adoption. The endometriosis needs to be managed first.

The answers won't necessarily come easily, and at this stage it is likely to be unreasonable to expect that you will see only one path of choice. You will need to do a great deal of talking, questioning, sharing. If each of you feels able to keep an open mind during these early explorations and is willing to try to reject nothing out of hand, if each of you will allow yourself to hear about options, to try them on and wear them for a while, to explore them with your partner before deciding whether or not this is an option you care to pursue together, you are ready for the next step in the decision-making process—gathering information about all the alternatives which you have not agreed to dismiss.

Educating Yourselves and One Another

Having agreed on whether or not to rule out certain options, you must obtain as much background information about each option which remains open to you as you possibly can. So that you can both feel confident that the final decision is mutually satisfying, both members of a couple should take responsibiity for participating in the information gathering process. You will find this an empowering experience, allowing you to regain an important measure of control. If your partner will not agree to take responsibility for some of this information gathering, stop the process and ask him or her to join you in some counseling sessions to determine what is causing the impasse.

Information is available from a variety of sources. Books, tapes, fact sheets, magazine and professional journal articles, seminars and symposia are sources of information. For referral to the most current and accurate written resources on infertility and some information on adoption, contact both the nearest local chapter and the national office of RESOLVE, Inc. in the U.S. and Infertility Awareness Association in Canada. For more specific information about various adoption options, your first stop should be Adoptive Families of America and their local member groups. For a nominal fee your local library can obtain nearly anything they do not carry through the interlibrary loan program. Hospitals and medical schools often make their libraries open to consumers for research. Your physician may be willing to have his staff do a computer search of professional literature on a particular topic for you.

Seminars and monthly meetings held by infertility and adoption support groups are another important source of information. Most RESOLVE chapters periodically hold an infertility symposium (often cosponsored with Serono Symposia U.S.A.) These are day-long events which offer a menu of presentations by medical, counseling, and social service professionals on most medical issues and treatments and some lifestyle alternatives. Similarly, in most major cities adoptive parent support groups sponsor adoption conferences or fairs.

Since these are often annual or biennial events, you may find that your own timing doesn't match that of the group. Don't despair! Frequently the sessions have been audio-taped and are available for borrowing or for purchase. Contact your local infertility support group or adoptive parents' group about this possibility.

On a national level, Adoptive Families of America holds an annual two day conference for adoption-built families and prospective adopters featuring national experts in the field and has every session taped by von Ende Communications. AFA makes these tapes available through *OURS: The Magazine for Adoptive Families.* Von Ende also tapes the biennial conferences of Indiana's Adoption Forum Coalition, the annual North American Conference on Adoptable Children, etc. and maintains catalogs and subject specific lists of their available tapes. Contact Brus and Diane von Ende at 3211 Margaret Dr., Golden Valley MN 55422 (telephone 612-529-4493).

I often speak to couples who are reluctant to reach out to an advocacy group. The excuse most often reported is, "We're feeling fine.

We don't want a support group." While I understand that many people do not wish to seek the support component of such groups, these groups offer much more than support. Such a reply reflects a misunderstanding of what adoptive parent groups and infertility organizations do.

These are the real experts in a field—those whose personal experience with it have taught them how important it is to be well informed. Volunteer leaders of mutual support groups have made it their business to gather as much data as possible and to keep track of the frequent changes not just in your own community but beyond it. Additionally, both A.F.A. and RESOLVE are becoming more and more involved in legislative advocacy work on behalf of their constituents. RESOLVE's chapters have won the battle for mandated insurance benefits in several states already. A.F.A.'s advocates lobby on the national level, monitor state legislation, and connect families sharing similar legal concerns from around the country. I believe that couples do themselves a serious disservice if they do not take advantage of the educational and referral and advocacy opportunities available through volunteer run advocacy and support organizations.

Inventorying Personal Resources

In creating a logistical plan for any purpose, an early step is taking an inventory of the resources available to be budgeted and expended in order to achieve a series of goals and objectives. Planning an assault on the infertility dragon is no different.

Resources at your disposal for this battle are all available in limited quantities and are for the most part nonrenewable, so they must be budgeted. Those resources are time, money, emotional energy, and physical capacity. I have found it helpful to use some visual symbols to represent each of these resources.

1

2

3
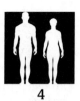
4

During your retreat weekend the question you will ask of yourselves and each other as you consider each step in putting together your personal plan will be, "How much of each of these limited resources—how much time, how much money, how much emotional energy, how much of my body's capacity—am I willing to risk on this step?"

56

In order to plan thoroughly, you will need to gather some practical, concrete information about your each of your resources before your retreat. Gather raw data right now. You will discuss it during the strategic planning retreat.

1   *Time*   Examine the restrictions imposed by your jobs. Is flex time available? Medical leave? Parental leave? Consider your ages.

2   *Finances*   How much money is available to you to expend for family planning in order to retain some financial resources for raising a family and pursuing other life goals? From what sources are loans an option? Gather specific information about any health insurance plans which cover you. What infertility treatments does it cover? Will it cover any adoption expenses? Get the details of your employee benefits plans. Is there an adoption reimbursement benefit?

3   *Emotional Energy*   Energy and emotions are not concrete. They cannot be objectively measured. Only through self examination and careful discussion with your partner can you assess the extent of this resource. Couples who have adequate outside support often find that their emotional reserves are increased as a result. This support may come from family and friends, from medical and mental health professionals, from members of a support group.

4   *Physical Capacity*   Just what is your diagnosis and what is the realistic prognosis for success in treating it? Have you seen a specialist in reproductive medicine—a board certified reproductive endocrinologist and/or an andrologist? Has your diagnosis been confirmed by more than one physician? How successful is the most successful local physician or clinic in treating infertility problems just like yours? Is there a more specialized treatment center within reasonable access to you? Where is the most successful clinic in your country or in the world located?

Building a Plan—The Retreat Weekend

After gathering a great deal of information, setting aside a weekend for the purpose of making some careful decisions and formulating a battle plan is a worthwhile investment in your family's future. The logistics require your willingness and commitment to giving undivided attention to planning your assault on the dragon. You will need a minimum of 48 hours for this phase of your planning process.

Your time will be most constructively spent without the interruptions of normal routine, so many couples have found it useful to plan such a weekend away from home—camping, in a hotel, in a friend's borrowed vacation home, etc. If your finances do not allow for escape, or if you feel that the pull of an escape location might distract you from the task at hand, your retreat can be successful from home base. Simply be sure that you tell your family and friends that you have plans for the weekend, hide your cars (so that no one will know that you are home,) unplug your doorbell (so that you won't be tempted to answer the door to friends who drop in unexpectedly,) turn your phone's ringer off and use an answering machine (with the screening feature turned off) to take messages for you.

Whether you are staying at home or leaving for your retreat, free yourselves of all normal weekend "must-do's." Change the laundry, marketing, cleaning and lawn care schedules for the week—or better yet, reward yourselves and one another by hiring these jobs out for this once. Give careful thought to meal planning for the weekend. If you will be staying at home, do all necessary shopping in advance and be sure to plan one or more meals out—you'll need the break. Plan to include time in the 48 hour retreat weekend for exercise and/or entertainment. Plan some walks or a jog together, take in a carefully chosen escapist movie or play or a concert (this isn't the weekend to rent the video *Immediate Family* or *Steel Magnolias*). If the location retains complete privacy, so that neither of you will be exposed to the observation of others if emotions rise to the surface, some of the talking you will do during the retreat weekend can easily be done while you are sitting on the bank of a river fishing, walking through a woods, lying on a quiet beach. Holding such intimate conversation in busy public places—city beaches, park benches, while walking down busy downtown streets or through a weekend art fair—is not recommended.

You will need paper and pencils, books and tapes and articles that each of you has already read and wishes to share with the other, staples to ward off the munchies, perhaps some tapes or CD's that you mutually agree are stress-relieving without being sleep-inducing.

This decision making process will be hard work—physically and emotionally draining. Take breaks as often as either of you feels a need. Let's go!

Setting Goals

The purpose of the weekend is to create a plan for managing your infertility experience—a plan that will allow you to reassert control over as many aspects as possible of your family planning, a plan that will take into account your dreams and desires, while realistically addressing your limitations. Using the information you have gathered, you will make long lists, transfer them to charts (some couples have found index cards helpful), and during the course of several hours you will add options and delete options as you discuss them.

Strategic planning—for battle, for business, for personal lives—presumes the setting of goals whose success can be measured in some fashion and which will be periodically re-evaluated. Broad general goals (example goal: An exciting birthday for Belinda), are achieved through a variety of possible objectives (example objectives: Party at home on Sunday the 24th; Dinner at La Tour; Friends pitch in on "the perfect gift;" etc.) Objectives are reached through the completion of highly detailed strategies (example strategies: Call caterers to find out how much a catered home party would cost. Arrange for florist to deliver flowers. Send invitations, etc.) In light of the success or failure of various objectives explored and strategies attempted, goals are evaluated and reaffirmed or restructured.

The first step in creating your personal plan for defeating the dragon of infertility is to decide together on your major goal. You will already have begun talking and thinking about your ranking and weighting of infertility's losses, and this will lead you to the task of determining through negotiation and compromise what the two of you as lifetime partners identify as your major goal.

Do you need to regain control? Do you want a pregnancy? Do you want to parent? What is number one?

Having identified your major goal, you need to examine all of the objectives that could help you to reach that goal. Brainstorm and be as expansive as possible. You can always delete objectives later.

For example, if your goal is to regain control, some of your objectives might be:

1   To become better informed about treatment
        alternatives.

2   To set a time table for continuing treatment.

3   To find other parts of your lives in which you **can** feel

        a full sense of control.

4   (Continue to add your own possible objectives)

If your goal is to become parents, your list of objectives might include a need to list and then rank and weight several alternative methods for achieving this goal, such as:

1   Becoming pregnant with a child genetically related to
        you both.

2   Using donor insemination (or adoptive embryo transfer,
        or contracting with a surrogate.)

3   Adopting.

        Beneath each of these objectives, brainstorm a list of all of the
strategies you can think of that would assist you in reaching this objective.
During this stage you should list every imaginable strategy—even those
that may seem initially unrealistic. For example, under the goal of
becoming parents, and the objective of parenting a genetically related
child, you might list:

1   Continuing standard treatments with a local gynecol-
        ogist/urologist.

2   Pursuing treatment with a nearby fertility specialist
        (reproductive endocrinologist or andrologist).

3   Finding the clinic most renowned in the world for
        expertise in our problem area(s) and traveling to this
        clinic for treatment

4   (Add as many others as you can possibly imagine)

        If you are working on a medical treatment plan, you should know
how many treatment alternatives there are for your medical problem(s)
and list them all. Beyond that, for future discussion, how many non-
medical alternatives are you willing to explore? List them all in a chart or
on index cards, and include there the symbols for each of your four limited
resources (time, money, physical capacity, emotional reserves) so that
you can begin to allocate those resources.

        What are the advantages and disadvantages of each alternative?
Do you have the resources available to pursue all of these options? Try
to regain as much objectivity about your situation as you possibly can.
Now is the time to get real. I have provided a sampling of questions to
consider in formulating your discussion, but my lists are far from
exhaustive. Your own list should be!

        How much **physical capacity** do you have? This involves first a
realistic assessment of the severity of your fertility impairment. Is giving
birth to a jointly conceived child an important enough goal and all other
alternatives so painfully second rate that you are willing to risk expending
all of your other resources for a very low likelihood of conceiving and
carrying a pregnancy to term? No? Well, how much would you risk? How
high must the odds for success be in order for you to be willing to try them?

How many attempts are you willing to make? What about your other physical abilities? How is your energy level? What about your partner's? What impact are various medications or treatments likely to have on your physical abilities to carry on in other parts of your life? Will you need and do you have available medical leave time? What reactions to medications can you expect? How do you plan to manage the physical exhaustion that might be produced by these options? What impact might each possible medical alternative have on your own future health? On the health of your future children? (For example, how carefully have you considered the risks to both yourself and your children if you experience a multiple conception and give birth to more than two children? There now exist in many large cities, support groups of parents of multiples who will be more than willing to share their experiences and concerns with you before you decide to take this risk.)

What about the **money**? Few of us have an unlimited supply! How is your insurance coverage? How is your savings? Can you afford to use money on a high risk, low rate of success medical option and still have reserves to spend on another option—say adoption or hiring a surrogate—if you are not medically successful? How many cycles can be attempted within your budget? Have you carefully and realistically considered the financial impact of a multiple gestation and/or a multiple birth? If you are pursuing either traditional or gamete adoption or even holding it in reserve as a next option, how specifically do you understand its financial impact? If adoption is one of the options you will be exploring you will want to consider allocating this resource in such a way as to creat a reserve for adoption, which is expensive, in the event that treatment doesn't work. What fees can you expect to pay to an agency or to the specific intermediary you have identified as able to help you? Would any costs be covered by your insurance? Can you obtain a loan for this purpose if necessary? Does your employer have an adoption assistance benefit? Remember that it takes a lot of money to raise a child. Be certain to keep in mind as you budget that you will need to have money in reserve for this purpose after your child arrives.

How much **time** can be expended? You will need to look at time from several angles: near term and long term. If travel is involved, can you take time from your work or are you willing to have the treatment impact negatively on your job? For how long? In pursuing an international adoption, would you be able to travel to and live in another country for several weeks?

Now comes a hard one. Most of us don't like thinking about how the consequences of our decisions to delay parenting, or the number of years spent in pursuing unproductive treatment have affected our future, but we must. You may need to stop for a while here and give yourselves time to recharge before seriously plunging into considerations about how to budget your time.

What about your future? How old are each of you now? In looking at your choices, you are going to need to consider whether you have passed a personal point of no return in planning to parent a child from birth. No matter how youthful both of you feel now, be realistic about where you are likely to be in ten years, in twenty years, and think about not just your own needs, but the needs of the children you want to parent. If you are considering adoption, you should know that some agencies do have age and length of marriage requirements, some countries impose such requirements on international adopters, and in adoptions where birthparents select adopting parents for their babies they may have strong feelings about age as well. If the answers to these questions produce a feeling that perhaps it is too late to begin with a baby, don't reject adopt before carefully examining the idea of adopting an older child. Consider as well that adopting without an agency is an alternative to agency adoption and may, if carefully explored and pursued, neutralize some of these restrictions.

Consider the **emotional energy** involved in each option being considered. How much are you willing to spend on this alternative? No matter which partner is in treatment, the stress of treatment is felt by both partners. No matter how physically or emotionally strong one partner feels after facing a disappointing change of mind in an adoption, the other may feel depleted and unable to go on. Can you come up with a mutually agreeable level of comfort beyond which point one partner has the right to call, "Stop!"

Barbara and Rusty spent their retreat weekend ensconced in the lake cabin of Barbara's parents. For three days they reflected, shuffled index cards, debated pros and cons, cried some in realizing that some dreams were being let go, and built a plan for themselves.

They wanted a child to parent, and they weren't getting any younger. At 33 and 38, they were beginning to watch their oldest friends emerge from the stresses of caring for very young children and find time for adult pleasures again. Their insurance plan had covered only the basic parts of their treatment. Now that they were involved in assisted reproductive technologies, they found themselves with ever mounting balances on their bank cards. Already they had had to cash in an investmant bond that had been earmarked for the downpayment on the larger home they would need in a few years when they did become parents. Rusty had been a loving a supportive partner of Barb's wish to become pregnant, but he was wearing thin. The drugs of each cycle of GIFT made Barbara moody and strident and sick. She produced eggs, all right, but only a couple each month, despite the high doses of hormones. They had never had a positive pregnancy test. Rusty was running out of energy and patience. He needed to move on. After the retreat weekend, Barbara knew that she did, too. They would stop GIFT and put their energies into adoption. Barbara would tell her doctor at her next appointment the following week.

The appointment went differently than she had expected. She tried to tell him about their decision to stop treatment, but her doctor had just come back from a professional meeting with exciting ideas about new things to try. The pump might be the answer—wearing a device which would constantly pump the appropriate levels of medication through a shunt in Barbara's arm might help induce better quality ovulation. He was so excited that it was hard for Barb not to get caught up in his enthusiasm. She went home having promised to talk to Rusty about it and get back to him.

But Rusty was full of his own enthusiasm. Part of his "homework" after the retreat weekend had been to make calls to two agencies, an adoption attorney, and a consulting service in town to gather preliminary information. On his second call, to an agency facilitating open adoptions, the workers had been excited to hear from him—did Barbara believe that?! It seemed that they were working with a birthmother who was Jewish. Five months pregnant, she wanted her child to be placed with Jewish parents, and, frankly, they had only two resumes on file, neither of which had intrigued this birthmother. She had asked Rusty to bring Barbara in for an interview in the next few days.

"Remember what we decided, Barbara? No more 'medical maybe's.' It's time to invest in a surer thing!" Rusty pleaded. And, you know, for the first time, Barbara didn't even hesitate. Their weekend of hard work had paid off. Both of them knew where they were headed now.

After you have thoroughly brainstormed and created what seems like an exhaustive list of options you will begin to delete those strategies that simply won't work for you. For example, you may feel that some strategies are morally or religiously offensive to either or both of you. Some strategies may demand more of certain resources than you are willing or able to expend. You may be unwilling or unable to travel for treatment, unable to afford certain treatments, or constrained by time from certain alternatives.

With a more realistic list of alternatives to consider it is important to constantly evaluate your reactions and your williness to compromise, expecting total openness and honesty from one another and considering questions such as:

1   Is this decision being considered after having thoroughly dealt with the loss of our assumed child?

2   What effects will the choice for this alternative have on our feelings about ourselves, on our moral or religious convictions, on our self esteem?

3   What effects will this alternative choice have on the feelings of my spouse?

4   What effects will this alternative choice on on my feelings about my spouse or his or her feelings about me? In other words, how will this affect our relationship with one another?

5   (If the alternative under consideration is not childfree living) What effects will the choice of parenting by this alternative have on the relationship each of us will have as parents to the child who will join our family in this way?

6   What effects will our choice of this alternative have on our relationship with family and intimate friends, and how do we each feel about this?

Strategizing

Your finished plan will probably include more than one alternative, each listed in prioritized order. Your first choice is your first objective; your second choice is your second objective, etc. The planning process presumes that because each objective is time consuming, you will want to accomplish some of the tasks of each objective concurrently.

For example, if adoption is one choice, but not the first choice, you still need to begin to explore some specifics like how long the wait is on the list of an agency you would like to work with. Perhaps the wait is long enough that you feel it wise to get on the list now, while you are still working on medical treatment.

Your strategies, then, will be very specific, and each of you will want to take responsibility for pursuing some of them (e.g. writing necessary letters and making phone calls, reading books and articles).

A word of caution. Conveyor belt couples may find it tempting to race from medical treatment directly to another option. Deciding to end treatment is a big step. Resolve to give yourself space from reflection and re-evaluation between the end of treatment and the agressive pursuit of either gamete or traditional adoption.

Borrowing Genetic Material—Special Issues

This is a book aimed at couples considering adopting children unrelated to either of them as an alternative route to parenthood after infertility. Therefore the rest of the book has been designed to lead couples considering this option step by step in exploring the many issues necessary to making an informed choice about adoption as a method of family building.

Many couples, however, after following the decision making process outlined here, will wish to pursue an alternative form of adoption: the conception of a child using the genetic material of someone from outside the marriage. This may mean using the sperm of a more fertile male either known or unknown to you in the process referred to as donor insemination. It may mean taking advantage of advancing technology which allows for the harvesting of ova from a more fertile woman, fertilizing it in vitro with the sperm of the husband in the infertile couple and reimplanting it in the infertile wife in a process most often called egg donation. Some programs offer the service of combining donor insemination and egg donation by borrowing the genetic material of both another man and another woman and having the resulting *in vitro* fertilized embryo transferred to the infertile wife for gestation and delivery, a process properly labeled embryo adoption. It could mean arranging to use a surrogate mother. Traditionally (and the practice goes back to Biblical times) a surrogate has been inseminated with the sperm of the husband in an infertile couple and has then given birth to a baby which she agrees to allow the infertile wife to adopt. Now a surrogate may also agree to carry and deliver an embryo genetically unrelated to her—conceived *in vitro* from the ova and sperm of an infertile couple (for couples whose wives are unable to carry a pregnancy).

Some of the material in the rest of this book will remain helpful to those couples—especially the material in Part Three about parenting issues. The resource section at the end of this section also refers couples considering quasi-adoption options to several books and fact sheets which can help in making the decision. This group of alternatives, however, remains shrouded in shame and secrecy, myth and misconception. It is unfortunately the case that the majority of physicians practicing in this field continue to deny the important reality that these alternatives are not medicines that cure infertility, but are alternative choices that result in forms of adoption.

This is a lengthy way of saying that I feel I would be remiss if I did not offer some specific suggestions for couples considering these alternatives. In making final choices about using donor gametes keep in mind that you are making a choice with the potential to throw the relationship into disequilibrium. Make sure you have discussed and made decisions about these factors:

1   Each partner must deal with the loss of the couple's assumed child. Make no decisions until each of you has had time to bury the child you would have created together.

2   Have you both acknowledged this as an alternative choice rather than as a medical treatment? This does not cure the infertility of the partner not genetically related to the child, though it does end the childlessness.

3   Have you discussed the ongoing impact of the fertile partner's gain in choosing this option (genetic connection) on the self esteem of the infertile partner (who experiences the permanent loss of genetic continuity and connection)? How might this affect the balance in the parenting relationship? Have you agreed on how to deal with this both now and in the future?

4   Are you certain that the decision has been made positively, rather than conceded to by a guilty-feeling infertile partner?

5   Will you tell others? Will you tell the child? If yes, have you discussed how and when? If no, have you thoroughly examined the ongoing burden on relationships of maintaining such a weighty secret?

66

In many cities, RESOLVE support groups or referral to a well qualified mental health professional running private groups or doing one-on-one counseling can be a helpful resource for couples examining quasi-adoption options.

Evaluation

Good planning calls for periodic evaluation. In fact, all goals and objectives should carry with them a projected completion date. Time, of course, is budgeted as a resource, built into the plan in such ways as your having decided to pursue three months' worth of a particular therapy before re-evaluating whether or not to continue or pursue another course of action or your planning to place an ad directed at birthparents in five issues of a national newspaper before evaluating whether to renew or revise it.

Your overall plan should carry the expectation for periodic evaluation, too. I recommend that part of your commitment to one another and to your jointly made plan should include scheduled promises to meet over dinner to discuss progress at least quarterly until your goal has been reached and, in the event that your initial goals have not been met, to plan another retreat weekend to be held one year following your first. At this time you can evaluate your progress, adjust your goals and objectives if necessary, and develop new strategies.

We'll still be stuck a year from now? I hear you exclaiming. No. If your plan has been made carefully and takes into account the limitations of your resources, the odds are that you will be successful and will not need to rework your plan. All good planning, however, contains a contingency measure for reevaluation and reexamination of the goals within at least a year if needed.

Following the Plan

Even couples facing what seem, on the surface, to be similar fertility impairments may make entirely separate decisions about how to proceed based on their individual and jointly shared values. Let me share with you examples of couples who have already worked through the decision making process outlined here...

Carmaine and Randy have been stymied by Carmaine's premature ovarian failure. Both want desperately to parent, but Randy is finding the idea of adoption particularly difficult because of his myth-filled but firmly held convictions (not shared by Carmaine, who is ready to adopt!) that bonding can be achieved only through genetic connection. Since Carmaine cannot ovulate, they can see no hope, and their relationship has become increasingly pressured by their blaming of one another for their joint failure to become parents. Almost serendipitously they approach their pastor just as he has recently met just the right counselor—a woman well versed in infertility issues, who, after spending several sessions with them working through their reactions to their individual and joint losses and allowing them to mourn those lost expectations, opens windows not even seen before: surrogacy and adoptive embryo transfer. They seriously consider both, find medical and legal advisors to answer their questions about each, and decide to pursue as first choice adoptive embryo transfer. If successful, this option will allow the two of them to experience the pregnancy and birth together. If not, and if they decide on surrogacy, Randy will have his genetic connection and Carmaine her child to love and nurture. There will be winners all around!

Sara and Matt are the owners and operators of a family farm. Together they are clear about their major interest—to become parents. They have pursued all of the least invasive medical treatments they can to try to prod Sara's stubbornly uncooperative ovaries. She responded best to a cycle of Pergonal—expensive for this uninsured couple with limited financial resources. The reproductive endocrinologist working with them at a major medical center sees GIFT as a promising treatment and has provided them with a great deal of literature, encouraging statistics of success for couples who try three cycles at the center's clinic, and a promise to work them into the waiting list quickly. Their doctor is convincing. It's tempting, and, frankly, they are having trouble letting this very nice doctor down, but they really don't see how they can afford up to three cycles of GIFT. Sara and Matt will more or less disappear from the clinic—not formally ending treatment, but just not coming back. Through their church, they learn of a young woman in another community who is parenting one child alone and is pregnant again. Within months they are the parents of her two children—a toddler and a newborn—in an open adoption. The birthmother's employee insurance plan has covered all medical expenses of the birth, the local department of social services provided their homestudy, and their total expenses involved minimal legal fees of an attorney specializing in family law who is also a member of their congregation.

———

John and Mary consider the losses of infertility and identify what they each wanted most from their original decision to become parents. For Mary, the need was to experience a pregnancy as well as to be a parent, yet she also mourns the loss of sharing a pregnancy and then a child with John. For John, on the other hand, individual continuity is just not important. John's dreams are of parenting—reading bedtime stories, coaching athletic teams. For this couple the carefully discussed choice to use donor insemination will be an attractive one—offering them each the opportunity to achieve their dreams and avoid infertility's most painful losses. If this option is successful for them, each of them wins what s/he wants most. Both, however, agree that their highest priority is shared parenthood, so that, should D.I. prove unsuccessful, John and Mary are ready to embrace adoption as an equally attractive way to build a family. They have begun to gather information about international adoption just in case.

———

Mark and Amy, on the other hand, acknowledge different needs. The grandchild of Holocaust victims and survivors, Mark mourns deeply his inability to provide another generation for his family. He is willing to go to dramatic lengths to improve his sperm count and to enhance his chances of impregnating his wife. Amy, too, wants a genetic connection, and initially sees clearly that she can have it, if only she can convince Mark to agree to D.I. Their physician, too, has endorsed this choice, reminding Mark that no one need ever know that Amy's child is not his by blood. With the help of a skilled facilitator, their communication leads each to see that for Mark to accede to such a demand from Amy would create a win-lose situation in the balance of their relationship and could impair his ability to relate positively to the child to whom Amy would give birth. The child would serve as a daily reminder that Mark had lost what both wanted most—genetic continuity—while Amy had achieved it! Additionally, for this couple, the interest in parenting is simply not strong enough in the face of their powerful interest in genetic linkage for either to consider that there could be a win-win after loss-loss in the compromise option of adoption. After careful reflection and a reaffirmation of their primary commitment to one another and to their marriage, this couple decides that their interest in a jointly conceived child is strong enough for them to spend significant amounts of time, money and energy researching and seeking out the clinics in the world with the highest rate of success in treating Mark's problem. After having pursued surgery, medications, and several courses of IVF without achieving a pregnancy, this couple chooses to embrace a child*free* lifestyle.

Each of these couples considers themselves successful in resolving infertility issues and making family building decisions. Their carefully considered choices were right for the two of them. Each was ultimately nurtured by a caring, helpful professional who accepted their personal needs, limitations and values and was able to feel personal success reflected in their joy. There could be more Mark and Amys, Carmaine and Randys, Sara and Matts, and John and Marys and fewer drifting, disappointed infertile people if all of the professionals working with fertility impaired people would make it a part of their practice to link services and provide a full spectrum of information and care for their patients and clients.

RESOLVE in the U.S. and IAAC in Canada can help you find a caring medical professional. The national offices of these two groups have developed fact sheets on choosing a physician. Your local chapter will include patients who will be happy to share their experiences with a variety of clinics and care providers in your community. Later in this book, in Chapters Five and Eight, we will talk about the qualities and qualifications to look for in selecting the right adoption professionals for you.

No one said that managing your fertility impairment would be easy. In making all of your decisions, setting all of your goals, following all of the strategies that will allow you to meet your objectives, be certain that the decisions you make now are made together and with enough care that you will remain comfortable with them ten, twenty, or thirty years into the future. It is always easy to look back and say "if only..." When decisions are made carefully, with complete knowledge, and with full communication between partners, they can last for a life time.

Helen Keller, a woman intimately familiar with profound loss, may have said it best,

> " When one door of happiness closes, another opens. But often we spend so much time looking at the closed doors that we cannot see the doors that have opened for us. We must all find these doors, and, if we do, we will make ourselves and our lives as beautiful as God intended."

Resources

This list of resources is designed to help you in making the decisions discussed in Part I of this book. It is not considered complete in any way. Important printed resources are introduced every year and at the same time valuable tools are taken out of print. This list is my personal selection of those consumer-oriented resources which I thought were most valuable, helpful and practical as this book went to press. You may very well have difficulty locating some of the books mentioned here on shelves in local bookstores. Your public library can help you borrow the books you need—often even those that are out of print—through the interlibrary loan system. The best way to keep yourself informed and current on what's new concerning infertility or adoption related subjects is to ask for current information from RESOLVE, IAAC, AFA, ACC, NACAC, NCFA, etc.

Organizations Offering Infertility Support and Information

RESOLVE, Inc. (1310 Broadway, Somerville MA 02144, telephone 617-623-0744) is a U.S. national nonprofit network of 54 chapters offering information, referral, support and advocacy services to infertile people. Dues of $35 annually (includes both national and local chapter membership). Their newsletters, fact sheets and symposia can be indispensable tools. Currently RESOLVE is putting a great deal of effort on a state by state basis into achieving mandated insurance coverage for infertility treatment. They have been successful already in Massachusetts, Maryland, California, and several other states.

Infertility Awareness Association of Canada (523-774 Echo Drive, Ottawa, Ontario K1S 5N8, CANADA, telephone 613-730-1322) is a Canadian charitable organization offering assistance, support, and education to those with infertility concerns by issuance of its bilingual publication Infertility Awareness five times a year; establishment of chapters to provide grass roots services; a resource centre; information packages; and a network of related services. Services are bilingual (English and French.) Membership is $30 Canadian annually. A complimentary information kit will be sent to interested Canadians upon request.

The Organization of Parents through Surrogacy (OPTS) (750 N. Fairview St., Burbank, CA 91505, telephone 818-848-3761) is a national non-profit, volunteer organization whose purpose is mutual support, networking, and the dissemination of information regarding surrogate parenting, egg donation, sperm donation as well as assisted reproductive technology including IVF and GIFT. OPTS publishes a quarterly newsletter, holds annual meetings, has a telephone support network, and actively lobbies for legislation concerning surrogacy. Membership is $40 annually.

Medical Information and Emotional Support

Healing the Infertile Family: Strengthening Your Relationship in the Search for Parenthood by Gay Becker, Ph.D. (New York: Bantam Books, 1990) Based on a series of interviews with infertile couples, Dr. Becker presents suggestions for coping and for moving on.

Without Child: Experiencing and Resolving Infertility by Ellen Glazer and Susan Cooper (Boston: Lexington Books, 1988). A collection of carefully linked personal experiences from infertile couples who have pursued the full spectrum of options and experienced a variety of outcomes.

and Hannah Wept: Infertility, Adoption, and the Jewish Couple by Michael Gold (Philadelphia: The Jewish Publication Society, 1988.) An infertile rabbi looks at infertility from a religious perspective.

Infertility: A Guide for the Childless Couple by Barbara Eck Menning
(second edition, New York: Prentice Hall Press,1988). The classic in the field. How could it not be a part of a bibliography on infertility!

Surviving Infertility: A Compassionate Guide through the Emotional Crisis of Infertility by Linda P. Salzer (New York: HarperCollins, rev. 1991). A well regarded handbook dealing with the psychological and social aspects of infertility

The Infertile Couple by Beth Spring. (Elgin, IL: David C. Cook, 1987.) A guide to the practicalities and ethics of making decisions about infertility written from the conservative Christian perspective. Written primarily for clergy, consumers, too will find it helpful.

Getting around the Boulder in the Road: Using Imagery to Cope with Fertility Problems by Aline Zoldbrod, Ph.D. (Lexington, MA: Center for Reproductive Problems, 1990). A booklet which offers professionals and consumers practical tools for using imagery to deal with the stresses of infertility.

The following two books are examples of the best in medical materials as of the date of this publication. Call RESOLVE for a referral to today's most current consumer oriented discussion of medical information:

The Couples Guide to Fertility by Gary Berger, MD, Marc Goldstein,MD and Mark Fuerst (New York: Doubleday, 1989).

From Infertility To I.V.F. by Geoffrey Sher, M.D. (New York: McGraw Hill, 1988).

Appropriate fact sheets from RESOLVE (See address/phone above. Order by phone with your credit card)

Enhancing Communication
Between Partners and Others

How Can I Help? A Handbook of Practical Suggestions for Family and Friends of Couples Going through Infertility by Diane Clapp and Merle Bombardieri (Lexington, MA: Fertility Counseling Associates, 1991).

Understanding: A Guide to Impaired Fertility for Family and Friends by Patricia Irwin Johnston (Indianapolis: Perspectives Press, rev. 1990).

You Just Don't Understand: Women and Men in Conversation by Deborah Tannen, Ph.D. (New York: Balantine Books, 1990). Clearly points out the differences in communication styles and interpretations between men and women, offering manageable techniques for improving communication between opposite sexed partners.

Getting the Love You Want: A Guide for Couples by Harville Hendrix, Ph.D. (New York: Henry Holt, 1988). Practical information on learning to defuse power struggles in relationships by letting go of self-defeating behavior, communicating more accurately and sensitively, and focusing your attention on meeting your own and your partner's needs.

Sweet Grapes: How to Stop Being Infertile and Start Living Again by Jean W. Carter, M.D. and Michael Carter, Ph.D. (Indianapolis: Perspectives Press, 1989). (see annotation below).

Childfree Living

Sweet Grapes: How to Stop Being Infertile and Start Living Again by Michael and Jean Carter (Indianapolis: Perspectives Press, 1989). Don't sell this book short! While it is the only book which provides information and advocacy for the option of childfree living (chosen by its authors), its excellent discussion of how to make good decisions makes it a good choice for all infertile couples and professionals working with them.

Appropriate fact sheets from RESOLVE (See address/phone above. Order by phone with your credit card).

Adoption
(A more detailed list follows Part II of this book)

Adoptive Families of America (3333 Hwy 100 North, Minneapolis, MN 55422, telephone 612-535-4829) is a 20 year old network of over 15,000 families built by or interested in adoption. Local affiliate groups number over 250. AFA publishes a bimonthly award-winning magazine, OURS: The Magazine of Adoptive Families, provides information and referral on all kinds of adoption (agency and private, domestic and international, infant and older child) to couples and singles interested in family building through adoption. AFA's Parent Resources store offers an extensive list of books, games, toys, etc. Active lobbyists, AFA is a respected presence in Washington.

An Adoptor's Advocate by Patricia Irwin Johnston (Indianapolis: Perspectives Press, 1984). This book's precursor.

The Adoption Resource Book by Lois Gilman (New York: HarperCollins, rev. 1988). The most comprehensive "how-to" available, this book by a journalist and adoptive parent also provides excellent decision making and consumer awareness information.

Ours Magazine from Adoptive Families of America (3333 Highway 100 N, Minneapolis, MN 55422— $20 annually) The most extensive adoption-related periodical in print.

Appropriate fact sheets from RESOLVE (See address/phone above. Order by phone with your credit card.)

Donor Insemination and Surrogacy

Having Your Baby by Donor Insemination by Elizabeth Noble (Boston: Houghton Mifflin, 1988) An exhaustive handbook covering every possible issue regarding D.I., this book takes a decidedly pro-openness view toward the issue of whether D.I. should remain anonymous.

Between Strangers: Surrogate Mothers, Expectant Fathers & Brave New Babies by Lori B. Andrews, J.D. (New York: Harper & Row, 1989). An attorney specializing in reproductive law and ethics looks at new technology and offers consumers issues to consider in their decision making.

New Conceptions: A Consumer's Guide to the Newest Infertility Treatments by Lori B. Andrews, J.D. (New York: St Martin's Press, 1984). An attorney specializing in reproductive law and ethics looks at new technology and offers consumers issues to consider in their decision making.

Surrogate Parenting by Amy Zuckerman Overvold. (New York: Pharos Books, 1988.) An in depth look at the many issues which arise in choosing to use a surrogate to achieve parenthood.

Understanding Artifical Insemination: A Guide For Patients by William Schlaff MD and Carol Frost Vercollone LICSW (Boston: RESOLVE, 1989). A helpful booklet introducing the most important issues.

Lethal Secrets: The Shocking Consequences and Unsolved Problems of Artificial Insemination by Annette Baran and Reuben Pannor (New York: Warner Books, 1989). These long-time adoption reformers (The Adoption Triangle)now take a critical look at traditional practices in donor insemination.

Appropriate RESOLVE fact sheets (See address/phone above. Order by phone with your credit card)

Coping with Loss

How to Survive the Loss of a Love by Melba Colgrove Ph.D., Harold Bloomfield, M.D., and Peter McWilliams. (Los Angeles: Prelude Press and Bantam, rev. 1991). A simple yet powerful handbook for getting through loss—of a person or of a dream.

Living through Personal Crisis by Ann Kaiser Stearns (New York: Ballantine Books, 1984). A practical guide to dealing with grief.

When Bad Things Happen to Good People by Harold S. Kushner (New York: Shocken Books, 1981). A reassuring approach to understanding loss and suffering.

General Decision Making

Yes or No: The Guide to Better Decisions by Spencer Johnston MD (New York, HarperCollins, May'92).

Overcoming Indecisiveness by Theodore Isaac Rubin, M.D. (New York: Harper & Row, 1985).

II

Making the Commitment to Adoption

4

Adoption's
Central Issues

Thank you for sticking with me! I know that many readers picked this book up already feeling that they'd heard as much as they ever wanted to hear about infertility, and that for those folks, reading two chapters which focused on the pain of infertility and communicating with your partner about it and then a decision making chapter that only alluded to adoption seemed like a real concession. You're no doubt chomping at the bit. The woman promised, after all, a book on adoption! When will she get on with it? ... Right now.

You've thought them through—those six losses of infertility—and you've talked them over with your partner. It seems clear to you that what you really want, more than a pregnancy, more than a child who can carry your and your partner's families' genes into the future, is a child to parent. Adoption is a road around the dragon. Are you ready to take it?

It isn't an easy road. Like infertility, it's a road you will travel for a lifetime rather than a side trip. It will get bumpy sometimes, because adopting is difficult today and adoption is an issue that will resurface for you and for your child at many key places throughout your lives. There will be many more decisions to make—baby or older child, healthy or with challenges, domestic or international, private or agency, open or confidential, this particular child or not? In order to achieve parenthood you'll likely have to hold your breath, bite your tongue and give up control again. It may make you angry.

In 1984 I wrote a book about adoption, *An Adoptor's Advocate*, to help humanize the process. It's dated now, and the book you are reading was written partially to take its place. But parts of it remain viable and have been included here. The first chapter of *An Adoptor's Advocate* was called "The Letter" and it included the following:

Dear Caseworker,

How perfectly furious it makes us that we do not have control of our own lives. Most couples decide for themselves when the time is right for a baby. Most couples need not ask for references from their parents, friends, neighbors, employers, or clergymen before planning additions to their families. Most couples have health insurance that helps to cover the financial strain of the arrival of a new child. Most couples decided on their own whether or not both of their children's parents should work outside the home. Most couples do not live each day of their lives over a span of several years of family planning with the anxious knowledge that any time, any day, the phone might ring, and, with no warning, no nine month wait, no gradual acquisition of correctly sized clothes and appropriate toys, no previous guarantees that carefully made vacation plans or education or job commitments could be carried out, a caller might say, "Are you ready? There is a one day/three month/one year old/boy/girl waiting to be yours if you say the word."

But we aren't most couples. We are an infertile couple. Frankly, we came to adoption as a second choice, our primary motivation a selfish one—we wanted a baby and we couldn't make one. But this wasn't something that we felt we could openly share with you. Nor could we share with you how humiliating it felt to need to prove ourselves to you and to those whom we had to ask to fill out reference forms for us before we could have a child placed in our home. Though in our private conversation with each other we talked about what financial strategies we would need to follow in order to save enough money to "buy" our baby from you, we feared that you would be horrified and insulted if we shared with you our feeling that the fee you need to charge us was a purchase price. We got all kinds of messages from both you and from society in general about the process we were entering, and because those messages were so mixed, we felt it safer to say nothing, even when we felt strongly about something you were saying or doing. Because we acknowledged your expertise and questioned our own, we smiled and nodded and agreed to whatever you asked of us without daring to question anything in your agency's process of adoption.

Surprised at the depth of our own reactions to our thwarted family plans, we found it difficult to trust that anyone could truly understand us and the trauma to an individual or to a relationship that comes of being found to be infertile and considering the alternative of adoption. The only way this can truly be grasped is to be infertile and to want children. How we'd love to insist that all caseworkers be adoptive parents, but we know that this is both impractical and impossible.

Though in most other aspects of our lives we are assertive people, we didn't dare assert ourselves with you, Dear Caseworker. You were too powerful. With you rested our only hope of being parents.

But now that we are parents, Dear Caseworker, we need to speak, because the system we dealt with, an old and beleaguered system entrenched in tradition rather than responsive to changing needs, needs revision. As it is it hurts too much, and, having satisfied our desire for a baby, even realizing that there are other, older children out there who need us, we can't quite bring ourselves to risk again the adoption system's humiliating pain. Fix it, Dear Caseworker. It shouldn't have to be this way.

An Adoptive Couple

"This letter," the book continues, "obviously written in great pain and at what the writer felt was some risk, was not responded to. Amazing, you say, that a social service agency would not have responded to a consumer's plea for sensitivity? Amazing, perhaps, but not uncommon. Was the caseworker insensitive? Absolutely not! She was simply too busy to respond. But because there was no response, this family, like thousands of others who make the same decision every day, voluntarily chose not to further expand their family by adopting one of the several thousand waiting children whose very existence make this caseworker's job so difficult, because the institutionalized adoption process and its system are simply too difficult and too painful to subject themselves to repeatedly. In light of the fact that a recent study indicated that over 50% of couples both fertile and infertile would consider adoption in expanding their families, this failure to communicate effectively is particularly sad."

There's something I didn't say when *An Adoptor's Advocate* was published in 1984. I wrote that letter. I really did—in 1979, and sent it to our caseworker at the agency on whose list my husband and I had waited patiently for several years. We had dutifully followed the rules and had kept our names off other agency lists. The out-of-the-blue-miracle adoption by private placement of our son had kicked us back to the bottom of the list again and, four years later, we had just been informed that it would be at least another several years before we would be "studied" for a child.

My husband had made it clear that enough was enough. He simply couldn't give up control over family planning any longer. We had waited at the agency's mercy for eight years or more, and rather than behave as supplicants any longer, he wanted us to make the decision to make our son an only child. I agreed reluctantly, sold most of the baby things in a garage sale, and, mourning another loss, wrote the letter. To this day that caseworker, who now knows me as an adoption and infertility activist and advocate, has never mentioned the letter. Her agency's practice has changed little in the nearly twenty years since my husband and I first attended an orientation meeting there.

I bring this up because if you are considering adoption seriously you need to know that it isn't going to be easy either! But, unlike battling infertility, this time your odds of success are much better. It is exceptionally rare for a couple who have carefully decided on adoption, responsibly educated themselves about its issues, and aggressively pursued a variety of avenues toward the goal not to be successful in finding a child to parent. I know some of what we will be reading together may sound discouraging, and that the process itself may at times seem overwhelming, but what I hope you might have learned from having worked through the process of decision making laid out in Chapter Three is that this is very much a manageable process taken one accomplishable step at a time.

Keys to success, however, include allowing yourself to be as flexible as you possibly can and developing a willingness to take charge, if necessary, rather than to abdicate all responsibility and control to an intermediary. Our job in the chapters in this section is to explore together as many adoption-specific issues as possible for you to consider in making your measured decision about and your commitment to adoption.

Our job is helping you to decide whether to make this second choice a best choice.

Oh, and, by the way—Dave and I adopted twice more. Once independently, once through an agency. We did so because in the interim, with the help of RESOLVE, a lot of reading, and a local adoptive parent support group which was affiliated with Adoptive Families of America, we learned to stop seeing ourselves as victims and we snatched back control of our family planning. When this book is published, our children will be 17, 11, and 8. We consider our family complete and our children perfect.

Is Adoption for You?

Whatever you do, be as sure as you can be, *before* that child arrives in your home, that adoption is for you. Oh, yes, you may be nervous and lacking in confidence at the beginning, but beneath that, you need to feel positive about adoption as a good way to form families.

———————

I remember lying awake for hours the night before we brought our son home, worrying. "Is this the right decision? ... Well,, I guess it has to be, we thought about it a long time... But maybe God was trying to tell me something when He made me infertile... Yeah, but so are a lot of other people and adoption works for them... No, I'll be an awful mother. I'll wake Dave up and tell him I've changed my mind... No, can't do that, he'd kill me ... What if being a mom is something instinctive that comes along with the hormones of pregnancy?"

But then they placed Joel in my arms. Gosh, he was scary! Red and skinny, with a puffy, very fetal-looking face, he had been born six weeks prematurely and weighed just four and a half pounds. We'd known about him since the day he was born, but he had spent the previous ten days in the preemie nursery, which was off limits to us, before the nurses decided that be wasn't going to gain weight fast until he had a mom and a dad to hold him. Now he weighed only four pounds, fourteen ounces, and he was so small that he easily lay in the cradle made by my cupped hands and my elbows. I look back at the pictures and realize that he was probably a pretty funny looking newborn, but to us he was absolutely beautiful, and his daddy and I felt instantly, ferociously, that he was ours.

Today he is 17, nearly six feet tall, brilliant and talented and handsome. Except for the fact that we are stricter than everybody-else's-parents, meaner than everybody-else's-parents, more conservative than everybody-else's-parents, have higher expectations than everybody-else's-parents (you know the litany, you were seventeen once) he figures that this is a pretty good place to be, that his life is going pretty well, that he belongs to us and we to him.

Shared Fate

It begins with a commitment to a life together.

H. David Kirk is a Canadian sociologist and adoptive parent who made a long career, beginning in the 1950s, studying adoption's impact on the people whom it touches from a sociological (pertaining to human behavior in social settings and relationships) perspective rather than a psychological (related to mental processing and behavior) perspective. After following a large number of adoption-built families in a study that encompassed the entire growing up years of their children he presented his Shared Fate Theory. First explained in the 1964 book *Shared Fate* (revised 1984, Ben Simon Publications, Brentwood Bay, BC) and expanded in the 1981 offering *Adoptive Kinship: A Modern Institution in Need of Reform* (Butterworth's, Toronto), Kirk's theory, condensed and simplified, is this:

All of us come to adulthood expecting to fulfill certain roles, one of which is parenthood. But every societal role also carries with it a set of societally-imposed expectations about that role, and the expectations about the roles of parent and child presume that these people will be genetically related to one another through the process of conception and birth. When people assume a role without being able to assume with it all of the expectations about that role, they experience what Kirk calls a role handicap. People touched by adoption—birthparents, adoptive parents, adoptees—all experience role handicaps. Both sets of parents are role handicapped—birthparents because they are parents without children to nurture; adoptive parents because they are parents but have not given birth and have no genetic resemblance or connection to their children.

Adoptees are role handicapped because they will be throughout life the
children of two sets of parents, and, while unrelated by blood to the nurturing parents who are their psychological parents, they are virtual social strangers to the parents who provided their genes and whom they resemble in many ways.

Sociologists, including Kirk in earlier work with other populations, have long observed that people who experience any kind of handicap (the preferred term today is *disability*) deal with it in one of two ways: they either accept the differences that it creates for them and look for ways around them, or they deny or reject the differences and try to pretend that they don't exist. Those who consistently accept difference are usually more successful at dealing with their disabilities.

Kirk's Shared Fate Theory, supported by his observations of hundreds of families over an extended period of time, notes that when adoptive parents and adoptees are able to consistently accept/ acknowledge the differences that adoption brings to their lives (he calls this practicing A.D. behavior) they eventually develop closer relationships, because they are able to empathize with one another about the losses each has experienced in living a role handicap and thus are inclined to communicate more intimately.

Now, I want you to think carefully about Kirk's position here and validate it for yourself through your observations of adoption-touched families. Many adoption-built families of infertile people tend to practice R.D. (rejection of difference) behavior most of the time. They try as hard as they possibly can—on the surface at least—to pretend that their families are "just like" families built by birth. They read little about adoption. They don't attend continuing education opportunities. They tend to distance themselves as soon as possible and in every possible way from the agencies and intermediaries who facilitated their adoptions. They don't belong to adoptive parents' groups.

Why is this? Let me explain it a little differently than Dr. Kirk did. Families who "match" are families for whom denial of difference is easy. For many of these families, this denial is a continuation of the loss reaction brought about by their infertility. By denying the differences in adoptive family relationships one can try to deny the discomfort of the losses of the pregnancy experience as a sign of their manhood/womanhood, of their genetic continuity and connection, etc.

Not all infertile adopters deny difference, of course. Families who adopt older children or children of a different racial or ethnic background than their own attend seminars, read books, subscribe to magazines and join parent groups in much higher proportionate numbers than those who adopt same race infants. The reason for this is clear. Every time such a family goes out into the public marketplace, enrolls a child at school, etc., it is obvious that their family has been expanded by adoption. The differences in their families are evident to society at large, so they couldn't deny difference if they wanted to!

Birthparents and adoptees have tended to practice R.D. behavior in the past, too. Adoptees often were afraid to hurt the adoptive parents they loved so much by asking questions or expressing interest in their families of origin. Birthparents hoped to be able to end the pain of the many losses they had suffered in the experience of an unplanned pregnancy and the choice to plan adoption by burying it rather than by resolving their grief and loss.

Today, in many places—though far from universally—the parent preparation process for prospective adopters and the support and facilitation process for people considering making an adoption plan is more supportive, more informative, more empowering of client choice than it was in the past. This has encouraged more straightforward communication between clients and social work professionals, which has resulted in less victimization, more confidence in decisions made, and thus less need to deny adoption's realities. And today, as more and more families are engaging in varying degrees of openness with birthfamilies in their adoptions of healthy, same race newborns, the percentage of families who are *able* to reject or deny difference in any consistent way is plummeting.

But for infertile couples, rejection of adoption's differences will always be tempting. There isn't one of us who hasn't observed, even when our losses are carefully resolved and we believe that we don't want to parent any other children than the ones we adopted, that life would be easier—for us, for our children, for their birthfamilies—if these children had only been born to us.

Nearly all of us waver back and forth in practicing A.D. and R.D. behavior, and this is *not* unhealthy. When our children first arrive and we circle the wagons and concentrate on the business of claiming each other and falling in love with one another it is almost essential that we spend some significant time in consistent R.D. behavior. The fact is that families built by adoption have more in common than they have differences with families built by birth, and in helping our children build a healthy sense of self esteem, it is important that we help them feel that they really belong to us.[1]

David Brodzinsky, a Rutgers University professor who also maintains a clinical practice with adoption-expanded families, has even noted that some families tend to go overboard in acknowledging difference, in essence making adoption the major focus of the family. He has added yet another term to the alphabet soup. He calls this coping pattern *insistence of difference* behavior (I.D.) and sees it as just as harmful to families built by adoption as is rejection of difference. A challenge, then, of healthy adoptive parenting, and one of the things we are going to discuss at length in part three of this book, is the need to learn how to balance ourselves on the tightrope of acknowledging differences without overemphasizing them.

Society's Reactions to Adoption

One of the primary reasons that we tend to wish we could pretend that adoption wasn't a factor in our lives is that we get such mixed messages about adoption from the world at large. Those whose lives have not been directly touched by adoption don't understand this process. Currently, the thinking of the general public about adoption pretty broadly includes a lot of myth-filled stereotyping, for example:

1   Adoption is a second best alternative for all involved because it means that birthparents don't live up to their **real** responsibilities, children don't live in **real** families, and adopters aren't quite **real** as parents because they have no children of their **own**.

2   Birthparents are irresponsible sleep arounds—our grandparents would have called them tramps—but even in today's more sexually permissive society where it is more acceptable than it has been in the past to become a parent outside of wedlock it is **not** acceptable to "give away" a child, because...

3   "No worthy, civilized person would give up their own flesh and blood."

4   The only acceptable reason not to parent a child to whom you have given birth is that you are too young to do so, and in such cases it is the generally accepted principle that family members should accept this responsibility, because "babies belong with their own families."

5   On the other hand, it is still generally believed that birthparents who do choose adoption can, will and should forget.

6   **Real** parents give birth, goes the common thinking.

7   And you **really** can't love a child unless you birth her.

8   The only logical reason to adopt is because you are infertile.

9   Yet, adoption is family building "the easy way"—just ask your co-worker.

10   **Real** children were not adopted.

11   But aren't adoptees "lucky" that someone as "good" as their adopters was willing to take them in.

12   I mean, really, adoptees wouldn't search if they **really** loved and were grateful to their adoptive parents.

13   Yet don't we as a society really eat up those often rather sensational adoption reunion stories that seem to be clustered at holiday times and which focus on the genetically tied people, rarely even mentioning the family members by adoption.

14   And it's commonly accepted knowledge that adoptees are less healthy emotionally than other people.

As we went through these myths did you hear the incredible set of mixed messages that birthparents, adoptive parents and adoptees are exposed to in this kind of thinking? For the adults involved in adoption these stereotypes seem to boil down to one public image of adoption: either we Did It when we shouldn't (and must suffer the consequences) or we Tried It and we couldn't (and must suffer the consequences). And at the center lies the innocent adoptee: poor baby, he'll never know **real** mother love, but isn't he lucky?

Widely promoting understanding of adoption issues is important for all of us touched by adoption, but most of all it is important for the children—the children who have been adopted as well as the children who are waiting for adoption. Only when society comprehends the roots of adoption issues will they become tolerant of, empathic toward and sensitive about them.

In Part Three of this book we'll spend some time looking at ways that we can begin to promote understanding of adoption issues and advocate for changed thinking. Right now, though, while you are still trying to decide whether or not to commit to adoption, a more important task is to acknowledge that such feelings exist and to determine whether or not you are willing and able to deal with these reactions to the family you are considering building by adoption.

They are difficult to ignore. From the day your child arrives the questions from those closest to you (let alone from strangers who somehow learn about the adoption) will include prying questions about how much you know about your child's birthfamily, whether or not you intend to tell him he was adopted, your future family plans (now you'll get pregnant) and more.

Your children will eventually be exposed to these mis-understandings, too. Are you willing to become prepared to comfortably and confidently deal with the teacher who feels that adopted children by nature have "problems," with the school yard observations about the "realness" of your family, with the myth-filled made for T.V. movies and sitcoms that your family will innocently stumble into? Of course, I'm not suggesting that you will ever reach a level of comfort with such insensitivity that you wouldn't mind it! Actually, the fact that you embrace adoption as a positive option and are its advocate should mean that you will always be offended by such stupidity, but, if adoption is for you, you will need to be willing to learn coping skills.

In later chapters we will discuss ways to practice reactions to such interference. Most adopters find that with time, response and reaction get easier and less bothersome. This is true in part because in living adoption you become part of a specialized learning curve. Spokane, Washington, therapist Jim Mahoney, in his wonderful trainings on adoption (he hasn't written a book yet, but there are excellent tapes available from several NACAC and AFA conferences), talks about the adult learning model as applied to adoption. Adults go through several steps in learning about any difficult issue. They begin with unconscious incompetence—just plain not knowing that they don't know anything about an issue. Gradually, they become consciously incompetent— understanding how much they don't know and feeling anxious about it. Tentatively they move toward conscious competence—working hard to deal with the realities of an issue on a conscious level every day. And the ultimate goal is to achieve the stage of unconscious competence, where one has learned so well that he no longer needs to consciously think about what he is doing. In order to demonstrate how this works, Jim uses an anecdote about learning to drive a car.

Think about yourself as a teenager, eager to learn to drive. First you expected to be able to just jump right in and do it (unconscious incompetence). Then, behind the wheel in driver's ed you realized that driving wasn't as easy as it looked (conscious incompetence). As the class progressed you learned to think carefully about every stop sign, every turn, every signal, every highway access and you were rarely distracted while driving (conscious competence). Finally, driving became so habitual and easy for you, that you have reached a stage of unconscious competence, where you get in the car, turn on the ignition and drive!

As you learn more and more about adoption, you and those who care about you will move from unconscious incompetence to unconscious competence. I want to make clear, however, that though these issues will come up from time to time, they are not a relentless, ongoing battle for most adoption-expanded families, whose daily lives are, for the most part, filled with the normalcy of being ordinary families!

Yes, it is true, adoption for you was a second choice in family building, but a task central to adoption for you and for your child is your ability to move beyond society's feeling that adoption is not just second choice but second rate to firmly believing that adoption is first best.

Building a Sense of Entitlement

In a 1981 book focusing on infertile adopters which was revised in 1987 as *You're Our Child: The Adoption Experience* (Villard Books, Washington DC) clinical social worker, Indiana University School of Social Work professor, and adoptive parent Jerome Smith offered his theory of *entitlement.* Smith observed that families built by adoption need to engage in the life long process of building a sense of vested rightfulness between parents and children—each coming to believe that they deserve and belong to one another.

Entitlement, says Smith, is a multi-step process beginning with recognizing and dealing with feelings about infertility (the issue we spent the first three chapters detailing), continuing with recognizing and accepting differences (Kirk's shared fate material), and including learning to handle reflections of the societal view of adoption as a second best alternative for all involved (about which we just talked).

Smith's book dealt with what are called traditional adopters—people who choose to adopt as an alternative to being childless because some medical problem makes their giving birth unwise or because they are infertile. The process of resolving infertility is a life long challenge, and it's the one step most likely to be ignored or denied by couples preparing to adopt. We'd rather bury it. We'd rather substitute for it. We want it to go away. Sometimes, the most unlikely people are the very ones who deny infertility's impact on them until years later, when, like moths in the darkest closet, it has had time to nibble away at the fabric of families.

Juanita was a family therapist who was delighted to discover that a RESOLVE chapter was

coming to her town. RESOLVE had not existed when   93
she was dealing with infertility—two nearly grown
adopted children ago. She volunteered to serve as a
support group leader and was accepted at once. What
qualifications!

But half way through the 10 week cycle of the
group, Juanita, like a carefully mended piece of china
soaking in sudsy hot water, came unglued. In helping
the others deal with their active grief over infertility's
losses, she realized that she had never even identified
them for herself before. Was that why she harbored these
unwelcome thoughts about her lack of connection with
her daughter? Was it less an issue of a lack of
psychological fit than a nagging feeling that her much-
wanted birth child would have been different, more
compliant, more like her mother? Family therapy
helped immensely.

―――――――――――

Building a sense of entitlement, however, is not unique to
traditional adopters. Fertile people who choose to expand their families
by adoption are called preferential adopters, and these families, too need
to develop a sense of entitlement. The process for them includes two of
the same steps: acceptance of difference and dealing with the second-
best reaction of society. But, rather than resolving infertility, the third step
for preferential adopters is the necessity to clearly identify and
acknowledge their motivations for adopting and how those motivations
may affect their parenting and their children's feelings about their adoptive
status.

Just as resolution of infertility's losses is not a one-shot, now-
we've-done-it-so-let's-get-on-with-it experience, neither is building a
sense of entitlement. People touched by adoption work on this and refine
it throughout their lifetimes. What's important is recognizing that this is
so and being committed to doing the work, because a poorly developing
sense of entitlement is at the root of many problems in parenting in
adoption: poor communication, super-parent syndrome, inconsistent
discipline, over-permissiveness, over-protectiveness, obsessive fear of
the birthfamily, and more.

It is also important to understand that entitlement building and
attachment building, while different, are inextricably interwoven, so that
problems in attachment can contribute to problems in building a sense

of entitlement and vice versa. We'll talk about attachment—the claiming process, the effects of earlier experiences, parent-child interactions and responsiveness to one another, the impact of psychological mismatching and more—in depth in a later chapter. Entitlement, though, is a separate goal—the key to successful adoption.

———

Paul and Ellen raised two children whom they adopted in the 1940s after many years of infertility and several pregnancy losses. Each child was about six months old at placement, and they were two years apart in age. This family consistently acknowledged adoption. From early childhood the children knew that they had been adopted. Paul and Ellen were warm, gentle, loving parents—both college educated—who raised their children in a lovely midwestern community and offered them many "advantages."

Their son, David, who was the older of the two, was always comfortable with the adoption. Close to his parents, but particularly his father, he never questioned their connectedness, and, while typically annoyed with his parents' conservative parenting style, experienced it as consistent. Quiet and smart, with a wry sense of humor, David was like his father in many ways. He grew to adulthood with an entirely confident sense of self.

The daughter always felt "different." Jane had some learning problems which made school a challenge, found that her interests and talents were a little "foreign" to the other members of her family, and didn't "look like" anyone at home. Her mother, very talented in most domestic arts, found a disinterested pupil and partner in her much loved daughter. Spunky and inclined to rebel, Jane's refusal to "go with the flow" of Paul and Ellen's parenting style made discipline a challenge. As a result, it was inconsistent, as her parents tended to experiment now and again. As an adult, this daughter continues to search for the answer to who she is.

As they prepared to sell the home in which the children grew up, Paul and Ellen asked David and Jane if there was anything in particular that they wanted as a remembrance from home. Paul had already divvied up a number of his family's heirlooms—a civil war sword,

some books and papers, his father's railroad watch, etc.
Ellen, on the other hand, had not. Jane made her list of
china, crystal, silver, etc. and it was sent. David, not
materialistic by nature, was thinking about mementoes
rather than relative value.

Two things stood out as memories from home.
A set of sleigh bells from his maternal grandparents' farm
hung in their hall. Every Christmas Eve from as long as
he could remember until he left for college, after the
children were tucked into bed, his father had taken those
sleigh bells down from the wall and climbed to the roof
of their house, where he rang then and called out, "Ho,
ho, ho!" What a wonderful memory. David wanted to
pass it on to his children. The second item was a
somewhat rustic sideboard in the dining room. It had
been brought to the Midwest from Pennsylvania by his
mother's great-grandparents in a covered wagon. He
asked only for these two items.

The answer from his mother was a shock. "I'm
sorry, David, but those belonged to my family. It didn't
occur to me that you'd want them, so I've already given
those things to your cousin, Bob; he's my only living
relative."

He's my only living relative? Paul and Ellen were wonderful
parents, their children well raised. But the two of them and each of their
children had quite different experiences in building a sense of entitlement.
Paul had thoroughly accomplished each step, and, in his relationship with
his son, had passed it on. But someplace deep inside, Ellen had some
unfinished business about genetic connection. She loved her children,
but she wasn't completely entitled, and so for her, neither were they.

This didn't have to be. The steps to building a sense of entitlement
aren't necessarily going to be easy, but with support, they are doable!
Most importantly, they must be done. Entitlement-building is adoption's
central task. In this section, as we lay out and ask you to work through
the controversial and unsettling issues that are unavoidably a part of
finding a child, having parental rights to that child legally transferred to
you, and then parenting that child, the question underneath it all is still **is
adoption for you?** But in order to answer that one you need to have a
sense of how committed you are to building a healthy sense of entitlement

with your child—resolving and successfully incorporating the infertility experience into your positive sense of self, accepting and acknowledging as consistently as possible that adoption is different from parenting by birth, and helping yourself and your family learn to respond to society's feeling that adoption is a second best alternative. Adoption has been a wonderful way to expand families for millions of infertile people! Is it the right choice for you?

5

You and the Adoption World's Professionals

By now, having worked through the decision making material in the first section of this book, I hope that you have come to see how important it is to good decision making that one has access to really good materials and outside assistance as needed. Having looked carefully at adoption's central issues, you must also see how very difficult it would be to proceed without competent professional assistance along the way.

Sometimes, but hardly ever, adoptions happen without any or with only minimal outside assistance. A step-parent adoption, for example, rarely involves any counseling or an assessment. Step-parent adoptions are relatively routine legal processes that may require only an attorney to file papers. Most non-relative adoptions, however, are much more complicated than this. Before we can go further in working our way towards a firm decision to adopt and then to decide what kind of child we are prepared to parent in adoption and what style of adoption best suits our needs, we need to spend some time focusing on the professionals practicing in adoption-related fields and the ways that they can assist prospective adopting couples.

There are three kinds of professionals who are likely to play important roles in your deciding to adopt and then achieving adoptive parenthood. They are adoption intermediaries, counseling professionals, and legal professionals.

Adoption intermediaries are the people who bring adopters and birthparents together to arrange an adoption, whether the parties actually meet each other or not. Intermediaries may be agency social workers, adoption attorneys, physicians, adoption consultants, or, informally, even family friends. Counseling professionals help those considering adoption sort through the many ramifications of this family planning alternative, pointing out options, providing information and education, and helping birthparents and adopters make careful objective choices. The counseling role may be filled by agency social workers, independent social workers, family counselors, mental health therapists, professional mediators, or other trained counselors. Finally, since adoption involves a legal transfer of parental rights from one set of parents to another, it is impossible to complete an adoption without the assistance of at least one attorney.

In the best of all possible worlds, each of these roles would be filled by separate people, each offering his or her own objective assistance to birthparents considering adoption and prospective adopting couples. Increasingly, however, the roles have become somewhat blurred, so that, sometimes because of a lack of information, sometimes because of an effort to save money, and sometimes in an effort to retain control, both birthparents and adoptive parents are refusing, avoiding, simply not being informed of the option of the assistance of one or more of these types of professionals—most often the counselors/educators.

Successful adoption is to a large extent dependent on finding the right resources to support a growing family. Your experience with other professionals in other fields has no doubt demonstrated for you that not all professionals are good at what they do—despite education and training, despite fulfilling licensing or specialization requirements. It is important that you, as prospective adoptive parents, understand and take hold of your power and responsibility if you choose this path to parenthood. In this chapter we will discuss the roles of various professionals and consider some ways to assure yourself that you have connected with adoption-knowledgable and infertility-knowledgable professionals and we discuss the gaps which exist in providing adequate services for couples considering moving from infertility treatment to adoption.

Who Is in Charge Here?—
An American Perspective

A Canadian friend who reviewed a draft of this book pointed out that she felt that "the system" might be perceived less adversarially by Canadians than my writing would appear that it did for Americans. It's true, the majority of Americans with whom I come in contact do experience adoption as a game to be played, a competition to be won. Perhaps this difference in American/Canadian perception is because of the competitive nature of modern American society, and perhaps this is one of the biggest differences between these two North American sister societies.

It is indeed the case that, in the U.S., prospective adopters have far less control and far fewer choices in terms of finding a licensed agency to help them in building a family by adoption than they did in finding medical assistance with their infertility. The media has also made most Americans very aware of some pretty scary issues for those hoping to "win" a child to parent: there are fewer and fewer healthy babies to adopt and more and more people hoping to adopt them, and among children not considered healthy babies the problems seem to be becoming more and more serious, challenging, and thus threatening and off-putting to prospective adopters.

In the U.S.'s free market society with a privately paid rather than socialized medical system, consumers are used to being able to do quite a bit of "shopping" for service, expecting that they can freely change providers if they are unhappy with results, and are rarely in a position to need to "qualify" for acceptance by a medical service provider. Canadian people deal with a different medical system. Since the system is socialized, there is much less entrepreneurialism and competitiveness, almost no financial incentive for physicians to train in highly specialized skills in the medical community in Canada and, indeed, Canadian patients queue up for long waits for many specialized services. Spoiled middle class American consumers would find such waits intolerable! While there is doctor shopping in Canada, it doesn't happen to the same extent that it does in the States, and patients tend to feel much less in control of their treatment in Canada than they do in the United States—partially because of the socialization of medicine.

While providing trainings in Canada I've noticed that Canadians seem to assume that all of the U.S. states are as wide-open in their approach to adoption as is a fabled and exaggerated place called California. In reality, of course, most Americans understand that, while the media does paint a rather strange portrait of what is going on in California, and while the California approach and experience to adoption may be slightly ahead of what is happening in other parts of the country, the media picture of California adoptions is far from accurate, nor is it typical of what is happening in the United States. Most of the U.S. remains rather conservative and traditional, though change is definitely occurring. The Canadian approach to adoption is probably only slightly more conservative, overall, than is the average U.S. approach to adoption. Consumers in Canada have similarly limited choices and similar "requirements" to meet.

The difference in perception concerning the adversarial relationship between consumers and professionals, then, may be in the different "conditioning" to professional intervention infertile Americans have had through the experience with an increasingly competitive infertility medical system before they move on to adoption.

Of course in some places in the U.S. there are adoption services and individual adoption practitioners that are so good at what they do that that adversarial relationship that many Americans feel to be an unavoidable part of adoption just doesn't exist! One of my hopes for this chapter and the rest of this book is that within the next decade there will be more and more such services!

Social Workers and Counseling Professionals

Who makes the match? In a traditional public or private agency adoption, birthparents and adoptive parents are brought together by an agency's staff—usually social workers. In independent adoption sometimes two sets of parents are brought together by an attorney or consultant or physician or other intermediary. In the hybrid called direct or identified adoption which will be discussed more fully in Chapter Seven, social workers do the assessment and counseling after the two sets of parents have matched themselves to one another in some other manner. Social workers are most often the professionals employed by courts to do pre-finalization assessments to provide a recommendation to the courts in independent adoptions as well.

In the United States, most of the time social workers have at a minimum a bachelor's degree, preferably in social work—a BSW—but often in an unrelated field. The most common degree in social work is the master's in social work (MSW). There is a doctorate in this field, but college professors teaching social work often hold Ph.D.s in related mental health areas. Some states, but far from all, require that social workers be licensed or certified, resulting in a designation such as CSW (Certified Social Worker). Beyond this, some states make available an examination which offers those who pass the designation LICSW (Licensed Certified Social Worker)—a step above CSW. Some social workers acquire even more specialized professional status by working to achieve the nationally recognized designation ACSW—as fellows of the Academy of Certified Social Workers conferred by the National Association of Social Workers.

This may not seem too unfamiliar a series of stepped qualifications to former infertility patients, who, before they ended treatment, usually became quite familiar with the training and certification steps physicians take from M.D. to graduate Ob-Gyn to board-certified Ob-Gyn to Sub-specialist in Infertility/Reproductive Endocrinology to

Board-eligible in Infertility and finally Board-certified Reproductive Endocrinologist/Infertility Specialist. What you will likely remember from those days with the docs, though, is that unless you were a careful consumer, most of them would allow you to presume that they had the highest rank of training and credentialing even whent hey didn't. The same is true in the field of social work. To know what your social worker's qualifications, experience, and training are, you are going to have to specifically ask, and it is entirely appropriate that you do so.

It may surprise you to learn that there are very few courses in schools of social work which focus just on adoption issues, and none which focus only on infertility. Infertility and adoption issues are normally covered as small parts of larger general courses on topics such as Child Welfare Issues or Marriage and Family. Most of what social workers learn about adoption or infertility issues is learned on the job or as a part of continuing education training through seminars offered by Child Welfare League of America or North American Conference on Adoptable Children or the American Fertility Society or Serono Symposia and by reading the journals of professionally related organizations and consumer advocacy groups. But seminars and journal subscriptions are both expensive and time consuming, so that many social workers whose employers do not reimburse for such continuing education are able to pursue it only on a small scale. It is not unusual, then, for well prepared consumers to be better informed about adoption or infertility issues than an inexperienced recent graduate of a school of social work.

The proper role of the social worker or other mental health professional is to build on a client's strengths. Not all counseling professionals are able to understand this concept and follow it, however. Finding the right social worker and/or the right agency will make an enormous difference in your ability to make the parent preparation process a positive experience and a productive one for your future family.

In the best of all possible worlds prospective adopters would shop for just the right agency and/or social worker, whose qualifications, experience, and interactive skills would be a perfect match. But in the real world of adoption, most of the time this is not an option. Because of the limited number of agencies, the size of their staffs, and the qualifications which may limit your acceptability from agency to agency, in reality, U.S adopters will probably feel that they have considerably less control over choosing their social workers than they had in selecting physicians during the treatment phase of their infertility.

Even if you are not able to apply at an agency whose policies and procedures make you feel completely enthusiastic, you can make the best of the situation by understanding what the process should be and filling in some of the gaps you find for yourself. Adoption education is available through many parent groups and through adoption consultants. RESOLVE chapters often offer support groups and symposia which are adoption focused. Subscribing to several adoption periodicals and reading as many books as possible will help you to move forward. More about this later.

Satisfying the Law

Attorneys practicing in this field are equally unprepared for adoption's intricacies when armed only with their law school training. Attorneys learn about the basics of the law and adoption in courses on family law, but most of adoption practice is learned on the job. While adoptions which are arranged by well regarded agencies usually involve fairly straightforward and simple legal work, independent adoptions are much more complicated and require specialized expertise.

Attorneys who choose to specialize in this field must truly be legal experts. In essence, adoption law is every bit as much a complicated specialty as is reproductive medicine. Of course you would not have had your brother-in-law the podiatrist perform tubal reconstruction surgery. Similarly, you will want to choose an attorney who has experience and expertise in this form of law to handle your adoption. The person who wrote your will or closed your real estate deal or defended your neighbor falsely accused of theft is probably not the person to finalize your adoption.

In all western countries, the termination of parental rights is a carefully regulated legal procedure. In the United States attorneys must assure the courts that both birthparents have agreed without coercion to this termination. In instances where a birthfather is either unknown or out of range of contact, attorneys must follow a specific legal process in order to terminate their parental rights.

There are no federal adoption laws in the U.S., so that attorneys who assist with adoptions which involve the residents of two different states must be familiar with adoption law in both states. The Interstate Compact on the Adoption of Children is an agreement signed by most of the states which regulates the placement of children across state lines. Each participating state has a compact officer who assures that that state's regulations are being complied with and assists the attorneys or agency representatives with necessary paperwork needed by both states. Similarly, in Canada, the federal Ministry of Health and Welfare staffs an Adoption Desk which coordinates all interprovincial and international adoptions.

One of the major criticisms about attorneys who serve not just as legal advisors on adoption but act as adoption intermediaries or facilitators has been that they are not trained in counseling or mental health fields but often seem to be practicing in these fields in trying to provide counseling for birthparents and preparation for adoptive parents. For years adoption agencies have felt that the danger of exploitation and poor preparation is exceedingly high in independent adoption.

In fairness, it must also be pointed out that as adoption in America becomes increasingly entrepreneurial, a not insignificant number of licensed agencies have begun to provide services which appear to be less than optimal. Agencies which advertise nationwide find it difficult to mandate birthparent counseling for clients who do not live in the state where the services is located, and so, increasingly, some agencies don't insist that the birthparents who plan adoptions through them receive options counseling!

Increasingly, attorneys concerned about developing a high standard of ethics in the field of adoption law are speaking out as advocates on controversial issues such as the need to refer clients to counseling services, the need for birthparents and adoptive parents to have separate attorneys each advocating for their particular rights, the need to bill for services on an hourly basis, and more.

The American Academy of Adoption Attorneys is a relatively new professional association which holds as one of its goals the establishment of guidelines and ethical standards for attorneys practicing in this field similar to the guidelines and standards established by professional organizations in the medical field such as the American College of Obstetrics and Gynecologists. Membership in this organization may someday be one of the criteria adopters and birthparents can look for in seeking the best of legal services in the adoption field.

Consultants—An Emerging Field

If you are using an adoption consultant as your intermediary, know that this is not at this time a quantifiable professional field. Instead, people from all sorts of educational and vocational backgrounds who have a strong interest in adoption issues simply set themselves up as adoption consultants. Consultants are often people who have themselves adopted and who wish to pass on their knowledge and experience about networking to find a baby, about how to write a resume, about what books and articles will provide useful information to prospective parents.

This can be a very useful service. However, it is important for consumers to understand and be cautious concerning the entrepreneurial nature of such a profession. One cannot take courses to qualify for such a position. There is no degree. There is no licensing. There is no specific form of continuing education. The result of this is that there is even more variation among consultants than there is among social workers and attorneys. Consultants, however, do not run agencies and therefore don't have lists of qualifying factors for their clients, so the choice to use or not to use a specific consultant is perhaps much clearer and more easily made than the choice to use a particular agency. The entrepreneurial nature of this emerging field results in rapid changes within it.

Finding the Right Intermediary

Recently the newspapers and tabloid format T.V. shows have been filled to overflowing with adoption horror stories: agency directors who abscond with thousands of dollars of adoption fees, leaving prospective parents stranded with neither children nor money to pursue another placement; intermediaries which operate across state or national lines and thus are less accessible to consumer protection advocates when they misinform or mislead prospective parents; independent intermediaries who, waving thousands of dollars, "snatch" new birthparents and their babies right out of the hospital and right out from under the noses of social workers and prospective adopters with whom the birthparents have been working for months. Adoption can be a scary world, and adopters are looking for guarantees.

Unfortunately, there aren't any guarantees. Deciding to work only with a licensed agency and not to consider independent adoption does not insure that all staff members are sensitive, well informed or competent; does not guarantee that fine quality education, decision making and support services are available to adopters and birthparents; nor does it insure that that rare embezzler won't be hired to the staff. Furthermore, licensing regulations for adoption agencies vary considerably from state to state, and in the majority of states they are not particularly stringent, nor do they include detailed procedural, financial, or assessment guidelines.

Adoption as an approach to family building has financial and emotional risks, just as did infertility treatment. Overall, however, instances like these horror stories are the exception, rather than the rule, and are statistically unlikely to happen to you. While there is no one way to insure that you won't be disappointed or victimized, there are some practical things you can do to lessen your chances of being hurt or disappointed in pursuing adoption.

First, recognize and prepare for the risks going in. Identify for yourself what you see as the positives and negatives of each style of adoption—domestic or international, agency or independent, open or

confidential. We will discuss each of these styles thoroughly in Chapter
Seven.

As a part of making this decision, assess just how much emotional risk you are willing to take. For example, some adopters are willing to invest a great deal of energy into developing a relationship with a particular birthmother because they feel that the benefits of openness for their child outweigh its emotional risks. Some adopters are willing to accept a role as foster care givers to a child they hope to adopt before the child is legally adoptable so that they and their child don't "waste" precious time spent in foster care. But some agencies and intermediaries are perfectly willing not to let adopters know that the adoption professional or a birthparent have chosen them for a placement until the birthparent has already terminated parental rights, thus protecting the adopters from the emotional risk of being disappointed should a birthparent change his or her mind about making an adoption plan.

When making decisions about intermediaries, think not just of yourself, but also of your child's birthparents. If you sense that an intermediary—whether social worker, attorney, consultant, etc.—is not providing good services to you, the odds are that the services he or she provides to your child's birthparents will be flawed as well. While you may be well enough informed to be able to "fill in the gaps" by seeking missing counseling or education or support services not provided by your chosen intermediary elsewhere, your child's birthparents may not be as well informed or as well connected.

Some have suggested that birthparent counseling is indeed a form of "insurance" for prospective adopters, significantly decreasing the likelihood of a birthparent's changing his or her mind after the placement of a child. If you find that you are not in a position to offer, to suggest, or to request supplemental services for your child's birthparents, you may wish to avoid using this professional entirely, understanding that, while on the one hand it is possible that this limits some of your opportunities, in the long run it is likely to result in two sets of better prepared parents. Accept the reality of the fact that birthparents do change their minds in adoption, and, while competent counseling makes this less likely, even the best adoption counselors have been part of several situations where birthparents had a change of heart after an adoptive family was already emotionally involved and invested and attached to a child.

Next assess how much financial risk you are willing to take. For example, working through a traditional licensed agency you are likely to be asked to pay only relatively small processing fees and the costs of the assessment/homestudy process before the placement, and your full placement fees will be due after the successful placement of a child. In most instances, if an adoption is disrupted before the placement, a traditional agency will place another child with you without expecting you to pay a second fee. Working through less traditional sources you may be asked to pay a large up-front fee in exchange for a "faster" process. In pursuing an independent or direct placement (and depending on the law in your state) you may be expected to pay significant medical, living, and counseling expenses for a birthparent—none of which are reimbursable if she decides to parent her child herself.

Choose the practitioners with whom you will be working carefully. Agree to work only with agency, social work, legal, medical, or counseling professionals with whom you feel confident that you can establish a relationship of mutual trust and cooperation. There are several steps you can take to make this assessment:

1   Ask for and expect to receive *in writing* as much information as possible about the details of the assessment process, the placement procedure, the financial commitment, and available post-adopt services for birth and adoptive families. This will help you avoid confusions and misunderstandings about your relationship with and responsibilities to and from your adoption service providers.

2   Contact local parent groups or infertility support groups and ask them what experiences their members and clients have had with providers with whom you are considering working.

3   Assess the availability and quality of education and support services for both birth families and adopting families the professional provides or refers to. If excellent education and decision making services are not a part of the services to be provided to you, they will not likely be part of the services provided to birthparents.

4   Just as you would have evaluated an IVF clinic's success rates before signing on for treatment, ask for the adoption provider's statistics concerning number of birthfamilies worked with in the last year, number of successful placements, number of birthparents who changed their minds after having once committed to adoption, etc.

5   Ask the provider to put you in contact with half a dozen or so other couples who have had a placement within the last year. Though some providers may beg off, citing confidentiality, most ethical providers will already have asked prior adopters for permission to use them as references.

While adoption is not without risk, it has been a successful way for millions of infertile people to become parents. Adoption remains a viable way to build a family despite rapid changes in the adoption community. Now, in the 1990s, when adoption is compared to high tech assisted reproductive technologies, per attempt, couples who pursue adoption as a route to parenthood are statistically more likely to be successful in their quest to become parents than are those who pursue IVF or GIFT. The best way to adopt successfully is to be a fully informed and conscientious consumer.

Building Effective Relationships with Professionals

In the end, it comes down to this: we are all responsible for how adoption works today, whether we are adopters or birthparents or whether we are adoption professionals. There are good and bad individual practitioners in every field. There are good and bad organizations as well. No matter what our role, we must accept individual responsibility for trying to make the "system" better. Actively trying to build solid, trusting, and cooperative relationships with the professionals who assist us, is an important part of the improvement of services.

All successful relationships—between coworkers, friends, family members, marriage partners, etc.—depend upon the development of mutual trust and admiration and a willingness to cooperate with one another. This is equally true in adoption. While you may see the system itself as adversarial, in order for adoption to be successful you must come to see yourself and your adoption facilitator (whether a social worker or an attorney or a clergyperson or whatever) as part of a team.

Recognize that the professionals with whom you will be working are human beings and they deserve your courtesy and respect, just as you deserve the same from them. Adoption workers come with strengths and weaknesses and, as we have discussed, may be well informed or misinformed. As individuals, these professionals have good and bad days. In many cases these professionals are employees taking orders from a "boss" with whom they may or may not have a positive relationship. While they are paid for what they do, in most cases they are not well paid! When you are able to see these overworked professionals as individuals, and to build individual relationships with them, you will be able to access their strengths to your benefit, rather than silently and resentfully suffering their weaknesses.

Keep in mind that it is the rare adoption professional today who actually sees himself in the role of screening people out of parenthood.

Most workers expect and want their clients to be successful adopters. Despite the adversarial feeling acknowledged throughout this book, workers are not in reality your adversaries. Work at attempting to build a team spirit rather than seeing yourselves at opposite ends of a playing field.

Good manners are at the heart of good relationships. Not only do we expect to be treated politely, but we must do our best to treat others politely as well. Nice touches (a friendly smile, a thank-you note where appropriate, compliments about the parts of the process that you particularly enjoyed or appreciated, consideration of feelings) will go a long way to enhance relationships.

There may indeed be times when you are not treated well. Ignore those instances which do not have long term consequences if you can. Perhaps you could write a furious letter and then not mail it. Keeping a sense of humor about petty annoyances can also be helpful.

When problems arise, however, that really signify a need for change either now or in the future, point them out, if you possibly can. At the very least keep a file of concerns you intend to raise and suggestions you will really make after your child arrives, so that you can help to assure that future clients will not face similar obstacles. Enlsit the help of a committee from your support group for issues that affect large groups of people. Never, however, under any circumstances, go along with allowing yourself or your child's birthparent to be grossly mistreated or exploited!

A theme of this book that you will by now begin to feel is being repeated over and over again must once again be stated. Adopting is complicated and it is hard work. One reason so much work is necessary before placement, however, is that the work you do now will help you to avoid mistakes with which you will have to deal later. The effort is worth it if adoption is for you.

Filling in the Gaps—An Aside to Professionals

In the best of all possible worlds, infertile couples would have available to them within any major city a stepped program that would offer them information, support and assistance with medical factors of infertility and its treatment; decision making help, support, and referral to service providers in dealing with options; and well thought out services within each of those options that would mean that for adopters, for instance, there was continuity in the education, decision making, placement, and post placement support and education services adopting families need.

As an infertility and adoption educator, one of my greatest

frustrations is that services for infertile people are so poorly linked with one another. Both the medical and social service systems seem to be so overwhelmed, understaffed and detached from one another that there tends to be quite a bit of confusion, a number of rather large holes for consumer to fall through, and little continuity. I've been looking pretty carefully over the last eight years since I wrote *An Adoptor's Advocate* for a model program in some community somewhere to hold up as an example of well linked services, and I haven't found one! Despite a large number of trainings I've done on this topic and the enthusiastic reception from professionals to the concept of linking services, evidently the hurdles have been too high to leap so far.

What are those hurdles? One, of course, is money. In the not-for-profit world hospitals and agencies have been cutting back on services rather than adding them. For a brief window of time in the early '80s it looked as if the competitive drive that makes a capitalistic society run might encourage the for-profit hospital system and the for-profit adoption practitioner system to lead the way in establishing new and innovative services, but even the for-profits are cutting back.

A second hurdle is the mobility factors in modern society which mean that not only are families more on the move and thus not as likely as families once were to be able to reconnect with their service providers should future problems arise, but workers are also more mobile, so that when families do recontact adoption agencies, for example, they are not likely to find a person on staff who is intimately familiar with their particular case.

A final hurdle is that credibility gap, the competitiveness that is so often perceived between consumers or volunteer advocates and professionals in fields related to infertility and adoption. I believe that the best way to eliminate this credibility gap is for professionals to begin to work more closely with the volunteer advocates in the field. Professionals often fail to understand the importance of peer links. As a society we tend to assign much more credibility to workers who are paid and services which are purchased than we do to the work of volunteers. Yet infertility and adoption oriented groups provide an amazing range of services for their members and clients using tiny budgets, kitchen table offices, and volunteer labor. Some of the best, most current, and most easily accessible information on infertility and adoption for lay people comes from the newsletters and magazines of infertility and adoption support groups. While professionally staffed organizations such as agencies and hospitals put on fine conferences, several of the largest and most highly regarded national and regional conferences for consumers on infertility and adoption are planned and implemented exclusively by volunteers.

Professionals must come to respect the value of the work that advocacy groups and their volunteers do, and to refer to them when appropriate rather than to compete with them by duplicating the education and support services that they provide so well. True respect means referring to them as early as possible after contact from the consumer, and consistently reminding the client of the availability of such services through their time spent with the agency or clinic rather than as a last ditch effort as the consumer departs the clinic after unsuccessful treatment or from the agency with a newborn in arms.

But, you say, your medical practice or your adoption agency does refer families to such groups, and it isn't your fault that they choose not to take advantage of them. Perhaps you need to reevaluate your approach to referral. What services do you describe or emphasize? Could it perhaps be only the support offered by such groups and not the education, the advocacy, the referral resources they provide? Please remember that there is a great deal of denial in operation in both infertility and adoption.

Infertile couples tend to deny their infertility for a long time, and it is not at all uncommon for them to refuse to identify themselves as "one of them" when thinking of an infertility support group unless they have been given a clear diagnosis of permanent sterility. Professionals who truly respect and appreciate the peer support and connections provided by groups such as RESOLVE or IAAC will be careful to endorse the education and information services and the advocacy components of such groups. These valuable programs are far less frightening and intimidating to consumers, and often provide the access to a group that can, if later needed, lead both to appropriate support and to transitional services to carry the client beyond treatment.

As we mentioned in discussing the Shared Fate theory, denial of difference is a common coping method for families new to adoption— even more so for couples who have not dealt effectively with resolving the multiple losses accompanying infertility. Being in control contributes mightily to a sense of well being. Adopters will often reject adoptive parenting groups while thinking "Those are for people with problems. We don't need help." Support is not the issue that will "sell" group participation here, either. Nor is social interaction. If a family is denying difference or refusing to identify with others in their same situation, they will not be interested in singling themselves out by socializing with other families who are also "outside the norm." *But*, nearly all new parents (no matter how their children arrive) are information hungry. They want to do a good job. They want to know about parenting methods, about programs of benefit to parents, about books to read and to share. Parent groups are especially strong at gathering and disseminating such information. Emphasizing this information and education component opens the door, allowing parents to discover for themselves the benefits of peer support.

Professionals need to have flyers on hand and to feel no qualms about offering them often and repeatedly. Waiting rooms so often supplied with subscription copies of magazines should also include copies of local and national newsletters and magazines which are infertility-related and adoption-related. Professionals might even consider plugging into local groups on the couple's behalf, making a first year membership in a local RESOLVE chapter or parent group one of the perks that accompany medical or adoption services for which the consumer is paying.

If professionals would stop competing with one another and with the volunteers in these fields, it wouldn't be that difficult to link existing programs and fill in the gaps to provide a comprehensive educational and support program for infertile couples. Hospitals and clinics and doctors could and should join with local RESOLVE chapters and mental health professionals and adoption practitioners to offer periodic and regular "When to Stop," "Is Adoption for You?," "Considering the Childfree Alternative," "Exploring Assisted Reproduction with Donor Gametes" seminars that allow consumers to explore alternatives in an environment that is anonymous and noncommittal.

The call came from a nurse who regularly teaches "Our Child—Preparation for Parenting in Adoption" classes for expectant adopters (based on Carol Hallenbeck's curriculum guide). She had heard from an agency worker in a nearby city who was looking for an adoption decision making seminar or class for several couples who had recently been in touch with her. The nurse had received a professional-courtesy mailing from a RESOLVE chapter in a state that neighbored her and knew that I would be doing a day-long class for that RESOLVE chapter soon. She wondered if I would be coming to her area or if I knew of something more local (the out of state program would involve a five hour or more drive from the city where the agency was located.)

We explored the problem together and were mutually frustrated to discover nothing available! In the capitol city (population over 1,000,000) of her state infertility support groups offer brief occasional evening meetings exploring alternatives and a few hospitals offer narrowly focused support groups for couples dealing with high technology treatments such as IVF or GIFT there. Every other year the RESOLVE chapter offers a day-long program focusing primarily on medical treatment but which includes some single hour sessions on alternatives, and on alternate years a whole coalition of groups and agencies offers an adoption seminar for those already committed to adopting and already parenting in adoptio. Local agencies provide orientation to their process for couples who have already made the commitment to adoption and education for couples who are awaiting placement with them. But nobody takes or shares responsibility for providing couples still in treatment but thinking about ending it with the opportunity for some extensive exploration of and decisions about alternatives beyond treatment.

Perhaps more importantly, the smaller cities and towns of up to 250,000 in the state have only the adoption agency services described above. There are no support groups, no seminars at all unless consumers are willing to drive several hours to the capitol. The links are missing, and they are important links.

Filling in the Gaps—Notes for Consumers

Of course what adopters want is to be the best possible parent to their child no matter how that child arrives. The intermediaries who assist in adoption will provide valuable assistance in preparation for parenting, but, parents, don't stop there! While you wait, read and listen to tapes—everything you can lay your hands on—beginning with the materials listed in the resource section. Attend adoption seminars and workshops sponsored by agencies, hospitals, adoptive parent groups, RESOLVE chapters. Join a parent group, at least to get their newsletter, but hopefully to spur your active participation (many of them have parents-in-waiting sub-groups or support groups).

There's an almost tangible difference in the air around infertile but still childless people who have finally committed to adoption.

An attorney and I found ourselves on the faculties of two separate symposia about six months apart in the same city. It was the first time I'd spoken to two different groups in the same city so closely in time. At lunch at the second program I ran into the attorney and we ate together. She had presented well received sessions on considering and pursuing private adoptions at both symposia. But something felt different. We were each fascinated by on our reactions to the crowds and were each surprised to have them confirmed by one another.

The first symposium, held in dreary November, had been an all day program on infertility issues—treatments, options, emotional issues—sponsored by the local RESOLVE chapter. It was attended by nearly 300 people who packed the rooms to listen to a high powered, well qualified faculty of medical and mental health and adoption experts. I did a keynote address called "Life at the Crossroad" where I presented a cheerleading-style effort to help couples re-empower themselves. I also did workshops on decision making, dealing with family and friends, and considering adoption. The evaluations for the symposium were excellent. Nearly everybody there felt they got just what they needed from the day.

Several months later, on a cold, grey February morning I was in the same city to keynote a seminar offered by an adoptive parent group—the local affiliate of Adoptive Families of America. Once again the list of offered sessions and speakers was impressive. Over 300 prospective adopters and adoptive parents attended. I was surprised at how many of the faces looked familiar from the RESOLVE seminar the previous fall. I spoke on promoting understanding of adoption issues and building a sense of entitlement and talking to kids about adoption.

Despite the fact that we were dealing with quite a few of the same people, the atmosphere was totally different on those two days. At the infertility conference attendees had been quiet and reserved; they hesitated to share with one another or to ask questions out loud. Interaction at lunch and at breaks was limited and somewhat muffled. The attorney and I had each felt what amounted to almost a pall over the day, despite the fact that it had been completely successful.

Today registrants had milled excitedly over

coffee and donuts waiting for the introductions to begin. The lunchroom buzzed and laughter pealed. Questions had been enthusiastic. The difference could be physically felt, and the difference here was hope!

Reach for that hope! Look for a preparation for parenting in adoption class in your community. Often based on Carol Hallenbeck's *Our Child: Preparation for Parenting in Adoption—Instructor's Guide*, these are the equivalent of Lamaze courses for adopters and they are wonderful! Often offered by RESOLVE chapters or adoptive parenting groups but sometimes by the parent educators at area hospitals or the Red Cross or at a YWCA/YMCA, these several week courses deal with the practicalities of getting ready to parent: bathing and diapering and other basic infant care skills, choosing a pediatrician, selecting nursery and clothing items and child-proofing your home, deciding whether to try to do adoptive nursing or to bottle feed. They also provide a completely nonjudgmental atmosphere away from the perceived judgmental process of the homestudy to share nagging fears with other prospective adopters, to explore concerns about reactions from family and friends, to talk about choosing arrival announcements and baby books. Most of all such classes make the coming child and your becoming a parent begin to seem real and exciting!

6

Making Decisions about Types of Children

So you've decided that adoption is a good option for you. Who might you adopt? Thirty years ago there would have been many children available, but few choices to make. Adoption agencies made nearly all placements then, and they made all of the decisions for both birthparents and adoptive parents. Agencies matched adopters and birthparents with little input from either. Adopters were under 40, well employed, married once, practiced the same religion. Most adoptions were of babies who matched their adopters as closely as possible—ethnicity, physical type and appearance, "background," religion, etc. Children considered adoptable were healthy (often spending several weeks or months in a foster home or a foundling hospital to assure this), and children with disabilities were routinely institutionalized. Confidentiality was the standard.

Today, most of this is flexible, and clients are empowered to make for themselves many more decisions than were theirs to make in the past. Adoption may occur either through an agency (public or private) or independently, either directly between birth and adoptive parents or with the assistance of an intermediary. Prospective parents are asked to consider carefully what health and developmental impairments they feel they might be able to handle effectively, and no child is considered unadoptable today. While many private agencies continue to have guidelines regarding age of parents, length of marriage, religion, etc., families who do not meet these guidelines will find that there are many other options open to them. While most adoption professionals still believe that race- or ethnicity-matching is the optimal situation for a child to be adopted, children are adopted both domestically or internationally who are racially different from their adopters.

At a minimum birthparents are empowered to develop a sketch of the kind of family they have in mind for their child, and often they make direct selections, either through confidential profiles or after face-to-face meetings. Some birthparents and adopting couples continue to want full confidentiality, but a spectrum exists from fully confidential through the one time exchange of anonymous letters to pre-birth meetings, to ongoing letter exchanges, and includes the possibility of ongoing direct communication and interaction and cooperation of birth and adoptive families.

Obviously, families considering adopting have many decisions to make. Each option has its own set of risks and benefits unique to the couple making the decision. There are two separate kinds of important decisions to make. The first is to decide what kind of child you are prepared to parent (baby/older, healthy/disabled or challenged, inracial/ transracial.) The second is to decide about the adoption process which is for you (domestic or international, agency vs. independent, confidential vs open). This chapter will deal with the first set of decisions. Now that you've decided to adopt, what kind of child is for you?

Most infertile couples who think about adopting wish to adopt a healthy newborn infant of their own race or ethnicity. This is a perfectly normal, perfectly healthy, perfectly acceptable expectation. After all, had they given birth to the child they initially expected to parent, the child would be newborn, would physically resemble one or both of his parents or their families, and, under average circumstances, would likely be healthy.

For many years—until the mid to late 1970s—this was a realistic wish, readily accomplished. The number of infants available for adoption and the number of families wishing to adopt were relatively close, and, in fact, during the '30s and '40s and '50s there were actually more babies in need of parents than families interested in adopting. In fact, in those years couples were often allowed to view and select from two or more healthy babies. Though treatments for infertility were less successful a generation or more ago, a solution to childlessness was easier. Couples who lost control of their fertility regained control of the family planning aspect of their lives by actually "choosing" their child.

Today there are still more children to adopt than there are potential parents asking for them. But those children aren't necessarily white, aren't necessarily babies, aren't necessarily healthy. Many factors have influenced this change: acceptance of single parenting as a lifestyle of choice, legal availability of abortion, a slight shift away from paternalism in social welfare policy, the move by disadvantaged groups of all kinds to demand empowerment, etc. For couples of African-American, Native American, or Hispanic origin, there remains a surplus of babies for adoption. For certain Asian ethnic groups international adoption can provide an opportunity to adopt a same-ethnicity infant. But statistics have changed dramatically for European-American couples. And for all couples the risks that a baby born apparently healthy may later develop problems brought about by poor prenatal care, in utero exposure to drugs and alcohol, or may develop AIDS are higher today than they were in the past. Today various sources claim that there are between 25 and 40 couples waiting to adopt every available healthy, Caucasian infant. This statistical swing has produced the need for couples to realistically examine their wishes and limitations about parenting and to consider whether they could consider expanding their horizons. But that is a hard thing to do, and it isn't the right choice for many people.

In fact, just in case no one else around you tells you this, let me make absolutely clear what I think about the push to get infertile never-before-parents to consider special needs adoption. Despite the changes in adoption that make inracial adoption of a healthy baby more difficult than it was twenty years ago, it is still perfectly normal, perfectly healthy, perfectly acceptable to make the decision that the right way for you to begin parenting is with a healthy newborn baby matched racially to you. Still ... it doesn't hurt to think about those other options, so that, if you do decide to reject them (for now at least) you will have done so not out of panicky fear and ignorance, but after reasoned exploration, discussion and decision making.

Boy or Girl?

Now here's a place where a couple can exert some of that lost control! You can indeed choose your baby's sex if you choose. This can be a real advantage to those for whom lost control is a big deal—or to some couples it can be absolutely unimportant.

Deciding to specify boy or girl will have only a small impact on your chances of adopting. In general, in North America slightly more boys are available for adoption than girls (might it be because a single birthmother feels she might be more able to parent a daughter alone?) In many parts of the world, however—Asia and South America, Africa and the Indian subcontinent—cultures where girls are much less valued than are boys, there are many more adoptable girls than boys.

It's not at all unusual for people to have a preference about the sex of their children. Actually, research shows that most parents expecting by birth do have a preference about whether their child will be a boy or a girl. But the attitudes toward sex selection of first children is opposite between parents who give birth and parents who adopt. When pregnant couples expecting a first baby are asked in opinion polls whether they prefer a boy or a girl, even in Western cultures, boy children still tend to be more desired than girls. But the reverse has been and continues to be true in adoption! More couples express a preference for girls than for boys. This is not true just in international adoption, where it has long been openly discussed, but also in domestic infant adoption.

Why would it be that adopting couples might prefer a girl to a boy, when birthing couples seem to prefer a boy to a girl child? It has been speculated that for some couples this is a reaction to their loss of genetic continuity. Boy children are still perceived as the continuers of family—carrying a family name from generation to generation. Girl children, whose names are still frequently changed at marriage, do not carry the same responsibility for family continuity. Is it easier for a man feeling the blow of the ending of his family blood line to adopt a girl than a boy? Is it easier for extended families to accept the adoption of girls than boys?

While couples adopting a first child less frequently specify sex, seeming to prefer instead to be surprised, just as couples are when they give birth, couples adopting a second child (either after a first adoption or in the case of those adopting after secondary infertility) very often find it empowering to make this choice. It is not uncommon for such couples who have children to specify a particular sex as their preference.

———

Karen had always seen herself as the mother of a daughter. Through all those long years of infertility she mourned what she feared would be the loss of the little girl with long hair to braid, a shared interest in flowers—all those things she'd dreamed about as a little girl playing with dolls.

On their third cycle of GIFT, Karen conceived twin sons born healthy. She and Roger were thrilled, but Karen didn't feel "finished." When the boys were five, Roger suggested GIFT again, but Karen knew what she needed, and Roger agreed. They adopted a two year old girl, Angelina, from Colombia.

———

Actually, there are some very practical reasons beyond just having the power to decide why many adoptive parents think about the sex of their children in relationship to one another.

●●●●●●●●●●●●●●●●

Barry remembered vividly how he was compared to his two-years-older brother Brian in grade school. Brian was smart and athletic and gregarious. Barry was quiet, awkward, and painfully shy. It seemed that almost every teacher remembered Brian, and Barry remembered their reactions as being *"You're* Brian's brother? Wow! I'd never have guessed!"* He had always felt that he was being negatively compared.

Barry didn't want to see that happen to his own children, and he figured two same sex kids were more likely to be compared than two differently sexed siblings. Furthermore, it seemed to Barry that if his children were genetically unrelated, the likelihood of their being very different from one another was even greater than it had been for himself and Brian.

Yes, Barry wanted this second child to be a son—not necessarily because he had always wanted a son, but because he didn't want his much-loved daughter, adopted at birth, or her younger sibling to feel the pain that he had felt as a child.

●●●●●●●●●●●●●●●●

It is probably a good idea for you to examine your motivations for wanting a child of a particular sex—not because having a preference is wrong, but because it is always valuable to understand why we feel as we do. In adoption, understanding our motivations contributes greatly to our ability to build a sense of entitlement.

A Baby? Maybe Not!

Of course you thought about a baby—it was logical. But what about an older child? Have you considered the older children who wait? Rumors abound, and the stories one hears are awful. Some are true. Some of these kids have indeed had horrible beginnings. Abandoned or willingly placed by birthparents simply unable to make it, or taken against their parents' will due to abuse or neglect, some waiting children have been moved from family member to family member or from foster home to foster home for years. But myth exaggerates fact. Some of these kids have had pretty good starts and relatively stable relationships with long term caregivers. Perhaps they started out in a stable birth family relationship which has now dissolved due to illness, death, divorce, unemployment or any one of dozens of other factors. Perhaps they've lived nearly all their lives in one foster home with a set of well trained interim caregivers while the agency tried to help the birthfamily get itself together.

Love does not conquer all, but the truth is that with appropriate education, parent preparation and post adoption services from a really good agency which will respect your need for full disclosure and honesty from them; with the support of a good adoptive parents' group; with a commitment on your and your partner's part to advocate for yourselves and your child, adopting an older child can be completely successful.

Before beginning to inquire about the photolisting books that catalog specific waiting children, begin the decision making process. In order to clarify your goals in parenting, and taking into account your personal fears, your personal needs, your specific situation regarding age and health, where you live, careers, etc. each of you should try to list any and all benefits you can think of in adopting a baby (e.g. having the opportunity to be the child's only psychological parent, babies are so easy for everyone to relate to, etc.) Then list the disadvantages that each of you sees in beginning with a baby (e.g. we'll be older than our child's peers' parents, we'd have to deal with day care problems, etc.)

Next list any and all benefits you can think of in adopting an older child (e.g. we get out of the dirty diaper and two o'clock feeding stage and go straight to the good stuff like Cub Scouts and making gingerbread houses, we won't have to interrupt careers with significantly long parenting leaves, etc.) and any and all disadvantages you can see to starting with an older child (e.g. we won't have control over what's happened in his past, our parents may not relate well to her, etc.)

Really investigate both your community and the agencies which specialize in special needs placements. Is there a strong post-adoption program? Are mental health providers in your town adoption-educated and adoption-sensitive? If you are considering a child with physical or learning disabilities, how are the educational and social services? What kinds of specially-focused programs exist for kids with problems, and how do parents using them feel about them? Speak to local adoptive parents groups and speak to the leaders of any local support groups which focus on the kinds of needs you are considering taking on.

In order to find the resources which can answer these questions, make contact with both Adoptive Families of America and the North American Council on Adoptable Children to ask for a referral to their affiliated parent group nearest you. Also strongly consider attending one of NACAC's annual North American Conferences on Adoptable Children, held every year in August at rotating sites throughout North America. This is the largest special needs adoption conference in the world. It is here that you will come in contact with the world's most well respected experts in the field, all of whom provide wonderful training, but several of whom have not written books or articles easily accessible to consumers. If you are seriously looking for the most expert information about adopting an older child, watch for and ask about the names Elizabeth (Betsy) Cole, Kathryn (Kay) Donley, Vera Fahlberg, Claudia Jewett-Jarratt, Jim Mahoney, Bernard and Joan McNamara, Barb Tremitiere. If you are unable to attend a specialized conference on special needs adoption, contact von Ende Communications about a catalog of audio tapes of past NACAC and AFA conferences which will allow you to take advantage of the knowledge and training of these professionals.

An agency which has expertise in special needs adoption and has a strong post adopt program should be mentioning the possibility of subsidies to help with any problems or ongoing counseling. Expect to hear terms like *life book, disengagement therapy, attachment disorder, attachment therapy,* and more. Expect to be referred to the books and tapes of some of the experts mentioned before. If you don't hear these things from your agency, bring them up. If you feel that your agency does not immediately understand what you are talking about and cannot actively engage in discussion about this, consider this a red flag!

———————

Leah and Ned lived in a small town served mainly by the public agency. There weren't many babies, but their caseworker was more than delighted to share the state's photolisting book of waiting children. Leah and Ned were swept into the adoption of Mia, a three year old described as bright, mischievous and affectionate, after waiting for several years and losing hope that there would ever be a newborn.

"Mia just needs undivided attention and a lot of love," the caseworker assured them. "You'll do fine."

Mia was affectionate, all right—indiscriminately so, and especially with men, even strangers. She masturbated in public—even at church. She was cuddly with her new daddy, but she was aloof from Leah. She was sneaky—hoarding food and seeming to deliberately look for ways to be naughty, which brought her attention—the negative kind.

Leah approached the agency, but no one there had any ideas, "Just be consistent and give her lots of love," they said.

Leah and Ned were dealing with a child who had been sexually abused—but they didn't know that. They needed special therapy—but none was available. Their child was unattached, though not unattachable—but no one was supporting them in getting the help they needed. Love was not enough. The adoption disrupted and Leah and Ned felt like complete failures—afraid to try parenting again.

Leah and Ned had not decided on a special needs adoption. They had settled for one. Furthermore, their agency had prepared them badly, withheld important information from them, and failed to provide the support and post-adopt services this family needed and deserved. The disruption of Leah, Ned, and Mia's adoption wasn't their fault. It was a failure of the system. But the system can and does work.

At 48 and 32, Rich and Maryanne were each in a second marriage. Neither had children and both wanted to parent, but Rich's age had been a factor which blocked them from applying for a baby at several agencies. They had optimistically pursued private adoption, but had given up when three birthparents expressed hesitance because Rich was older than their own fathers, whom they sure didn't want to parent their babies. On investigating international adoption, they discovered that Rich's age was a factor with nearly all of the countries local agencies could help them with.

They were about to give up when they ran into an adoption worker they knew socially at a party and she laughed, "Have I got a ten year old for you!" She was kidding, of course, but it got them thinking.

At 48, Rich still harbored a desire to be a Little League coach for his son's team. He wondered if he'd be as physically fit at 55 or 60. Maryanne had spent a lot of time getting her small business off the ground. She was its key employee; it was going to be difficult for her to arrange to be home full time with an infant for a while and then juggle day care for six years.

Looking through the photolisting books, they found Morrie, an eight year old boy from a state half way across the country. He was healthy and handsome, but hyperactive and dyslexic. The foster mother with whom he had lived since the age of four months was elderly and ailing. He had to move.

It sounded challenging, but they decided to check it out. Their research produced some encouraging news. Their city had a well respected private school that specialized in dyslexia. A significant proportion of its graduates went on to college. A subsidy which was a part of Morrie's adoption planning would help to offset the tuition. The local agency put Rich and Maryanne in touch with an active adoptive parents' group, and they discovered that there was a smaller support group within the group for families of children adopted at an older age. Their pediatrician spoke with Morrie's current doctor and was reassured that drug therapy effectively managed his attention deficit/hyperactivity disorder. The Little League needed another coach. Morrie, Rich and Maryanne became a family.

You do yourself a serious disservice if you don't realistically look at the option of adopting an older child. But do so in light of what you know about your resources—time, money, emotional reserves, physical capacities—and about your community's resources as identified from your research. It is perfectly reasonable that the result of this soul searching might be to decide that you want to parent a baby.

Sure, healthy is easiest, but health is a relative thing. What represents compromise to you? Where is the line over which you just can't go?

First, be realistic. It is utterly impossible for an agency or intermediary or a birthparent to guarantee you a completely healthy child. Children who are born apparently healthy, whose gene pools do not indicate the likelihood of impairments, regularly develop illnesses and conditions that could not be predicted. This happens in families of the sturdiest stock and to mothers with the best of prenatal care. There are no guarantees in parenting. Your ability to be as flexible as possible in this area will significantly increase your odds of becoming a parent sooner and of a younger child. And, you know, that flexibility is going to come in handy when you do become a parent—by birth or by adoption!

Agencies will definitely ask you to carefully consider your limitations regarding the health and abilities of a child. They will likely provide you with checklists filled with the names of illnesses and disabilities and ask you to check off yes or no or maybe. What they will not likely do is offer you any specific information about the problems on those lists.

Here's more homework for you! Once again consider AFA and NACAC and their referrals to local parent groups your first line resources. Contact your local United Way or other community clearinghouse and ask for referral to agencies and support groups dealing with the health problems which you would like to further explore. Talk directly to parents dealing with these problems. In doing so you will discover that the vast majority of things on those lists are problems that can range in severity from quite minor to overwhelmingly disabling. But as well, some things that could appear on the surface to be fully correctable or purely cosmetic can be symptomatic of far more serious conditions.

━━━━━━━━━━

Jessie and Vic were pretty clear—perfectly healthy babies were what they wanted. Three of them— as closely matched to them as possible. To assure that, they were pretty certain about their expectations from a birthparent, too. She wasn't to have drunk or smoked or taken drugs during pregnancy. They wanted a full family social and medical history on each birthparent.

Because of their clearly defined limits, they had ruled out international adoption (too many of those babies were abandoned, so health and prenatal history weren't available). They had ruled out parent-initiated private adoption because they were unwilling to commit to a birthparent during her pregnancy—they wanted to be sure the baby was healthy. So Jessie and Vic were waiting in line at a traditional private agency practicing confidential adoption.

Their group homestudy included four other couples, all of whom were told to expect that they would likely receive a baby within a year of approval. The first couple to adopt got a gorgeous little boy. The second couple's little girl had bright red hair. The third couple received tiny twins born four weeks prematurely. The fourth couple adopted a biracial boy.

Sixteen months after the end of their home- study, Jessie and Vic still waited. They had discovered that couples who had been in the group following theirs had already received placements! They went to see their caseworker. "Well, we wouldn't have been able to deal with the biracial baby," Jessie said, "but those other kids would have been perfect! When will it be our turn?"

"To be honest," came the reply, "we didn't think of you for any of these children. The backgrounds of all of them included something on your listed limitations. The first boy's birthfather's family had a strong history of strabismus (crossed eye), but the baby didn't appear to have the problem, and this couple figured that was correctable if it showed up later. The little girl with red hair sure wouldn't have looked like you at all, and would have drawn comments from others. Besides, we couldn't make contact with the alleged birthfather and so we had no medical history on him. The twins were so small and so early that there was a significant risk of problems. They spent some time in the preemie nursery, where their adopting parents were able to visit daily to feed and hold them."

Vic and Jessie reevaluated their list, and one month later they were the parents of a little girl. When the call came, they had been hesitant. Hers had been a difficult birth and she had a dislocated hip. But they called the pediatrician they had preselected and asked him to look at the records and the family history and he was encouraging. APGAR scores were good. Baby would be in a cast for a while, but she would be a fully functioning, rambunctious toddler in no time.

My advice is this: the more *maybes* you check, the better! If your answers are mostly *no's* you're going to be called only when pure perfection is available. If your answers are *yes* or *maybe*, you'll probably be on the short list for a lot of possibilities. Remember, you can *always* say no to a specific situation that just feels wrong. This is something over which you have absolute control. (No, it won't necessarily be easy to allow yourself to do this.) You can always take the time to fully investigate the health issues presented to you before saying yes or no to the adoption. On the other hand, you can't say yes to something you don't even know about!

If possible, establish rapport with the physician who will be your child's pediatrician before your child arrives. Choosing a pediatrician who is knowledgeable about adoption issues can be important for any family. It may become even more important if you are adopting a child with emotional problems or a child from another country. Speak with other adoptive parents about their pediatricians. Ask if s/he would be willing to review health and birth records and offer a medical opinion before you accept a placement. If you are adopting a newborn, sometimes your doctor will be willing and able to check the baby out in the hospital—even in situations where you yourself are not yet allowed in. If you are not able to engage a pediatrician before your child's arrival, ask your own primary care physician if he or she would be willing either to examine these records or to refer you to specialized help if need be.

Race or Ethnicity

The issue of race matching in adoption inspires—a better word may even be *incites*—both a political and moral debate. The facts are clear. While European-American babies are at a premium and Caucasian adopters are lined up 25 to 40 deep to adopt them, there are significant numbers of minority children—particularly African-American, Hispanic, and Native American—waiting for adoption in the United States while minority families are not at the same time waiting to adopt. Throughout the world in third world nations and now in the European countries struggling from behind what was once the Iron Curtain, millions of babies and children cry out for parents.

minority families, who experience poverty and lack of education in much higher proportionate numbers than do white families, are more at risk for the problems that lead to separation of parents and children. While minority families have been reluctant to adopt through the system (partially because recruitment among minority families has been poorly done at best) minority communities have, historically, practiced informal adoption—"taking care of our own"—at a high rate.

Keeping in mind that society looks upon adoption as a service for children, not a service for adults, the solutions to the problem of waiting children are controversial. While a number of European-American couples have expressed interest in adopting minority children, professionals in the minority community are resistant to such actions. Is transracial adoption in the best interests of a child?

Native Americans concerned about the large numbers of children adopted by whites and removed from their cultural heritage successfully lobbied for the passage in 1978 of the Indian Child Welfare Act, a special law which, recognizing the sovereignty of Indian nations, gives tribes the absolute power to make foster and adoptive placement decisions about their children and discourages the placement of Native American children with families who are not themselves Native American. The National Association of Black Social Workers has called transracial adoption a form of cultural genocide and has fought unsuccessfully for similar protection. While child advocates in some states, such as Michigan, have successfully defeated official policies which require the placement of minority children in minority homes, some states, notably Minnesota, have passed cultural heritage acts which mandate that agencies must go to tremendous lengths to place children in families of like ethnic backgrounds. Several states, including my own, Indiana, have been threatened with civil rights suits by prospective adopting parents angry about policies on placement of minority children.

Elizabeth Bartholet, an adoptive parent who is a professor of law at Harvard University, met the issues head on in an article she wrote for the *University of Pennsylvania Law Review* (Volume 139, Number 5: May, 1991). Ms Bartholet writes in "Where Do Black Children Belong? The Politics of Race Matching in Adoption." Her article has inspired much needed discussion.

My thesis is that current racial matching policies
represent a coming together of powerful and related
ideologies—old fashioned white racism, modern-day

black nationalism, and what I will call "biologism"—the idea that what is "natural" in the context of the biological family is what is normal and desirable in the context of adoption. Biological families have same-race parents and children. The law and policies surrounding adoption in this country have generally structured adoption in imitation of biology, giving the adopted child a new birth certificate as if the child had been born to the adoptive parents, sealing off the birthparents as if they had never existed, and attempting to match adoptive parents and children with respect to looks, intellect and religion. The implicit goal has been to create an adoptive family which will resemble as much as possible "the real thing"—the "natural" or biological family that it is not. These laws and policies reflect, I believe, widespread and powerful feelings that parent-child relationships can only work, or at least will work best, between biologic likes. They also reflect widespread and powerful fears that parents will not be able to truly love and nurture biologic unlikes. These feelings and fears have much in common with the feelings and fears among both blacks and whites in our society about the danger of crossing racial boundaries. It is thus understandable that there would be much support for racial matching in the adoption context.[1]

But all of this has been politics! Most infertile people aren't adopting out of any political motivation. They are adopting in order to become parents! It is easy for couples desperate to adopt a child to make an idealistic leap of faith. "A child is a child. Kids grow better in families, and these are kids without families. Give me this child to love."

The reality of transracial or transethnic adoption is really much different. Love does not conquer all. The problems inherent in interracial dating or interracial marriage are also a part of interracial adoption. In either case, the result is a multiracial or biracial family.

In Chapter Four I mentioned Jim Mahoney's discussion of the adult learning model (moving from unconscious incompetence to conscious incompetence to conscious competence to unconscious competence.) In his trainings he often applies this concept to racial issues. Most well educated North Americans of European heritage are completely unaware of the extent of racism in this culture.

Many couples who would not even consider adopting an
American Black child adopt internationally from Asia, India, South America without considering it a transracial or transethnic placement. Often these decisions are made in a state of unconscious incompetence about racism in North America. Since much of American racism is based upon an often unacknowledged hierarchy of skin shade, these adopters believe of their children adopted from overseas that because they are not of African Negro heritage (not true of most adoptable South American children), and because they will be lighter of skin than American people of African heritage (also frequently untrue) that these children and their families will experience little if any prejudice. It is not until their growing children run smack into racism that such naive adopters are brought up short.

Dave and I adopted Lindsey, of African-American and Hispanic heritage, feeling comfortable that we knew what we were doing. We knew other transracial adopters, we knew people of color, we lived in an integrated community and were committed to continuing to do so.

Thinking that we were consciously competent, I realize now that we were probably somewhere between unconscious incompetence and conscious incompetence in our understanding of racial issues. Truth be told, in making the decision, early on we focused a lot on the fact that her birthmother, with whom we would have an open adoption, was after all, Hispanic, not Black. Lindsey, we reasoned then, was Hispanic. Wasn't that "easier" in the part of the country in which we live?

The fact is that Lindsey looks exactly like her handsome African-American birthfather. While her Hispanic heritage is an important and wonderful and positive part of who she is, to the world at large she will always be recognized and reacted to as an African American person, so that it is really important that she comes to identify herself positively in this way.

We were quite unprepared for the silent blatancy of racism until we became a family of color. Early on we were not surprised to find that when we went out as a family—white Mom, white Dad, two white children and black baby—there was a great deal of positive attention of the aren't-you-people-wonderful, isn't-she-cute variety. On the other hand, we were shocked to find that when one parent went out with baby, reactions from both black and white people were cold and standoffish. There was a definite unspoken criticism, which we finally came to understand came from the assumption that they were observing an adult involved in a transracial sexual relationship.

It is one thing to share, as I still do, the family-of-man ideals of many transracial adopters, who loudly—and accurately—point out that biracial children are genetically no more black or brown or yellow or red than they are white and argue for an acceptance of biracial people as a group separate and equal to either of the races of which they are blended. It is quite another to deal yourself and help your children learn to deal with day-to-day racism based on their perceived minority heritage.

In her article Bartholet refers to a number of studies which have attempted to measure the success of transracial adoptions. These same studies are also cited in Cheri Register's excellent book on international transethnic adoption *Are Those Kids Yours: American Families with Children Adopted from Other Countries* (The Free Press, 1991). Most of these studies produce similar results: transracial adoptions are successful (when measured by children's self esteem and cultural pride) to the degree to which adopting parents are willing to make themselves culturally competent—willing to learn about, live within, and embrace the culture and the people of a child's minority background. If you are considering a transethnic domestic or international adoption, you should read the studies that Register and Bartholet digest for you, you should speak directly to local families who have adopted transracially, and you should either attend an AFA or NACAC conference or you should listen to the appropriate audiotapes from recent conferences on these issues.

Developing cultural competence means being sensitive to the issues surrounding moving an Asian child to a rural American community. It means understanding the problems inherent in sending an African-American child to an all white private school. It means developing a willingness—no, an excited interest—in living in an integrated community, eating ethnic foods, extending one's circle of support and friendship to include people of color, and more. For most middle and upper middle class people of European heritage, developing cultural competence will not be easy, because the fact is that most of us are much more racist than we care to believe.

No matter how hard we, her white parents, work to develop cultural competence, to a large extent Lindsey will grow up precisely what the derogatory term *Oreo* refers to—black on the outside, white within. I've heard similar terms, *Twinkie* and *banana*, used to describe Asian people who are immersed in white culture.

I quite like the approach of adoptive parent (of Korean-born children) Gregory Gross on this issue. Writing in the March/April 1992 issue of *Interrace*, Gross says that he sees his task as teaching his children to value their outside coating so that they can value their inside core. The banana skin (or the Oreo outside) will be tough, the filling soft and sweet.[2]

We desperately love our child. She is ours in the same gut-wrenching, I'd-die-for-her way as are our other two children. We feel that we are good parents, and you would never get us to go so far as to say that we were not the best parents Lindsey could have. On the other hand, we are ready to admit that we were typical educated white liberals—very idealistic, very naive. We are working as hard as we can.

Adopting transracially can be a beautiful way to form a family. It has been a successful way to form families for thousands of parents and thousands of children. But for exactly the same reasons that interracial marriage is not for everyone, transracial adoption is not the right choice for every couple. It is perfectly reasonable for you to decide that you wish to pursue an inracial adoption.

Muddied Thinking about Choosing a Type of Child

One of the most important reasons for the inability of many infertile couples to consider special needs adoption is that they are normal. Like everyone else they have fears, doubts, and prejudices. As a group they have the same needs, dreams, and values as do fertile couples. Proportionately, then, they are no more likely to see special needs adoption as a family building option of first choice than are their fertile counterparts.

Since friends, neighbors, family members look at adoption as second best and for the most part reject it as a family building alternative for themselves, infertile couples are frequently unable to see themselves as potential adopters of waiting children either. They often hold a buried feeling that they are being treated as "second class citizens" offered what society sees as "second rate goods" rejected by everyone else, but seen as "all they can get" or "all they deserve." This too-negative-to-voice feeling is a part of the traditional adopter's feeling of powerlessness, but it is fed by the approach to special needs adoption taken by most agencies.

Special needs adoptions are usually faster than infant adoption; there are fewer requirements and qualification to meet; agency fees are often lower or nonexistent; subsidies often exist which appear to "pay" people to accept such children. To the couple looking from the outside, not able even to get close enough to the realities of special needs adoption to be properly educated, and thus primed to misinterpret what little they do know, such facts and fantasies are frightening and even demeaning.

Parenting is never easy, but it becomes more difficult when the baggage of several years spent with other families, racial differences, or profound disabilities is added to it. This is the primary reason that the vast majority of parents considering family expansion prefer to do so by giving birth over and over again rather than by adopting children already born and in need of homes. All of society accepts this reasoning on the part of fertile couples and do not think poorly of them when they choose not to adopt.

The common value system declares that birth is superior to adoption as a method of family planning. Most people, then, are delighted but somewhat surprised by the fertile couple who chooses to adopt rather than to give birth to some of their children and tend to heap praise and admiration on such adopters ("Aren't you people wonderful to take that child! I don't know how you do it. I don't think I could, but I'm sure glad that there are people out there like you!") while at the same time viewing their motivations as somewhat suspect. ("Why would you want to take someone else's reject when you could have a baby? You're asking for trouble.")

Because infertility often damages self esteem, infertile couples, who have not had the opportunity to parent by the traditional method, often harbor the unexpressed fear that they will be unable to do a good job. Some even feel, as I did briefly, that their infertility was a signal from God that they wouldn't make good parents. They desperately want to get as close to the "real thing" as they can in order to test their fitness for parenting. Children with special problems, such couples feel, need special parenting skills, and they question whether they have the ability to acquire such skills. Some professionals question this as well.

And finally, adoption is often difficult for extended families to accept in principle. Couples sometimes feel that they have let their families down with their infertility and thus fear being rejected by them. They feel that a baby—one of their own ethnicity—might be more easily accepted by their families, allowing both themselves and their children to experience the "realness" of multigenerational family dynamics that they might miss out on if their family did not accept a special needs adoptee. While this is a solvable problem, and indeed we will spend some time talking specifically about bringing families along in the adoption experience, the fact that this fear is rooted not in myth but in reality makes it a difficult fear to erase.

The facts are clear. Waiting children, who were once seen as unadoptable and shuffled off to institutions with little attempt to find adoptive homes for them, exist in large numbers. In the last couple of decades child welfare advocates have done an admirable job of changing professional attitudes about such children, Now, permanency is the goal for every child, and caseworkers are pressured to find homes for these children.

Many prospective adopters comment that they felt uncomfortably pressured by their agencies to consider special needs adoption. Rarely is such pressure intended or consequential. In most cases the sense of pressure comes as a result of adopters feeling their own sense of guilt in response to the reasonable suggestion from agency workers that couples give at least careful thought to all of the options open to them in building a family by adoption.

Sometimes, however, the pressure is real. Social workers are real people, normal people. They share the same value system held by the majority of the society in which they live, and thus some of them send the same set of mixed messages to infertile couples that they are receiving from family and friends. Frustrated by the need to find homes for children in need of them and faced with increasing numbers of potential adopters inquiring about the almost nonexistent "Gerber baby," adoption workers wish that the ideal could be met: that children in need of homes and couples who want children could meet each other's needs. Faced with this practical crisis, adoption workers sometimes subconsciously buy into the old adage "beggars can't be choosers" as they consider infertile couples in the adoption approval process. The message goes out, this time not just from the uninformed neighbor, but from the most powerful person in their lives, "If you really wanted a child, you'd take one of those homeless kids they advertise in the papers."

So the double standard which has always been at work in society at large has filtered down to some social work professionals. An adoption worker who would not judge negatively a fertile couple's decision to give birth rather than to adopt an older child reacts impatiently toward, and even questions the motivation for parenthood of, the infertile couples seeking a healthy infant, and the credibility gap widens.

Just as you carefully explored all of your choices in medical treatment, it makes sense that you would do yourself the service of fully exploring the entire range of adoptions, but understand that ultimately only you can decide whether to adopt a baby or a waiting child.

Adoption itself is an enormous leap! Few fertile people have the courage to make that leap. Leaping even farther—to create a multiracial family, to accept the challenges of parenting a child who comes to you with several years' worth of less than optimal parenting experiences—takes superior courage. Since infertile people are perfectly normal people, there is no reason to presume that they will be prepared to make this leap in numbers proportionately higher than the fertile population.

Obviously, the decisions to be made are enormous, and they are made more difficult by the complexities of infertility and the process of adopting itself. In order to make these decisions, you will find it helpful to work on the decision making process of developing goals and objectives, examining alternatives and strategies, and allocating resources again. In addition to the material I share here, at the end of this section you will find a selected list of recommended resources which will help you in the data collection process that is part of your decision making routine. These materials will help you to examine in more detail the various adoption options which you find yourselves willing to explore, and they will offer quite practical advice for pursuing your objectives.

Adopting a Second Child

For first time parents, decisions about sex, about age, about ableness, about ethnicity of their children are probably more complex and difficult to make than are those same decisions for couples who are adopting for the second or third or fourth time. Oftentimes, though certainly not universally, second time adopters find that they are feeling much more flexible about many of these issues.

There are a number of reasons for this common change in flexibility, but the big one is clear—experience. The lack of experience about parenting that made infertile non-parents so needy of getting as close to the "real" thing disappears when one has successfully parented for a while. Babies grow quickly, and, usually, so does love. It becomes easier, with experience, to imagine being successful with a slightly older child, to understand falling in love with a child of a different skin tone. It is clear, for most, that adoption is a real and solid way for families to be formed.

This is often less true for secondarily infertile couples adopting after having given birth to a first child. For these couples, adoption itself remains the great and frightening unknown. While they are often more confident in their competence with parenting skills, they are often every bit as frightened as are infertiles who become parents for the first time through adoption about those nearly unspeakable fears—Can I love a child not genetically related to me? Can the rest of my family? Will I be a real parent to this child? For couples dealing with secondary infertility, perhaps the best resources for exploring concerns and finding support are not infertile couples who have already adopted (but have never given birth), but instead preferential adopters—fertile couples who have chosen to expand their families by adoption despite their continued ability to expand it by birth.

The final decisions about the sex, age, ableness, race of your child are yours. Beyond the unforeseen circumstances that become a part of any parenting experience you have enormous control and power here. In order to exercise that power and control, you must be well informed and willing to demand your right and the right of your child to full disclosure of any and all pertinent facts from the intermediaries involved in your adoption. You are *not* a beggar, you are a *chooser* in this case! Be sure that you make careful and clear decisions that you will be able and willing to claim as your own, whatever they may be.

7

Choosing a
Style of Adoption

Deciding how to adopt involves understanding the variations of process and style that are available. Having covered some important issues about the professionals who work in the field of adoption and carefully examining the options in deciding what kind of child to adopt, this chapter will look at the choices open to you in selecting a style of adoption.

To begin, a word of caution. Laws vary from state to state or province to province, and most assuredly from country to country. Additionally, terminology varies from place to place and differences in various local usages can cause some confusion. I have tried, whenever possible, to choose to use most consistently the labels and terms which will be clearest to the largest number of potential readers of this book, while at the same time at least mentioning the alternatives which might be considered synonymous. You must understand from the outset that before you can choose a style you must be absolutely clear about what is legal in the place where you live!

Agency Adoption or Independent Adoption

In general, the term *agency adoption* refers to the situation in which adopters and birthparents are brought together because each came independently of one another seeking the services of an agency licensed by the government to facilitate adoptions. There are both public agencies and private agencies. Until recently all licensed adoption agencies were also registered not-for-profit organizations, though now in the U.S. a few states do provide for the licensing of for-profit organizations as adoption agencies.

Public agencies are supported by the tax dollars of a state, province, or municipality and may also receive federal funds. Often these agencies carry names like Whatever County Department of Family and Children's Services or State Children's Services or Department of Welfare, or Children's Aid Society, etc. Public agencies serve the public at large, but this does not mean that they do not have requirements and prerequisites for adopters. Those prerequisites, though, are generally more flexible than those of many private agencies. Though public agencies rarely directly accept applications to adopt from people who are not legal residents of their tax base service area, they do work cooperatively with agencies in other geographic locations to arrange placements of special needs children.

Agencies referred to as *private agencies* are supported by funds other than tax dollars from sources such adoption fees or United Way or a religious or fraternal or family foundation benefactor (for example Jewish Social Services or Latter Day Saints Social Services or Lutheran Family Services or Salvation Army Adoption Services or Spence Chapin Agency, etc.) Sectarian private agencies are religiously connected and may or may not serve only clients of that faith. Nonsectarian agencies have no connection with a particular religion. Private agencies do not serve the public at large, but most often do serve a rather large pool of people who meet requirements set by their boards of directors.

Both public agencies and private agencies facilitate both the adoptions of healthy babies and the adoptions of children with special needs, although some private agencies do specialize (for example Aid to Adoption of Special Kids focuses on special needs placements and Homes for Black Children recruits minority adopters for minority children). With increasing frequency more agency-arranged infant placements are occurring through private agencies (which are often able to offer the birthmother more financial support and/or private medical care as opposed to clinic care) and fewer through public agencies.

Fees at agencies are set by their boards of directors, and vary widely. Some publicly supported agencies charge no fees at all and others charge minimal fees. Some private agencies are able to keep fees lower by subsidizing them through private donations or contributions from sponsoring religious bodies. Fees may be figured as a percentage of income, as a flat fee, or totalled from a fee-for-services menu.

Agencies, public or private, set their own policies about openness and there is a wide variation among these policies, some of which are influenced by the laws of individual states. Some agencies facilitate open adoptions and many also provide for full confidentiality.

An *independent adoption* is one which occurs outside of the licensed agency process. (In the U.S., this process is also often called a *private adoption.* I have chosen not to use this term to describe non agency adoption, however, since in the large Canadian province of Ontario the term *private adoption* involves non-agency "licensees" who are both attorneys and social workers and the process is more akin either to what in the U.S. is most often called direct adoption or to our private agency adoption, though on a much smaller scale).

In a non-agency or independent adoption either the birth and adoptive parents found each other directly, or they were put in touch by an intermediary who does not work for a licensed child placing agency. Intermediaries may be friends and neighbors, members of the clergy, physicians, attorneys, independent social workers, and, increasingly, people who call themselves adoption consultants. Sometimes independent adoptions are the result of serendipitous connections between friends of friends. Adoptions without the assistance of an agency are prohibited in several U.S. states and Canadian provinces. Sometimes this means that residents of states where adoption without an agency is not sanctioned cannot adopt independently in other states, either. At this writing only Connecticut, Delaware, Massachusetts, Michigan, and North Dakota completely prohibit independent adoptions, but adoptions without agencies are an issue of such concern to many people that bills to prohibit them are introduced every year in dozens of state legislatures. Be certain to check your state's current law before investing your self too heavily in an independent adoption.

Some adoption intermediaries who operate as businesses do maintain a matching service much like that of an adoption agency, though, in the U.S., at least, they are not licensed as adoption agencies. More and more often independent adoptions occur as the result of adoptive parents themselves spreading the word about their interest in adoption until they are contacted directly by a birthparent. This contact may be arranged in a way that maintains anonymity and confidentiality, or the adopters may choose an open adoption arrangement involving varying degrees of communication between birth and adoptive families.

Financially, because independent adoptions involve negotiating the transfer of parental rights directly from a set of birthparents to a set of adopting parents, most of those working in adoption believe that independent adoptions should always involve payment only for direct services and that suggested flat fees ("I can get a baby for you for $20,000") are morally and ethically wrong. Flat fees may even violate many states' laws.

This may initially seem confusing, since adoption agencies commonly charge flat fees or percentage of income fees. When fees which are collected by a licensed agency represent a "surplus" over and above the actual expenses for a particular adoption, that "surplus" is not considered a "profit", since it used to help defray the cost of state licensed services provided to birthparents who did not make adoption plans. State laws prohibit either unlicensed intermediaries or birthparents from profiting in adoptions. Attorneys can charge their normal hourly rates for legal services, counselors for mental health services, physicians for the medical care they provide, consultants for training they may offer, but no one can charge something in the nature of a "finder's fee" for the service of bringing adopters and birthparents together. Furthermore, states have specific regulations about just what expenses of birthparents may be reimbursed. Some will allow for the payment of living expenses or clothing allowances and others will not. Birthparents are prohibited in every state from exchanging their parental rights for money or cars or tuition, etc. Before agreeing to anything, be absolutely certain of your own state or province's law!

Whether you adopt through an agency or independently, you will in every U.S. state need to have some kind of official assessment of your home, your qualifications for adoption, and your readiness to parent (see Chapter Eight.) In agency adoptions this always occurs significantly before placement and continues after the placement of the child with several months of what is called a supervision period before the adoption is finalized. It is becoming increasingly common for courts in places where independent adoption is an alternative to require a pre-placement homestudy for independent adopters, too, though in many places the homestudy in a non-agency adoption continues to occur by court order after the placement of the child and before finalization.

In recent years, in response to the needs and wishes of birthparents and adopters living in states where independent adoption is illegal, a hybrid of agency and independent adoption has been developed. This hybrid is sometimes called *direct adoption* or *designated adoption* or *identified adoption*. What this means is that adoptive parents and birthparents who have come in contact with one another directly or through an intermediary go together to a licensed child placing agency or licensed social worker and ask for the services of that professional in obtaining the counseling, preparation, and legal services necessary in order to arrange a legal adoption.

Since this hybrid mandates the involvement of government licensed or sanctioned service providers, U.S. designated adoptions come closest to duplicating the form of adoption which in the Canadian province of Ontario is called private adoption, and which should not be confused

with U.S. independent adoption, which is also often referred to as private
adoption.

Because of the wide spectrum of options within both independent adoptions and agency adoptions, deciding whether to adopt through an agency or without one requires careful soul searching and more specific information gathering. For example, the decisions you make about domestic or international adoption, about confidentiality vs openness, about your interest in being directly involved in the process vs having someone else do the negotiating and the matching, can influence the decision to use an agency or not. The requirements and the style of the agencies at which you qualify may influence this decision. How strongly you feel about being able to control the relative health of your child may mean that an independent adoption which involves a direct commitment to one pregnant birthmother is not for you. The amount of emotional or financial risk you are willing to take may influence this decision. Your feeling that time is limited may direct you away from long agency waiting lists and prompt you to actively pursue an independent adoption on your own. Money may influence this decision depending on the relative fees and expenses at the agencies or intermediaries with which you put yourself in contact. And more. Here is another place to gather as much detailed information as you possibly can and then to use the process outlined before to set goals and objectives, develop strategies, and allocate resources.

As Ron and Julie faced their infertility they came to realize that, if they had to make some choices, parenting a child from infancy was what they wanted more than a pregnancy. They evaluated their options and decided to invest their energies and financial resources into pursuing adoption. With the help of their RESOLVE support group they were guided to books to read, Adoption Forums to attend, and people to consult. They became omnivorous learners.

After having initial meetings with two adoption agencies, Ron and Julie decided that they were not comfortable giving so much control of their lives to the agency social workers, so they began pursuing independent adoption while they waited for their names to move up on the agency waiting lists.

They assessed their skills and talents and decided to write letters in search of a child. They began the process by reading more books, selecting an attorney, buying a printer for their computer, and composing letters to doctors, attorneys, college fraternities and sororities, school counselors, and anyone else they thought might come in contact with birthparents who wanted to make an adoption plan. They felt they regained lots of lost control as they spread the word of their search to family, friends, and acquaintances.

Within a year their efforts led them to an independent adoption that worked out beautifully. They brought home their healthy, same race infant directly from the hospital in an adoption which happened to cost several thousand dollars less than what would have been their agency percentage-of-income fee. They were able to develop some openness with the paternal birth family which brought them lots of satisfaction in the years to come.

Two and a half years later, they were able to adopt a second child delivered by the same doctor in the same hospital with the same attorney at about the same cost as the first adoption. Their family building complete, they proceeded to preschool, soccer, and swing sets.

At about the same time as Ron and Julie began to explore adoption, in another state Chris and Wade were considering adopting, too. They had been in treatment for a long time, and the results had been three miscarriages, the premature birth and death of a son, and a tremendous dent in their financial situation. They, too, made many calls, attended several programs, and read books.

In examining their own resources, priorities, and limitations, they came to realize that the best style of adoption for them would be a confidential one arranged by an agency. The churches of their religious faith supported an adoption agency as part of its ministry in the pro-life movement. Part of that ministry included the commitment of the churches to subsidize the costs of providing agency services to all birthparents who approached them. This meant that adoption fees were kept very low. As well, Chris and Wade did not want to risk what they feared would be the emotional devastation of the loss of another child should a birthmother change her mind after placement. The emotional protection offered by the church agency, which would make a placement only after both birthparents' parental rights were terminated, would alleviate this fear. Furthermore, they did not want to have contact with their child's birthfamily.

In Chris and Wade's case adopting through this agency would be financially and emotionally accessible to them, while the independent adoptions they had explored would not. The wait would be three years, but, looking back, they feel that the investment of that time was worth it to them. Their daughter is living proof.

At Issue

The controversy over agency vs independent adoption centers around the perceived possibility for exploitation of both birthparents and prospective adoptive parents, which of course can certainly determine whether an arrangement is made that is in a child's best interests. Vocal opponents of independent adoption are most often those who believe that only social workers, practicing not independently but in an agency where they can be properly trained and supervised can offer the education and counseling needed by birthparents and prospective adopters in considering and following through on an adoption. Critics also point out that without a licensing entity to monitor what goes on, there is the possibility for exploitation. Critics claim that birthparents can be poorly advised of their options, promised more than can be delivered. In effect, the critics say, babies can be snatched away from birthparents. Adopters, too, desperate for a baby, are at risk for exploitation. Opponents of independent adoption fear that there is a genuine risk of black market baby selling, auctioning infants to the highest bidder, or creating babies as products, when independent adoption is allowed to exist unregulated.

Those who support non-agency adoption reply that among the reasons that independent adoption has existed and has come to flourish are that too many agencies establish unnecessary or illogical hoops for adopters to jump through, that not all agency professional provide competent and compassionate service, and that not all birthparents and not all adopters want the education and counseling services of social workers. These clients feel that they should not be required by law to submit to this control over their family planning when couples who choose to become pregnant and give birth do not. They point out the courts are responsible for monitoring both the expenses in an adoption and the proper termination of parental rights by birthparents and thus can and should prevent the inappropriate termination of parental rights or the sale of babies.

There is much to be said for all of these arguments—pro and con. Licensing by a state does not a good professional or a good agency make! In addition to the handful of exploitive independent intermediaries out there, there are some terrible agencies licensed to do adoptions in this country and there are a great many poorly trained social workers employed by relatively good agencies. No matter how you adopt, you must choose your helping professionals carefully and wisely!

My own reservations about independent adoption are limited and specific. They concern counseling and education or the lack of it. Though increasingly the professional intermediaries (attorneys, and physicians and adoption consultants) who facilitate large numbers of independent adoptions are ensuring that their clients get good preparation services—either by referring them to professional services, or in many instances by hiring professionals in the mental health or social service fields to work with them—there remain far too many attorneys and adoption consultants who are attempting to practice social work and doing it badly or ignoring the need for it at all. While poor social work is being practiced in some agencies, there is more abuse of this issue in independent adoptions than in agency adoptions.

A well done parent preparation process—I'm not talking about the old-style but still prevalent homestudy (more in Chapter Eight)—can be one of the most valuable steps parents can take in getting ready to parent in adoption. I fear that attempting to avoid this process is too often a rejection-of-difference behavior (remember Kirk?), too often a knee-jerk attempt to snatch back lost control (remember infertility's losses?), too often a reflection of an obsessive need to get a baby—any baby—and get on with life after infertility. Adoption is different. All of us who parent through adoption need help to learn about this clearly in order to become really good parents in adoption. And all of us who wish to be parents at all want to be really good parents.

Beyond and perhaps even above the preparation needs of adoptive parents, I've come to understand much more clearly over the years how vital it is to our children's birthparents that they get proper education and options counseling services before making an adoption plan. Adoption is a forever decision, and it cannot help but represent an enormous loss to birthparents who choose this option. It is absolutely not the correct choice for all people dealing with an untimely pregnancy.

Historically—whether their adoptions were made through an agency or independently—far too few birthparents actually made *an adoption plan* (the "correct" positive adoption language terminology). The old language that we optimistic (and defensive) adoptive parents and adoption professionals want to eliminate as part of our drive to promote the use of positive adoption language really did fit many birthparents in years past and continues to accurately describe the experience of a minority of birthparents today. Too many of these birthparents were not shown clear choices! Nobody actively supported the possibility of their parenting their children themselves! Far too many of these anonymous, faceless birthmothers (unknown to their children's adopting parents because confidentiality was mandated and there were no other choices) really did *relinquish* their children to adoption. They really did *surrender* to a paternalistic system. And, while this happens in agencies, too, the odds are higher that those birthparents whose adoptions have been arranged outside of an agency had no options counseling or mental health services of any kind and thus may not have actually made an adoption plan.

This does not have to happen in an independent adoption, though! Whether the adoption is to be confidential or open, objective counseling is important. Neither you nor an intermediary who is not a mental health professional is in a position to assess how fully informed your child's birthmother is about her options. But, even more if the adoption is to be confidential, you should advocate for this preparation and counseling. In a confidential adoption, over the years you will think often about your child's birthparents and wonder how they are doing. Having the knowledge that you did all that you could to ensure that they were supported in making the best possible decision for themselves as well as for the child you share will be valuable to you and to your relationship with your child.

Whether you are adopting through an agency or without one, you can, and indeed you *must* if you care about your child's birthfamily, willingly and actively offer to provide objective outside counseling services for a prospective birthmother who is considering placing her child with you. If the agency or the independent adoption intermediary whom you have contacted reacts negatively to this idea, consider this a red flag and look elsewhere!

Finding a Birthparent on Your Own

Another term you will begin to hear more and more frequently in the adoption community is *parent-initiated adoption*. This is not a separate type of adoption, but a style. It refers to the situation wherein prospective adopters or birthparents seeking adoptive parents for their baby, actively seek out a match in adoption. Parents may advertise or send letters or circulate resumes, etc. The point is that they do not rely exclusively upon an intermediary or an agency to locate the other set of parents for them. Birth or adoptive parents take an active role in creating an adoption plan. Key to this process, and what can make it most different from a traditional confidential agency adoption, is the active pre-birth commitment of one particular set of adopting parents to one particular birthmother. From an ethical, moral perspective, this should mean a willingness on the part of an adopting couple to parent the baby born to this birthmother no matter what the sex or health of the child she bears.

Mythology has it that independent adoptions are always parent-initiated. This is not true. Many adoption intermediaries do all the bush-beating for prospective private adoptions. The same mythology says that agencies don't like parent-initiated adoptions. This is also untrue as a blanket statement. Increasingly agencies are becoming involved in parent-initiated adoptions—whether through the process called direct/designated adoption or in response to their clients' interest in exerting more choice and control in arranging an adoption.

Decisions about parent-initiated adoption involve weighing what are, substantially, emotional risks. There is the risk of putting yourself out there in a public marketplace to be judged. Some couples are comfortable sending resumes, printing business cards, placing ads and others are not. Some prospective adopters are comfortable coming to know a birthparent before delivery and trusting that she will indeed make an adoption plan, and others are not. Some adopters, and indeed some birthparents, need their intermediary—agency or independent—to serve as a buffer, while others want control to remain with them.

Domestic or International Adoption

Deciding whether to adopt a child born in your own country or one from another country is a very complex and personal decision. If you are thinking that international adoption may be a fast, cheap way to adopt a healthy white infant, you are completely misinformed. Throughout Canada, Western Europe, Israel, Australia, New Zealand, etc., Caucasian prospective adopters find a shortage of healthy same-race babies to adopt. American couples who travel to adopt from other countries are often shocked to run into large numbers of non-American people of European heritage there hoping to adopt, too.

Although recently the raising of the Iron Curtain and the discovery there of many young European children in Romania, Russia, etc. in need of homes has seemed to produced at least a temporary new source of white children[1], most international adoptions for the past two decades have involved the adoption of children of color. East Indian, Asian, South and Latin American Indian or mixed race children, Filipino, Caribbean Black, African Black and other babies have been adopted by U.S. citizens at the rate of 5,000 to 8,000 per year over the last decade. Americans have adopted older special needs children from overseas as well, though in much smaller numbers. Between October, 1990, and September, 1991, Americans adopted a total of only 7,801 children from 79 different countries outside the U.S. The largest number—2,287—came from Romania, whose current government has now banned international adoptions. The second largest number came from South Korea. Where once over 4,000 children a year came to the U.S. from Korea, changes in government policy and social attitudes resulted in only 1,534 Korean adoptions to the U.S. in 1991. India sent 397 children during this period, the Philippines 341. All together, the South and Central American countries of Peru, Colombia, Guatemala, Chile and Honduras accounted for 1,753 adoptions.

International adoption can be both complex and expensive. It may be a parent-initiated adoption arranged directly through an agency in the child's country of origin, or it may be an agency adoption arranged and facilitated by a U.S. agency with connections in one or more other countries. International adoption involves a homestudy (sometimes through a private agency and sometimes done by an independent social worker), the gathering and translation of many documents, the cooperation and approval of the U.S. Department of Immigration, and more. Some countries require that adopters travel to that country and live there for a few weeks before they will grant an adoption. Other countries allow children to be escorted by agency workers, airline personnel, etc. to meet their new parents in their new home country. Current how-to information is available to you from a variety of sources— AFA, Adoption Council of Canada, local and regional parent groups (such as Families Adopting Children from Everywhere in Maryland, Latin American Parents Association based in New York state, the Open Door Society of New England, Adoptive Parents Committee of New York and many, many more), agencies such as Holt and Dillon which specialize in helping couples throughout the U.S. adopt in other countries, etc. Gather this information and then apply the decision making process for yourself.

If you are considering adopting from outside the U.S., first carefully consider all of the issues raised in Chapter Six about transracial/ transethnic adoption. Your child will likely be a child of color and will be exposed to the prejudice of many people. Your child should feel proud of his cultural and racial heritage, and you will need as a family to embrace that culture, to work hard to introduce and inform your child about that heritage and to bring it alive for him. Read the books, listen to tapes, speak to experienced parents, and explore as carefully as possible the culture of the country from which you are considering adopting before making a decision.

Be prepared as well to deal with two further, oft expressed concerns. The first may come from people here at home: why are you adopting a child from overseas when there are so many waiting children here? (A very common criticism of those who hurried to adopt white babies briefly available from Romania was that AIDS infected and otherwise unhealthy babies waited here as "border babies" in U.S. hospitals and should have been given first thought from people who were supposedly rushing in to help.) The second comes from those who see citizens of developed and prosperous Western countries as exploiters of the world's famine and unhappiness. More and more the governments of countries who once allowed many babies to be adopted in North America are finding the exportation of children to be an embarrassment and are making adoption more difficult, demanding instead to know why the U.S. and Canadian governments, if they truly care about children, do not offer them humanitarian aid to care for their own children. Are there right or wrong answers to questions like these? No. Perhaps they are not even appropriately asked. But once again, understanding your own private motivations will help you in building a healthy sense of entitlement.

Access to Information

We need to take a little side trip here to a discussion of the history of adoption and some philosophical debates going on today in order to be prepared to discuss the newest optional style—confidential vs open adoption.

Before adoption was formalized and institutionalized in the earliest decades of this century, illegitimate or orphaned children in need of parents were cared for by extended families or members of a community. There was little secrecy about the issue then. But, when adoption became a structured social service which matched parents and children previously unknown to one another, things began to change.

The new way of looking at things first suggested that children be transplanted from one family to another and not even know that they had not been born to the parents who raised them. Then it was decided that children did need to be told of the adoption, but that, in order to protect both adoptees and birthparents from the shame of illegitimacy and to protect the wounded egos of infertile adopters, birth certificates would be amended to pretend that adopters had given birth to these children. Under this system, in order to prevent competition between parents and confusion in children, adoptive families and the birthfamilies would never meet one another or have identifying information about one another. Even as societal changes made the stigma surrounding either infertility or illegitimacy all but disappear the majority of adoption agencies have continued to support the idea that birth and adoptive families should not be in communication with one another throughout the child's growing up years, but there has been a slowly shifting attitude about whether or not adult adoptees should have access to identifying information about their birthparents. An increasing number of people—adult adoptees, adoptive parents, birthparents, and professionals—are challenging the wisdom of maintaining secrecy and anonymity across the life span. They point out that many adoptees experience significant confusion during their adolescence and later as they struggle to understand who they are and why adoption was planned for them.

This has led to an ongoing discussion about whether there is a need for more *openness* in adoption. Although the debate often gets muddled, in reality there are several separate issues involved here. One issue is the debate over opening records to adult adoptees and/or to the birthparents of adult adoptees. A second issue pertains to just how much information families should be given about the birthfamilies and the earlier life experiences of older children who are being adopted. And finally, there is the debate over whether birthfamilies and adoptive families should be in communication from the beginning of an adoption and perhaps throughout a child's growing up years. In order to deal with the last, which is an emerging style of adoption, we need to have given careful thought to the other issues. While extremist proponents of one view or the other often see these issues as one and the same, many adoption educators— and I am one of them—feel that, while they are interconnected, they are indeed separate, and that it is possible to feel quite differently about each matter.

Opening adoption records to adults continues to frighten many people. The central issue is no longer the fear that there is something intrinsically harmful to anyone in the adoption triad when they have contact with one another as adults. Contacts have been made outside of the system and records have been open in some official way in several countries and in some U.S. states for a long enough period of time now that there are some things we know. We know that the majority of adoptees and birthparents living in places where records are accessible to them if they wish do not choose to make use of this access. But we also know that for the adoptees who do wish this access and are denied it, the ramifications of this lack of control over an issue as basic as the facts about their genetic identity can sometimes be overwhelming and almost disabling. We know that in the overwhelming majority of meetings between adult members of birth and adoptive families not only has there been the relatively successful formation of new relationships, but also the relationship between adoptee and adoptive parent has been strengthened rather than impaired. On the other hand, we also know that there are a shrinking number of birthparents who do not wish to have contact with their adopted-away children, who have been promised privacy and wish to keep it, who may not even have told anyone else (parents, husbands, subsequent children) about the adoption.

It is this last bit of knowledge that is causing the debate. Those who rally for the continuation of closed records see themselves as vocal advocates for those birthparents and adoptees and adoptive parents who wish to have their privacy maintained. To date, the compromise position has been to advocate what are called voluntary registries in each state. A voluntary registry operates only with consent. In other words, if both a birthparent and an adoptee have registered, a match is made. If one or the other has not registered at all or if they have registered in the negative (asking not to be identified) no match is made and no information released.

Concerns about this system are several. First, in some states adoptive parents must also grant their approval for such a match to be made. I must say that as an adoptive parent I am downright offended by this concept that my adult child would need my permission to do this when he no longer needs my permission for anything else—marriage, buying a sports car, electing to have cosmetic surgery, etc. I support entirely the concept of voluntary registries, but do not support the idea that adoptive parents should have a veto power in a match. Second, there is the argument about whose rights are paramount in the event that either one of the birthparents or adoptee says no to a match. This is a tough one. I tend to think that one birthparent should not be able to prevent a desired meeting between the other birthparent and the adult adoptee. Then there is the question of whose rights should prevail between adoptee and birthparent. I found this issue harder to decide, but as my children's advocate, I have come to feel that the adoptee's rights should prevail. After all, he was the only one given no choice at all in the original decision which transplanted him from one family to another. This needs more discussion and the development of some alternatives.

Ultimately, however, I believe that the solution to this debate can and should be solved by a substantial change in focus of adoption education coupled with the passage of time. It is difficult for me to believe, after having been convinced by the agency system that adoption is a service for children and is practiced in the adoptee's best interests, that it could ever be in an adoptee's best interests to deny him as a reasoning adult access to the facts of his heritage, if he wishes it. If, from now forward, adoptive parents and birthparents were to be counseled to understand that even if the adoption is to involve no contact between birthfamily and adoptive family through the growing up years eventually the adoptee would be given full identifying information upon request, I believe that the problem would be solved in a generation. Of course, one solution for some birthparents set on perpetual anonymity might be to abort, rather than to make an adoption plan. This opens an entirely new can of worms. This book will not enter the debate over abortion rights.

The second openness issue being debated is just how much information adoptive families should be given about the children who come to them. I have a very difficult time understanding why there is a debate! How can adopters effectively parent when there are significant issues being kept from them? How can the holding back of information from parents—no matter how negative—be in a child's best interest? In fact this so-called debate has recently been the substance of a number of legal suits wherein adoptive families have sued adoption practitioners who did not tell them about genetic problems, about a history of drug or alcohol abuse, about sexual abuse, about a history of violent behavior in an older child and more. The suits are malpractice suits. May the adopters and their children win!

All of which leads us to the question most debated of all...

Confidential Adoption or Open Adoption?

The type of adoption which involves no sharing of identifying information between birth and adoptive families is called by its supporters *confidential adoption.*[2] Most agencies which practice confidential adoptions do feel that it is important to provide adopting families with as thorough as possible a medical and social history of the birthfamilies of an adoptee at placement and to pass on any pertinent information which they discover later, while at the same time protecting the privacy and confidentiality of both families at least through the growing up years.

Proponents of confidential adoption argue that not all birthparents and adoptive parents would be able to form successful relationships, that there is a danger that a child who has two sets of parents to deal with concretely rather than in the abstract will have difficulty understanding who are his "real" parents, that adoptive parents may find it difficult to build a sense of entitlement when the birthparents hover in the background, that birthparents will find it difficult to finally grieve the loss of their children and move on. There is merit to each of these concerns.

On the other hand, opponents of confidential adoption who support openness argue that children can benefit from having direct and concrete answers to the questions about adoption which are a normal part of their growing up years, that adoptive parents who actually meet and know their children's birthparents need no longer fear the fabled knock on the door by the unknown birthmother and so can be more relaxed as parents, and that birthparents who have direct information about their children's families can indeed move forward more confidently, not having to worry each time they see a sensationalistic media report about an adoption tragedy. There is merit here, as well.

For about the past ten years, a number of agencies have been offering varying degrees of communication between birth and adoptive families in what has come to be called *open adoption*. The spectrum of openness ranges from a one time exchange of letters without identifying information at one end to what the experts in the field define as *continuing open adoption*: the ongoing back and forth sharing of information between an adoptee and his families of birth and adoption designed to foster communication and cooperation for the adoptee's benefit throughout the lifespan.

Dr. Marianne Berry, in her article "The Effects of Open Adoption on Biological and Adoptive Parents and the Children: The Arguments and the Evidence" (*Child Welfare*, December, 1991) divides openness into four different categories:

1   Restricted open adoption, in which the adoptive family shares pictures and non-identifying information with the birthparents for a limited period of time after placement, with the agency or intermediary acting as the liaison between the families.

2   Semi-open adoption, involving a face-to-face meeting between birthparents and adopting parents but no further sharing of information.

3   Fully open adoption wherein the adoptive family and birthparents meet and share information for a limited time.

4   Continuing open adoption, a style in which the birth and adoptive families plan to contact each other over the course of the adopted child's development.

At this particular time, most adoptions involving openness fall somewhere in the middle of the range of communication, involving periodic letters or picture exchanges, but little visitation back and forth between families.

Since agencies have only been offering openness options to birthparents and adopters for about a decade, we do not yet have clear data about whether or not this form of adoption is preferable for most adoptees and their two families. Most of what has been written about open adoption comes not from objective academic observation and research, but from clinical practice experience. Kathleen Silber, first with Lutheran Social Services of Texas, then with the Children's Home Society of California and most recently with the Independent Adoption Center, is a clinical pioneer in this field and has written for consumers (*Dear Birthmother* and *The Children of Open Adoption*) and trained professionals extensively. Sharon Kaplan Roszia, of Parenting Resources in Tustin, California, has developed a trademarked form of open adoption which she calls Cooperative Adoption, described in a book of that same name. As I write, Sharon is in the process of co-authoring with Lois Melina another book on openness, due to be published in the fall of 1993. These women and Patricia Martinez Dorner of Texas and Jim Gritter of Michigan are active clinical advocates of open adoption. The most articulate and convincing opponents of open adoption are Bill Pierce and Mary Beth Seader of the National Committee for Adoption, whose member agencies offer clinical evidence supporting confidentiality.

Careful objective analysis may at some point in the future give us clearer answers about the long term effects of openness on children, birthfamilies and adopting families. Several studies are in progress already. The work of professors Ruth McRoy (University of Texas) and Hal Grotevant (University of Minnesota) is ongoing. Preliminary findings seem to indicate that families operating in the mid range in openness tend to be more satisfied with their arrangements than are the families on either end of the spectrum.[3] On the other hand Marianne Berry's study suggests that, while adoptive parents are often uneasy about open adoption, those who practice it feel more settled over time, and, in fact, the more direct and the more frequent the contact, the less worried the adoptive parents were about being entitled to the child.[4]

What is important for us to keep in mind as we sort through whether openness or confidentiality are appropriate for us, is that what is best for the child who was adopted needs to be central to the decision. Frankly, it matters little whether birthparents would like an open adoption if it is not in the child's best interests. It matters little if prospective adopters want to put the birthfamily behind them and pretend that they don't exist if it is not in the child's best interest. Children are the most important clients in adoption.

What we do know for sure about openness in adoption is that it generates a great deal of debate and that there is a considerable misunderstanding and mythology surrounding it. Open adoption is not co-parenting. It is not at all like shared custody in a divorce. Even in the most communicative open adoptions it is clearly understood that the adopting family are the legal, psychological, and practical day-to-day parents of the child.

Most openness arrangements work quite well. Of course there are awkward moments, and Berry's research indicates a clear need for the continued involvement of professionals serving in a mediating role. In agreeing to an ongoing relationship, adoptive couples and birthparents are creating a new kind of extended family relationship. In some ways, a fully open adoption is like a marriage. It demands respect for one another and a commitment to maintaining a positive relationship. But marriages are hard work, and, usually they involve two people of similar ages and backgrounds and value systems. In fact adoption often matches people who would not have much in common if it were not for the adoption.

The two sets of parents are almost always of significantly different ages. This can be particularly difficult when the birthmother begins to see the adopting couple as surrogate parents for herself. Sometimes this goes unnoticed, when the adopting couple, focused so on the excitement of the coming baby, fail to understand the tenor of the relationship as viewed by the birthmother.

Pete and Nancy went through several months of Sandy's pregnancy with her, driving her to doctor's appointments and offering her a lot of emotional support. Sandy was far away from home, and she became dependent on the warmth and caring of Pete and Nancy's friendship. Nancy was her Lamaze coach and was with her when Aaron was born.

But then they were gone, caught up in parenting Aaron, and, while grateful to Sandy, much less inclined to spend long hours on the phone with her, have her over for dinner, listen to her problems at work. Their caseworker, Camille, played an important role in helping Sandy deal with what really had become two losses— the loss of her baby, and the loss of an intimate relationship with Pete and Nancy—and to help all of them negotiate a comfortable relationship for the future.

Sometimes the birth and adoptive families are of different
educational and/or ethnic or socioeconomic backgrounds—backgrounds
that would not lend themselves to naturally occurring ongoing friendships.
Skilled facilitators can be helpful in mediating misunderstandings and
helping both families develop the tools for building a successful long term
relationship.

At Issue

Because more and more birthparents are requesting openness
as a condition of making an adoption plan, some prospective adopting
couples are finding themselves pushed into what still feels like an
uncomfortable corner, forced to agree to openness or be denied the
opportunity to parent. Perhaps nothing in the changes which are afoot in
adoption frightens me more than this trend. I am meeting more and more
parties to adoptions who have in some way failed to live up to the bargains
they made in negotiating with the other family in open adoptions both
agency arranged and privately parent-initiated. The great majority of
these situations have involved adopting couples who agreed to some form
of openness before placement and then decided at some point after the
finalization of the adoption that they didn't want to continue with the
communication. Some of these situations have involved semi-openness,
where families maintain anonymity and communicate only through an
intermediary. Others have involved fully open adoptions, where
birthparents and adoptive parents have been in frequent direct contact
with one another. In either case, the pain of betrayal felt by birthmothers
in such situations is intense.

Liz, the single mother of one child, was in her
mid-twenties when she became pregnant again. Very
aware of how difficult it was to be the effective parent of
one small child on her own, she did not feel confident
that she could mother two children in the way she wanted
her children to be parented. She sorted through her
options with great care, and decided on adoption only
after finding an intermediary who would help her to
arrange an adoption which involved some degree of
openness.
    Without sharing last names, addresses or phone
numbers, Liz met her child's prospective adopters and

developed a warm relationship with them. During the last portion of her pregnancy they shared a great deal with one another. Together, Liz and Jeanette and Jim agreed that once each year during the month of her child's birth, Liz would receive a letter and pictures. Liz would also write annual letters to his family, and Jeanette and Jim agreed that they would keep these for him and share them with him when he turned 18. When her son was born Liz lovingly placed him in Jeanette's arms and dealt with her personal grief and loss, confident that she had made a good plan for herself and for her son Dean.

Problems began quite early. Jeanette and Jim weren't sure about those letters. They wanted to put conditions on the pictures that they sent, asking that they be kept in their attorney's office rather than be taken home for Liz to keep. Liz worked very hard to negotiate with them, providing them with solid adoption information, finding a mediator to help the three of them sort through their concerns, and things got better, though they remained awkward.

It was when Dean was seven that the bombshell hit. The letter was very late, and what it contained was a shock. Liz learned that the son she had thought (somewhat sadly, for him) was an only child, was the oldest of three children. Jeanette had been pregnant when Dean was born, and she conceived again quickly after that birth. Jeanette and Jim had been afraid to tell Liz about the pregnancy before the birth because they had feared she would change her mind. After the adoption their lie had simply snowballed on them. They had not known how to correct it.

Liz took it hard. So, in essence, all of those letters, the counseling sessions and a couple of social meetings since the adoption had been lies. Nothing she thought was true was true. She had been so honest with Dean's parents that she felt incredibly betrayed by their lack of trust. Up to this point she had been an ardent advocate for adoption as an option for an untimely pregnancy. Now she wasn't so sure.

———————————————

Max and Cathy adopted through an agency in the southwest which arranged only open adoptions and would not work with couples who wished confidentiality. They met Marcy during her sixth month of pregnancy, and were thrilled when she decided that the match was perfect. They communicated closely, and were able to be in the delivery room when Jillian (a name the three had chosen together) was born.

After the birth, Cathy and Max were less eager to have Marcy remain a part of their day-to-day lives, but, as the social worker explained to Marcy, this was typical. They were very much involved in claiming this child as their own and building attachments within their newly expanded family. Marcy tried to be patient.

Shortly after the adoption was finalized, both Marcy and the agency were shocked to find that Max and Cathy had moved! There was no forwarding address for their mail, no forwarding phone number. Max's employer refused to give out information about where they had gone. In fact they had moved to Chicago—a plan they had had in mind, and which the large national corporation for which Max worked had agreed to, since just before Jillian's birth. Marcy and the agency had both been betrayed. Max and Cathy had played a game with them and changed the rules after they had possession of the most valuable piece.

———————————————

If any one thing has made me open to the idea that confidentiality may not be the best way to practice adoption, it has been coming to understand that there was a great deal of deception practiced in many old-style confidential adoptions. Birthparents were often given assurances about the adopting family that were not kept. Adopting parents were too often given inaccurate or incomplete profiles on the birthfamilies. Our first adoption was a traditionally confidential one, as were Dave's adoption and that of his sister. Maybe my husband's birthmother, now in her sixties or seventies, had no other choice and has lived her life filled with regrets.

Maybe my son's birthmother, now in her early thirties, has been unable to manage her grief and move on productively with her life. Or maybe both of these women are confident in the decisions they made and are doing well. How do I know? Is it important that I know? By the same token, sometimes I feel a sense of disappointment when we don't hear from our youngest daughter's birthmother in a while. She's moving on with her life. Do we expect too much from her and of ourselves in trying to maintain contact as our lives diverge and we are all so busy parenting young children?

What I do know is that all three of my children are doing quite well in three quite different forms of adoption. We have very little information for our seventeen year old, but we have made it clear that we stand ready to help him obtain whatever he wants to have. So far, he isn't too interested—not an atypical reaction from male adoptees. We have identifying information about our eleven year old, though we have never had direct contact with her birthfamily. (By Berry's definitions where does this fit? The communication was restricted at her birthparents' request to just before and after the birth, yet we have full identifying information.) We answer our daughter's questions and have shared what we know—including a picture. Thus far, this has satisfied her needs. The adoption of our eight year old is a continuing open one. We are in at-will direct contact with her birthmother, though we do not visit back and forth with one another. Our daughter has received a few gifts and cards and she has seen pictures of the children we refer to as her birthmother's children, who are younger than our daughter and were born in a marriage to a European-American man. Our daughter isn't particularly interested for now.

All of these children are doing well, despite the diverse kinds and amounts of information we have for them. I am convinced that this has nothing to do with the confidentiality or the openness of their adoptions, but with the commitment we have made as their parents to believing in them and in our relationship with them—the degree of our mutual senses of entitlement to one another. We have clearly sent the message to our children that without question we consider ourselves a family, that we respect each of them as unique individuals, and that we respect their birthparents and their decisions. Or course they have questions! And we answer them honestly and straightforwardly and with no reservations.

There are birthparents for whom confidential adoption remains the best option and birthparents who should have openness. Similarly, open adoption is right for some adopters and confidentiality better for others. Some children will do better with openness and others with confidentiality. The menu of options must remain open to the clients who are empowered to make the choices right for themselves. And key to

the success of adoptions is the matching of birth and adopting parents
who agree on and choose the same level of confidentiality/openness.

As for me, I come down squarely in the middle. I believe that when adopting parents have confidence in their intermediaries' honesty with them and thus feel confident that both they and their child's birthparents have freely made a choice that feels right for them their shared child will flourish in whichever environment—confidential or open—his two sets of parents create for him.

If you decide on an open adoption, do so only if you are absolutely certain that you are able to commit for your lifetime to living up to your promises and working on ways to negotiate through problems. This isn't just a matter of ethical responsibility to your child's birthfamily. It goes much farther than that. What is Dean going to think when Liz contacts him at age eighteen and learns as their relationship progresses that the parents whom he loves and who love him lied to her? What if an adult Jillian searches for and finds her birthmother, only to learn how Max and Cathy betrayed her? No matter how strong the attachments, no matter how fully entitled parents and children feel toward one another, how will these parent-child relationships be affected by such news?

In choosing an open adoption, be prepared as well, for the ongoing changes that must be negotiated in any working relationship. Rather than look upon these negotiations as promises carved in stone, so that you risk being disappointed when either of you is unable to live up to those promises, but instead look at the agreement less as a contract and more as the beginning of a flexible relationship based on trust that is similar to a marriage. What you and your child's birthparent want and need now may not be what either of you feels you want or need later. Open adoption pioneer Kathleen Silber wrote in an article in *Adoptnet* (March/April, 1992) that birthparents nearly always decide later that they want more rather than less contact with the adopting family than they thought they would during their pregnancies. Therefore, she suggests that it is nearly always better to agree to an arrangement which is more conservative than you feel you could live with (for example a birthparent seems to think she only needs one picture a year when you know in your heart that you would be comfortable with more frequent communication than that) rather than one which stretches you to what you believe are your furthest limits.

The question remains, is openness the right style of adoption for your family?

The looming fear which casts its shadow over far too many placements and which causes prospective adopters not to count too much on happiness is that the baby's birthparents will change their minds. I've often heard people not touched by adoption comment that they "know how it feels," that, they, too, worried that their baby would not be healthy, that something would happen at birth. They compare failed adoptions to miscarriages or to neonatal deaths.

There are certainly some similarities, but this is not the same fear, nor are the losses equivalent. Of course prospective adopters do indeed worry about whether or not the baby they are waiting for will be healthy, but this particular fear is different. The fear we are talking about here is that a perfectly healthy baby, one which adopters have spent several months allowing themselves to fantasize about and plan for, will be born, will thrive, will fill their lives with temporary joy, but will ultimately be taken from them when a birthparent has a change of heart.

It happens. In no U.S. jurisdiction can a birthparent terminate parental rights before a child is born. Birthparents, and no one else, have total control over whether or not an adoption plan will come to pass until a legislatively set time hours, weeks, months after the birth of a child at which time their termination of parental rights becomes irrevocable.

How does one deal with such a fear? The first step is in acknowledging it. If you find this fear immobilizing, it need not stop you from adopting, but it will mean that your choices about style of adoption will be narrowed. A couple for whom this is an overwhelming fear will want to avoid direct adoption and open adoption, where they would have knowledge of the expected child and a relationship of some sort with birthparents. They will want to avoid at-risk adoptions. Instead, they will want to seek out an agency or intermediary operating in the most traditional, confidential way—where matches are made by professionals rather than by birthparents, where adopters are not told they are being considered as parents for a particular child until after it is born, where the child remains in substitute care until after the court hearing which permanently terminates his birthparents' parental rights, where they will receive the call to pick up their baby only after all danger of a change of heart is past. While this may limit opportunities, it is a realistic goal to set which takes into account the couple's resources of emotional energy and how rapidly and thoroughly they feel they would be depleted by a failed adoption.

There are several ways in which couples who feel cautiously able to take this risk may make the decision to do so. Couples who are involved in confidential adoptions may agree to a placement before parental rights are terminated if they feel relatively confident that the agency with which they are working would use traditional foster care if they felt the birthparent was wavering. These couples take such a risk knowing that their conservative agency is not going to put them in deliberate emotional jeopardy. Couples who are pursuing open adoptions sometimes factor into their decision for openness the knowledge that a personal relationship with the birthparents tends to result in far fewer changes of heart than happen in confidential adoptions where no relationships are formed.

The fact is that most birthparents who seriously explore adoption and then reject it do so long before they have made a commitment to a particular set of parents. While horror stories abound on the adoption gossip line, the removal of a child from his adoptive home after placement is still a relatively uncommon occurrence. Armed with this knowledge, some couples are able to take accept the risks with little uneasiness.

But knowing that it doesn't happen often does not lessen the intensity of the pain when an adoption does disolve. Here again is a loss unacknowledged by society as one deserving of the trappings of mourning that surround a death. While people who suffer miscarriages or neonatal death often point out the relative insensitivity of people who comment that "at least it wasn't a real baby" or "at least you didn't know him," couples who lose a child in an adoption gone awry often hear "well, at least it wasn't your own child" or "well, at least he's with his real mother."

Ironically, the loss experienced by those who must give their children back to birthparents may be much more akin to the loss felt by birthparents who follow through on confidential adoption plans than to the loss felt by couples who experience a pregnancy loss. Their losses are similarly invisible and misunderstood and may even subject them to criticism. Their roles as parents at all are similarly unacknowledged. The losses of disappointed adopters and the losses of birthparents are both for a child who is not dead, but who remains somewhere out there—happy or unhappy, healthy or not—a ghost child inaccessible to them, possibly forever. As I read the beautiful poetry written by my friend Wendy Williams, who only recently lost her second child when his birthmother changed her mind several weeks after his birth, and then read the exquisitely pain-filled poems of Mary Anne Cohen, a New Jersey birthparent who is a vocal and articulate leader in the adoption reform movement, I am struck by their similarities.

Enhancing the Odds

It's tempting, after having been unsuccessful in trying to build a family for so long, to enhance one's odds by continuing treatment long past the early stages of exploring adoption and into the active pursuit of a particular placement. Yes, it's tempting. After all, this way the odds of coming out with a child to parent are greatly enhanced. Besides, you're not getting any younger and you've always wanted more than one child. Why not two at a time—it would be like twins!

It's tempting, all right. But is it reasonable to pursue pregnancy and adoption at the same time? Is it ethical? Is it moral? My opinion—not a popular one with couples still operating in an obsessive mode (those couples who would do anything and everything to get a baby to parent)— is that it is not. Hear me out. I have several reasons for feeling so strongly.

First, this isn't fair to your children. Every child deserves to be wanted for who he is. Not as a replacement for someone else. Not as a substitute for what one hopes still to have. For himself—unique, individual, and wonderful. This requires fantasy, time, attention, preparation. It means dreaming far beyond an immediate goal—to acquire a child— toward dreams for a future together—one in which, at least for the nine months time it takes to grow another baby, he will be the center of your universe.

Even more than the more traditionally spaced adoption-built family, the existence of two obviously dissimilar children so close in age makes the adoption-built family more vulnerable to the scrutiny of strangers. This means that you will be questioned even more often than other adoption-expanded families. Eventually, this can become very awkward not just for you, but for your children.

It is tempting for society at large as well as for parents who are raising two children closer to one another in age than the length of a nine month pregnancy to artificially "twin" them. But these aren't twins. Not only are they not the same age, and therefore are likely to be at startlingly different stages during the rapidly changing first two years of development, but they aren't even genetically similar! Genetic twins often have some of the same paces and rhythms, but pseudo-twins are likely to be strikingly different from one another. During school years, the time during which adopted children are most likely to begin to deal with their grief and loss and to feel awkward about the differentness of their families, artificially twinned children are even more susceptible to the unfair comparisons from teachers and peers than are differently aged adopted siblings. The parents of multiples—whether twins, triplets, quads—will be happy to tell you how challenging it is to raise genetically related twins. To artificially twin unrelated children does them both a disservice.

Professionals in the adoption field have not come to a clear consensus on this issue. Dr. David Brodzinsky cautions that if children are raised as if they were twins there can be drastic consequences, but

he points out that when parents of back-to-back children are realistic, 163
most families function quite well. According to Dr. Joyce Maguire Pavao,
a family therapist specializing in adoption who was herself adopted,
however, "It's difficult, if not impossible to fulfill both children's needs."
In an interview with the *New York Times* (December 26, 1991) Dr. Maguire
Pavao noted that adolescence may be a particularly difficult time for
artificially twinned adoptees.

Second, pursuing a pregnancy and an adoption or two adoptions
at the same time is not fair to your child's birthparents. A couple who has
experienced the trauma of an untimely pregnancy and decided on
adoption is showing enormous courage. They are likely to receive little
support from the world at large for making such a decision for themselves
and their child. In making an adoption plan they are presenting you with
a priceless gift—the greatest gift you will ever receive. Most birthparents
given the power to do so select their child's adopting parents with great
care, looking for the parents they believe to be most likely to appreciate
this gift and treat it with the utmost love and respect. While they do indeed
most often wish that their children will be placed with a family who will
give them the possibility of a sibling, the majority of birthparents are likely
to be put off by the perceived "baby greed" of couples intent on adopting
two children at once.

Given the fact that there are so many couples waiting to adopt,
why would a birthparent deliberately choose a couple who was already
pregnant or hoping to be any day—a couple who would be distracted from
giving their baby undivided attention by a second needy infant? Even
more, why would a birthparent choose a couple pursuing two adoptions
at once? It is unlikely that couples working on two separate adoptions at
a time can allow themselves to be fully committed on an emotional level
to both. Could such birthparents fully depend upon you to remain
committed to them no matter what?

Well, maybe not. Maybe an agency wouldn't place a baby with
you if they knew you had just conceived or were about to receive a second
baby through a private adoption. Maybe two birthparents wouldn't both
willingly offer you their about-to-be-born children expected within days
or weeks or months of one another. So, you could always lie! Just don't
tell them! Ah, yes, and remember Liz, the birthmother who discovered
after seven years of deception that her son's adoptive parents had a son
six months younger than the one she had placed with them and another
only a year younger? It wasn't so much the fact that they had those children
that angered Liz, she felt betrayed by the fact that they had deceived her
for all those years. Someday the son they share will know of this deception.
What will he think?

Third, this isn't fair to *you*. Preparing for parenthood is a multistep process, and people preparing to adopt who allow themselves to embrace the adoption and truly believe in its successful outcome go through a series of role transitions very much like those undergone by couples who are pregnant.

The Psychological Pregnancy

During the nine months that expectant biological parents wait for birth, they become very introspective, communicating with one another in joint fantasy while sharing common fears and anxieties, and they begin the practical steps of nest building: creating physical and emotional space for the new phase in their lives as they grow to love the particular child with whom they are pregnant. Pregnant women experience four developmental stages during the pregnancy, and their parenting partners usually experience these stages along with them. They are

1   Pregnancy validation—accepting the pregnancy as a reality.

2   Fetal embodiment—incorporating the fetus into the mother's body image.

3   Fetal distinction—seeing the fetus as a separate entity in order to make plans for him.

4   Role transition—preparing to take on the parenting role.

Both Cathy Floyd (in an issue of the *American Journal of Nursing*) and Carol Hallenbeck, R.N., a childbirth educator who is also an adoptive parent, have observed and written about comparable stages experienced by adoptive parents who allow themselves to participate in a psychological pregnancy. These stages are

1   Adoption validation—accepting the fact that their child will join the family by adoption rather than by birth.

2   Child embodiment—incorporating the child by adoption into the parents' emotional images.

3   Child distinction—beginning to perceive of the child as a reality in order to make plans for him.

4   Role transition—preparing to take on the parenting in adoption role.

It is impossible to experience a psychological pregnancy related to a particular adoption when one still has enormous amounts of time, energy, emotional reserves, and money committed to becoming pregnant biologically.

So many decisions. They are yours. Make them carefully and well. They must last a lifetime, and if they are well made, they will.

8

Winning the
Seal of Approval

You've decided to adopt. You've made decisions about the age, sex, relative health and ethnicity of the child you are hoping to parent. You've thought through the various approaches to adoption and decided on whether to pursue an agency or non-agency adoption, whether to look for confidentiality or openness. What you need now is the piece that grates and rubs—offcial permission to become a parent, societal approval to add a child to your family.

Homestudy. Assessment. Evaluation. Approval process. There is old style thinking reflected in these, the most commonly used terms which describe the way in which government-licensed adoption agencies or social work professionals learn about prospective adoptive families, educate them about adoption, and make recommendations to the courts regarding their suitability and readiness for parenting in adoption. These terms feel judgmental and seem to imply a gatekeeping responsibility on the part of paternalistic professionals. Increasingly, professionals are changing the process and taking a new view. The preferred term today is *parent preparation*, which is softer, more inclusive, more positive.

For many people considering adoption the process these older terms describe is the single most intimidating factor in deciding whether or not to adopt—can I submit myself to the white-gloved inspection of a homestudy by an authoritarian social worker who will pass final judgment on whether or not I can be a parent? In this chapter we will try to accomplish several things. We will talk about the purpose and relative value of required special preparation for parenting for adopters. We will look at some of the common factors about traditional assessments that have been most disheartening and corroding for prospective adopters and offer professionals some suggestions for change. We will consider some ways in which prospective adopters can become appropriately prepared for adoption if circumstances do not bring them in contact with sensitive and well informed professionals. And, while we're doing all of this, we'll invite adoption professionals to read over our shoulders and take heed, taking with them ideas which will result in the replacement of those still existing homestudies with the fresh new wind of parent preparation.

Why a Homestudy?

It is important to remember that the official societal view of the institution of adoption is that it is a service for children, not a service for adults. That being the official stand, gatekeeping is indeed a part of society's responsibility. It is the judicial system's role in adoption to make decisions which are in the best interests of the child in deciding about terminating or assigning parental rights. This is the legal principle which gave rise to the concept of studying the home, the environment, the character and the relationship of prospective adopters in order to determine which, of multiple potential parents, would best suit a particular child. The role of the social worker, then, is to make a recommendation to the courts about the assignment of those parental rights—a recommendation based on professional evaluation.

All who adopt will go through an assessment/preparation process of some sort. This is a legal requirement in all U.S., Canadian, and British jurisdictions. Some assessments are more intensive than others. Generally, in most parts of the U.S., the assessments which are done by agencies which are arranging the placements of children under their own care by matching them with people who have applied to that agency to adopt are more detailed and demanding and are accomplished over a longer period of time than are the assessments done by court order before the finalization of independently arranged adoptions. Additionally, the goal of the process differs substantially from agency to agency.

Now, some of what follows in this chapter may sound a little ethereal. What you would like most to have, I know, is a rulebook that explains exactly what a homestudy is and how to play the game successfully enough to pass Go and collect your baby. But the fact is that if this is to be likened to a game, it is a game without standards and rules! I doubt that you would be able to find any two unconnected agencies anywhere in the world whose assessment processes were the same.

To make matters even more confusing, right now, at the end of

the twentieth century, the approach to assessment used by professionals
is undergoing dramatic, almost revolutionary, change, and in some
pockets of the western world practice is so radically different than it was
ten years ago that indeed it is appropriate to re-label the approval process
parent preparation.

In my view, and in the view of most adoption advocates and
parents who have familiarized themselves with adoption issues beyond
the limited circle of their own family, the concept of parent preparation
is an important, necessary, and even exciting part of becoming an
adoptive parent. There is much to be said for the benefits of an up-to-
date parent preparation process. Good parent preparation begins with a
supportive and positive relationship between client and professional which
is built on trust and allows the professional to help clients build on their
strengths toward the goal of being really effective parents. In parent
preparation you will meet other couples and share concerns. You will
probably meet some birthparents (even if you are going to adopt
confidentially) and have a more realistic picture of what birthparents are
like. You will be introduced to parent groups, literature, and other
educational and support opportunities which you are otherwise quite likely
to miss. You will be offered parenting tips and practice in dealing with
societal reaction to adoption and answering your child's questions. You
will have an opportunity to polish the rough edges left on your feelings
about infertility with a trained facilitator and to try on some adoption
options that you may not know how to explore without committing to
them. You will explore ways to bring your family aboard in embracing
adoption. You will be encouraged to make an important first step in role
transition—from non parent to parent—with the support of some folks
who can really make it happen. While I encourage you to avoid if at all
possible an old style homestudy, I urge you not to avoid true parent
preparation, but instead to actively seek it out.

Still, it is unfortunately the case that the majority of social service
providers in the English speaking world continue to operate in a
paternalistic, gatekeeping style under which it is the role of the social
worker to know what is best in assessing readiness to adopt—as if there
were some objective set of standards for doing so. Whether this is
deliberate, out of force of habit, or because of incomplete training varies.
One of my hopes is that those who are working this way out of habit or
out of ignorance can and will change when shown good reasons for
developing a new way of interacting with clients.

While there is little standardization in the old-style process (some
agencies prefer a series of private interviews with couples, who may never
meet another couple involved in the process at the same agency, while
other agencies use group work in combination with private interviews),

there are certain common elements to the processes of agencies operating in the older style. It is the existence of these confusing, unexplained and therefore misunderstood common elements juxtaposed against the absence of standardization (which would indicate professional agreement) which makes it so difficult for adopters to feel that the homestudy makes sense or has any real value for them. If a step is important at one agency, why is it left out at another? If one agency feels it unnecessary to require a certain procedure, why is the other so adamant about requiring it?

Rarely do adopters feel confident enough in their "approvability" to openly question the process. Through consumer advocacy groups, however, they have, throughout the last decade, continued to raise questions about a number of issues, including those to follow.

I raise these issues here for two reasons. First, for the consumers of adoption services reading this book, I hope that by becoming aware in advance of some of these issues and allowing yourselves time to think them through carefully you will be better prepared to deal with them. I hope that you will feel empowered to diplomatically question issues that are unclear to you. You can, if need be, train yourself to be stoically tolerant of those unavoidable issues which you find particularly offensive before you enter the process. You will be able to seek out and focus on the valuable parts of the process and even to look elsewhere for important missing pieces—in effect creating your own parent preparation experience even if your agency still thinks it does homestudies!

Second, for professionals reading over the shoulders of my consumer audience, it is my hope that I can help you to see how really unproductive the old style is, so that you will be encouraged to initiate change from within!

Fitting the Mold

Just getting *to* the homestudy is a challenge. Having to qualify by meeting an agency's standards and requirements—especially when there is such a variation from agency to agency in those standards and requirements—is the first hurdle. While we may be able to understand rather easily some requirements—being a member of a certain religion if the agency is sponsored by that religion, for example—other requirements really hurt. Why would a previous divorce, for example, in this era when well over 50% of marriages end in divorce, preclude parenting? As couples are marrying later and later, setting arbitrary numbers of years for length of marriage can mean that couples who made careful decisions later in life may fail to qualify by virtue of their age after being married long enough! And, speaking of age, how old is too old? In this era when it is more and more the rule, rather than the exception, for couples to delay childbearing into their 30s, where couples are succeeding at infertility treatment into their early 40s, how realistic is it for an agency to say that they will not place babies with couples where one parent is over 40? At a nonsectarian agency, how can one require that applicants "practice a religion" when many people have an active and fulfilling spiritual life outside of organized religious denominations?

It's enough to drive a couple away from agency adoption! And it often does. The fact is, though, that such agencies expect that some clients will voluntarily turn away from such restrictions.

The truth, were it told, is that for many agencies, strict requirements such as these serve one purpose and one purpose only— they are effective gates which serve to slow the flow and make the work manageable. It isn't anything personal. It is simply an issue of supply and demand that if there are forty to one hundred couples waiting for each available newborn (varying numbers are quoted from reliable sources) there has to be a way to weed the lists of applicants down to a manageable size. It is more acceptable in a society which claims on the surface at least to be embracing of socioeconomic, cultural, racial, and educational diversity to set qualifications about length of marriage, about age, etc. than to require a certain level of education or of income or to exclude people because of race.

From the perspective of those who promote agency adoption and are critical of independent adoption, however, such gatekeeping regulations and qualifications become counterproductive to their goals of ensuring that all couples are properly prepared for parenting in adoption. When couples are turned away at the intake door, they don't necessarily stop their efforts to adopt. They keep looking! And in an age of increasing entrepreneurialism in adoption, they are highly likely to find some intermediary somewhere who will help them adopt—with or without an "appropriate" assessment and preparation process! Furthermore, there is little doubt that a significant number of what might turn out to be the very best possible parents for an agency's client children are lost because of arbitrary qualifications.

The Relationship of Caseworker and Client

It all begins with a personal relationship—the one that must be forged between prospective adopters and social worker. Successful parent preparation results from trust built between client and professional, and building that trust is itself a challenge. Adoption workers are threatening. It goes with the territory. No matter how understanding, how knowledgeable and how compassionate he or she is, the caseworker is still perceived as a threat by nearly every client—fertile or infertile prospective adopter, man or woman dealing with an untimely pregnancy—who walks through the office door.

Control is one of the issues that makes this so. In modern society a feeling of being in control of one's destiny is vital to a sense of well being. Losing control through illness, accident or uncontrollable circumstances is very difficult. Even people who consider themselves to be devoutly religious often have difficulty turning over control of their destiny to a supreme being. Yet this is what the concept of religious faith demands. To be asked to turn over to another human being complete control of an area of their lives which most people take very much for granted—family planning—is particularly hard for preadoptive parents of the birth control generations. Yet this is what adoption often demands—of both adopters and birthfamilies.

There is no license to parent. There are controls on marriage and divorce which require societal intervention to do or to undo. We must meet certain requirements to complete education, to drive a car, to obtain a job, to qualify to vote, to buy property, but if one is biologically able to reproduce one is not required to qualify to become a parent. Our laws and social customs assume that the biological relationship between progenitor and offspring is inherently inviolable except under the most dire of circumstances, that society generally has no business interfering in the parent/child relationship.

When adoption is looked at from the point of view of the would-be parent, who is asked to defend personal values, plans, goals, motivations, relationships, finances under examination by one who has the absolute power to grant parenthood (whether of a first child or of a fifteenth), perhaps it isn't too difficult to understand why preadoptive parents find it hard to relinquish this control. After all, who is this person more powerful even than the physician who could try to help, but had no absolute power to ensure that we would become parents? What specific qualifications, educational or personal, equip him or her to hold this God-like power? Since most parents aren't evaluated and licensed, how will our suitability be determined? Where are the written criteria for what constitutes parental fitness, and if such criteria are not written, what qualifies this person (perhaps young and/or unmarried and/or not a parent or at least almost never an adoptive parent) to decide whether or not we are parent material? If we are approved, what qualifies this person to decide which child, how young or how old, what sex or what color, how healthy or unhealthy, we are qualified to parent?

All preadoptive parents ask these questions silently—and it's important to note that birthparents considering adoption have a similar list and a similarly suspicious view of the caseworker. Few of these clients, however, openly question the social worker. To other clients, such questions seem perfectly logical. To some adoption workers such questions seem insulting and even threatening. I am a professional, such workers say, qualified by training and study to do such work. Would you, they ask, seek only a diabetic doctor to treat you for diabetes? No! You would choose your doctor on the basis of his educational qualifications and trust his knowledge. If you didn't trust him you would change doctors. The same, then, should be true of your relationship with me.

In the crux of this argument—that one places trust in a professional by virtue of his education and thus his expertise and that in the absence of this trust one finds a new professional—lies the heart of the problem as perceived by many potential adopters. Adoption is a difficult and slow process. Potential adopters don't feel that they have the power to pick and choose their agencies as they would a doctor because there are fewer and fewer agencies facilitating adoptions, and because due to restrictions on age, religion, length of marriage, etc. they do not qualify at all agencies. They may not feel that they have the power to pick and choose social workers within an agency because many agencies don't have a large number of adoption workers. As well, unlike the situation of a patient electing to see a doctor who practices in a group, where the patient is allowed to decide with which physician he wishes to make an appointment (and I might point out as a valuable aside that infertility patients are notorious for doctor hopping!), at an adoption agency couples are usually randomly assigned to a worker and then may fear that a request for a change in worker may be negatively received and thus cause them to risk general disapproval by the agency.

Would-be parents feel powerless whether they actually are powerless or not. The degree of powerlessness they feel is in many cases directly proportional to their perceived need to adopt. The infertile couple or single person with no children at all and a deep desire to parent may feel most powerless. The couple with four biological children who have also adopted six times and are being asked to consider a sibling group may feel least powerless. Yet all of them probably do feel or have in the past felt the frustration of losing control to a social worker.

Traditional adopters feel vulnerable. Unlike preferential adopters, who come to adoption with the biological capability of expanding their families as a kind of insurance should adoption not work out, infertile couples know that adoption may be their last chance to achieve parenthood. Because society does perceive adoption as a second best alternative for them, they may, too, and it may have taken a great deal of careful introspection as they went through the process of dealing with infertility's losses for them to have been able to feel positively about this compromise to their original life plans.

———————————

Ashley and Del felt that they were lucky. Unlike many of their friends, they had forged a friendship with the social worker who had facilitated their first adoption, and, as a result of these warm, trusting feelings, they expected the second adoption to flow more smoothly for them emotionally. And it did, until the disaster.

Ashley and Del's second placement was disrupted after several weeks when their child's birthmother had a change of heart. They and their older child grieved for months, and were comforted by the fact that many people, including their social worker, were able to offer them empathic support.

Throughout the grieving, Ashley and Del, who had earlier worked very hard to understand the losses which accompanied infertility for themselves, experienced real clarity about what was going on for them. They grieved the terrible loss of the actual child, of course, but beyond that, this loss had reopened the old wounds about lost control. They had rediscovered just how out-of-control their family planning was.

After grieving for her lost child, Ashley grieved her empty arms and her inability to do anything about filling them. Five months had passed and she was eager to adopt again, but she was dependent upon the caseworker's assessment of her readiness.

It did not even occur to Ashley that the caseworker would misinterpret her feelings, and so she made no attempt to hide her loneliness and longing for a child to fill the waiting nursery. However, the caseworker was concerned. "You sound far more sad than you were the last time we spoke," she said. "We must make sure that your grieving has progressed sufficiently; we don't want to place an unfair burden on the new baby. Let's work together on this to help you get ready."

Ready?! What would ready mean? Ashley and Del were frightened, and for the first time in their relationship with their caseworker, wondered if they had

come to an impasse with her. Perhaps they shouldn't
have been so open with their feelings after all. Perhaps
that old-style thinking—the one that labels all loss in
infertility the loss of a dream child, the one that expects
there to be a finite point at which one's losses are
"resolved" would enchain them indefinitely.

There is no way for adoption workers to completely erase the
adversarial relationship that traditional adopters may experience. This
perception is part of the situation, and much of that can't be changed.
There are ways, though, for caseworkers to ease the tension, and many
workers and agencies today are in the process of doing this.

Primarily these new ways of looking at the process involve the
professionals first accepting that they may be expecting too much from
themselves in thinking that they alone can adequately prepare an adopter
for parenting. In seeing oneself not as the grantor of children, but as the
preparer of parents, a professional becomes himself an adopter's
advocate. If professionals truly see themselves in this role, they are eager
for continuing education and they work toward flexibility and humanness
in the system, more responsiveness in and justification for policy, better
training of social workers and foster parents, less theory and more
practicality in parent preparation, better communication with and referral
to other helping professionals and adoption-related services. Adoption
professionals have always seen their primary client as the child in need
of parents. But only in forming a positive relationship with those parents
can they protect the child's best interests. Working on building that team
spirit first discussed in Chapter Five is a way to begin.

After the initial panic, Ashley and Del decided
that they had to clear the air with their social worker
somehow. They knew that the heaviness of waiting
would only increase if they could not speak freely to their
worker and they valued the friendship with her far too
highly to let the relationship slide. Knowing that their
worker was sensitive to their vulnerability, they arranged
another meeting with her to talk things over. Though
nervous and awkward at first, they managed to discuss
their fears and concerns, and the caseworker was able

to reassure them that she was in support of another placement as soon as circumstances made it possible. Everyone felt much better afterwards.

The caseworker and Ashley did not come to a complete agreement on a model for grieving after an adoption loss, but they continue to work together on understanding the issues. Ashley searched for material on grief and adoption loss, but found little. She soon realized that this is one of the "silent" topics of adoption, and she is committed to furthering understanding of this issue.

It has not been easy for Ashley and Del to take the initiative here, but it would have much harder to continue second guessing their worker's thoughts, and to risk losing the mutual trust and support that had been built up between them over the years.

In order to work toward forging those solid relationships, professionals need to understand how adopters perceive certain aspects of traditional assessment. Adoption professionals, please read over our shoulders, your clients' and mine, as we examine some elements of traditional assessment...

Sharing Intimacies

As I write, an amusing commercial for a laxative is being shown frequently on television. Maureen and Roger sit on their front porch, Roger absorbed in his newspaper while Maureen carries on a conversation with the camera. She proceeds to tell us that when Roger is feeling "you know, irregular" she offers him this product. Roger, amazed at what he is hearing, appears from behind the newspaper to express his indignation. "Maureen!" he cries.

"Well, it's true," she replies.

"But you don't even know these people!" cries Roger as he hides his face again behind the paper.

We are not a culture in which we are raised to feel comfortable sharing the facts of our most intimate lives. Why, in many marriages (I don't know, is it most?) couples married many years consider their bathroom functions every bit as private—if not more so—than does Roger.

Imagine yourselves, then, being asked by a perfect stranger about the frequency and the satisfaction of your sex lives. Beyond imagining, expect that this may happen. A part of the assessment process for many agencies includes private discussions between each of you and your social worker and then the three of you together about many very intimate issues: your relationship with your parents and your siblings, your relationship with your partner, your feelings about religion or spirituality, your private value system, your goals for yourself, your sex lives.

Anna and Joe were frightened. Had they blown it? Totally unprepared for the fact that their caseworker might ask them about sex, each had answered his questions differently when they went in for private interviews. Joe had figured that it probably wasn't a good idea to admit to a social worker who was a priest that they had been intimate before they were married. Anna, on the other hand, had been unable to lie to a priest, of all people! Now they were worried. What would it mean that their answers were different? Did it matter anyway? What was the reason for asking these questions?

I've always wondered, and as I result I've asked many caseworkers I've met, what they do with the information they gather about sexuality. I've asked by what standards they evaluate this data. I've asked who trains them for this work. With the rarest of exceptions, the answers are strangely negative and noncommittal. Few adoption workers have received training on how to evaluate the answers to intimacy surveys, few agencies have standards. Perhaps even more shocking, far too many adoption workers are so uninformed about the practical realities of infertility that they are unaware of how common temporary sexual dysfunction is for couples who have ended treatment and are simply too exhausted after years of scheduled intercourse to care about having intercourse for pleasure for a time. Since most couples are unaware of this common reaction, too, the result of this mutual lack of knowledge is that the very people (mental health professionals) who might be able to assist a couple feeling frightened of this element of their reaction to infertility is in essence unavailable to offer help in working it through!

Beyond sexual intimacy issues, in this enlightened age of getting in touch with our feelings, most prospective adopters have at least a passing familiarity with such terms as *dysfunctional family, inner child, co-dependency,* and many more frightening and controversially defined issues such as what constitutes child abuse (though we all seem to know that the tendency toward it is passed on from generation to generation). These are issues which may or may not be important to share with an adoption worker.

The deciding factor in whether or not these intimate issues will prove valuable if shared is simple and straightforward. If the professional knows why he or she is asking the question and on what basis it will be interpreted, if the worker is qualified to assess the information and to provide assistance if merited, if s/he can help couples to understand how it will be a valuable part of preparation for parenting, it can be important to share this information. It is perfectly reasonable for prospective adopters to ask about these things before answering uncomfortably intimate questions. Of course you will want to do so in a pleasant, cooperative, and positive way, rather than to challenge the professional in a manner which serves to put him or her on the defensive.

References

The need to provide personal references, while perhaps the most easily justified and understood requirement of the approval process, is often uncomfortable and agonizing. Numbers and types of references required vary considerably among agencies, as does the form in which they are to be submitted. References from some or all of the following may be requested: the prospective adopter's parents and siblings, employers, friends and neighbors, clergypersons, the school of other children in the family.

The need to supply references destroys completely and forever any remaining privacy the prospective parents may have had concerning their family expansion plans. While couples contemplating becoming pregnant may never need to make this known to others until they are successful in their efforts, the reference gathering aspect of the adoption process requires that adopters ask for the cooperation of others in gaining agency approval. It can be humiliating to ask for references for such a purpose, as it may seem as if one is requesting permission to do what for others is a totally natural and independent action—building a family. This

enhances the adopter's feelings of being out of control. After all, what
prospective parent by birth must depend on the positive reactions to themselves and their family plans from parents, neighbors, employers, etc. in order to add a child to their family? Buried deep within the discomfort of asking for such a reference is the adopter's nagging fear that he may indeed be rejected by the agency and then be placed in the position of having to explain this to those who have supplied references.

When Rashid and Esther applied to adopt, Rashid still felt a little reluctant. Concerned about what others would think and say about their inability to conceive, he resented having to get a social worker's approval. Things got worse when he was asked to send out reference forms. "From that point on," said Rashid, "it felt kinda like someone was watching us in bed. Everybody knew we were trying to start a family, and they might as well have been asking us about how the sex was going as asking us how the homestudy was going."

The format in which references are to be supplied can also be a cause for concern. Some agencies request general letters of reference with few if any specific guidelines, while others supply a highly detailed questionnaire to be completed. Most often there has been no attempt to design individual reference models for each type of reference supplier, so that the adopter is placed in the awkward position of asking people to supply information about which the referrer may not have knowledge.

Most of those asked to supply references are uncomfortable doing so. Aware that they themselves have not needed such public permission to parent, they feel awkward. When information is requested to which they feel that they cannot or should not appropriately respond, they feel the weight of responsibility given over to them by the person needing the reference, and, to a certain extent intimidated by the authority of the system, they would be hesitant to question the agency's procedure and thereby risk jeopardizing the adopter's chances.

Brenda and Stan were adopting for the first time. Their agency asked them to forward copies of a single standard reference form to each of their parents, two friends, each of their employers, and their pastor. They complied and waited.

Brenda, a teacher, was called to her principal's office one afternoon during her prep period, where she faced an embarrassed man. "Ah, uh, Brenda, I, uh, got this form, and I sure do want to help you out here. Adoption is a great thing and all that. I guess I just don't quite know what you want me to say on a couple of questions, though.... like 'How would you describe the stability of the marital relationship of this couple?' What would you think I'm supposed to say there? I don't know your husband."

He didn't mention specifically the other question that had stood out to Brenda as a toughy, 'Would you be feel comfortable placing your own children in this couple's care?'"

After an awkward silence, they agreed on some "right" answers. A day or two later, Stan's boss placed a photocopy of his response to the agency in the interoffice mail. Some questions had been left blank.

The development of a specific written policy about references would have helped both agency and client here. What does the agency hope to learn from each type of reference requested? Have they made that clear by designing tools which take into account the differences in viewpoint of each referrer? What will be the agency's reaction to a questionable reference or an entirely negative one? Is a system of checks and balances in place that will guarantee the adopter the opportunity to defend himself while at the same time protecting the confidentiality of the referrer? When references are well justified and carefully developed tools are used, agencies will receive more helpful information and couples will be feel less awkward about asking for references from others and less resentful of the need to supply them.

Often used screening tools include psychological tests such as the Minnesota Multiphasic Personality Inventory (MMPI). In concept such a tool has real merit. In practice, clients often react negatively to them when agencies do not have clearly defined policies delineating their reasons for such testing and defining how results are to be used.

Who will evaluate the results of such a test? How will those results be used in determining the approval or rejection of a client? What follow up might be suggested for a client whose test results reflected poorly upon them? Has the agency chosen an instrument which is considered up-to-date, well respected and reflective of current values? (Many older tests still in use today are criticized for their sexist overtones.) Will test results become part of a permanent record? If so, who will have access to this information, how long will it be retained, and under what circumstances and to whom might it conceivably be released?

Rebecca and Bill had given birth to more than one child before deciding to expand their family by adoption. They were adopting out of preference rather than giving birth again. Well respected in their community as involved and active parents, they were working on their third adoption of a waiting child when routine results of psychological testing suggested that Bill was a poor prospect for adopting due to apparent risk factors for substance abuse and impulse control problems.

Bill and Rebecca were shocked and frightened at such a result. Their caseworker, however, simply decided to ignore the test. No confirming test was administered. No suggestion was made that Bill be screened by a mental health professional. The child—an unattached and character disordered 8 year old—was placed.

Bill had many concerns about this situation. "How could she just ignore such results?" Bill asked. "It was almost as if we were talking about my horoscope and deciding that, while it was kind of fun to look at, it wasn't to be taken seriously. If this test was an important enough part of the adoption process to take up several hours of my time and add a significant charge to my bill, how could such results be dismissed so casually?"

Certainly if psychological screening tools are to become a standard part of any agency's homestudy process, the agency should establish specific policies regarding their use and application. To prevent misinterpretation and misunderstanding, such policies should be put in writing, so that couples can read and reread them, ask appropriate questions, and be referred to them. This written information should include a thorough discussion of the strengths and weaknesses of the instrument being used, a statement about how the results will and will not be used, and should include an established route of appeal should applicants strongly disagree with the results of their testing. Above all, agencies who do choose to administer such testing should do so consistently, and clients should be able to expect that their results will not be taken lightly.

Medical Screening

Wendy was raised in India and was exposed to T.B. there. In Ontario, where she now lives, the provincial agency, C.A.S., requires T.B. screening, and Wendy will always "fail" this test. Because there is no written standardized policy concerning what is to be done with the results of medical screening, Wendy's fear is that some uninformed "bureaucrat" will wipe out her chances for adopting a child with a stroke of his pen. While her fear may have no basis in reality, without written policy, her fear is logical!

Once again, there is no standard, but nearly all courts and/or agencies require some sort of medical screening for the people involved in adoptions—adopters, birthparents, children to be adopted. At issue is how such tests are to be used. People who are involved in adoption have a right to be told in advance how the results of such screening will affect them.

Cassandra and Craig applied to adopt a healthy Caucasian infant at an agency which had no written policies concerning health. They went through an initial group process with several other couples and then began to gather their "paperwork"—references, auto-biographies, medical exams, etc. They expected to pass with flying colors and were shocked to find that they were not approved because the agency considered Cassandra "morbidly obese" despite her doctor's statement of her relative health. At the same time, a minority couple in the same study group were approved, despite what appeared to Craig and Cassandra as the husband's similar weight problem. Craig and Cassandra wondered: is this an issue of health or an issue of cosmetics? Are health standards different for choosing the parents for children of different races?

Aside from medical issues about themselves, adopters have the right to know whether they will be given all available information about their children-to-be and about their birthfamilies. For many years traditional social workers resisted telling prospective adopters about birthfamily health issues that they feared would prejudice the adopting family about accepting the placement of a baby who appeared to the workers to be healthy. But we realize now that the appearance of health can be deceptive. We are coming to understand that it is important that social workers be better trained to understand the importance and significance of such items as APGAR scores, a history of ADHD in the family, etc.

As we come to know more and more about the damaging effects of in-utero drug and alcohol exposure, about the effects of exposure to sexually transmitted diseases, about the genetic links to various learning disabilities and to heightened distractibility and hyperactivity, it has become increasingly important that parents be given all information about their child's birthfamily medical history, pregnancy and delivery history, and early experiences. This goes far beyond the issue of whether or not couples will say no more often to children they might have parented successfully had they been kept in the dark. Yes, some couples will indeed say no to certain risks. But more than this, parents cannot be expected to parent effectively if they are not given full information about the children they adopt. All of us deal more effectively with the known than with the unknown.

My own state, Indiana, conservative in many other ways, was

the first in the nation to **require** the gathering of and passing on of a relatively extensive non-identifying medical history which is to be presented to the adopting parents before finalization of both agency and independent adoptions and a copy of which is to be placed in the court files. I was privileged to serve on the Attorney General's task force which drafted this document. But other states have been slow to follow suit. It remains the case that far too many agencies, through either ignorance and/or bad policy, do not pass on significant medical information to adopting families.

The bottom line, then, is that agencies have no right to keep any information from prospective adopters. This is more than my personal opinion. It is emerging social policy. Several lawsuits contending that agencies which deliberately or out of ignorance withheld medical data from prospective adopters were guilty of social work malpractice are in progress and a handful have already been heard and decided—in favor of the parents!

Money Matters

Perhaps no issue incites more debate than the issue of fees in adoption, and the rhetoric involved in such a debate is schizophrenic at best. People working in adoptions are highly offended at the mention of the word purchase when applied to the placement of a baby, yet it is a fact that healthy, white infants command the highest fees. Minority children, older children, and children with disabilities wait to be adopted, and in order to promote their adoptions, agencies are forced to recruit parents from outside of their approved-and-waiting lists, to waive fees entirely, and to ensure that children with problems which will require professional intervention and assistance are accompanied by federal adoption subsidies.

In the real world of adoption the healthy white babies most traditional adopters seek are a valuable commodity. Because the pool of waiting parents for healthy Caucasian babies is large and the supply small, there is competition among prospective adopters. Agencies and intermediaries placing babies can be picky about qualifications and unyielding about fees, which can be and are high enough to cover the costs of these adoptions and as well to subsidize other less lucrative services.

Public agencies usually handle both infant adoptions and the adoption of older children, but because public agencies are able to offer birthparent clients only clinic-based and publicly-assisted medical care, far more birthparents seek the help of private agencies or of non-agency intermediaries (adoption consultants, physicians, attorneys), who, when local law allows, are often able to offer private medical care and support and living assistance.

Private agencies and non-agency intermediaries, on the other hand, are far less often involved in the placement of older children or sibling groups, and they often refer babies born with disabilities to the public sector agencies. This, coupled with the fact that most older adoptable children become available because their families have become in some way embroiled in the public "system," means that public agencies are saddled with enormous expenses that private agencies rarely experience. Who pays for these expenses?

Many public agencies do not charge fees at all, but are instead supported by public funds—your tax dollars. Nearly all private agencies do charge fees, but the size of the fee and the method by which it is determined vary considerably. Private agency fees may be based on a flat across-the-board sum for all applicants, on direct costs of services, or on a percentage of income with or without a ceiling. At some agencies fees include everything from the homestudy through the legal costs of finalization, which will be processed by the agency's law firm. At other agencies each service is paid for piecemeal, beginning with an application fee and following up with a specific fee for each counseling session or group workshop.

The allocation of funds collected from placement fees varies considerably from agency to agency, too. At some agencies, fees become part of a general fund which supports the expenses of a wide range of community and social services. At other agencies, adoption fees remain exclusively within the adoption program. Some agencies further divide their adoption program so that funds collected from adoption fees are not applied to expenses incurred in providing services to birthparents who do not make adoption plans. However, it is more common that the services supplied to the over 95% of birthparents who do not make adoption plans are paid for from the fees collected from those who adopt the children of the 5% of birthparents served who do choose adoption.

Agencies usually try to explain that there are expenses in adoption services and, since somebody must pay for them, why not adopters, who benefit most from their services? On the surface this is logical, but adopters ask themselves, how do we benefit from services supplied to non-placing parents? Of course there are expenses in adoption, but no one involved in special needs adoption suggests that adopting families should reimburse custodial agencies for several years of counseling and foster care in making these placements, so at what age or in what condition do children cease to become worth paying for? How is it logical that a percentage of income is a "fair" assessment as a placement fee when parents by birth do not pay for the professional assistance they use in their children's arrival in this manner?

Few adopters would argue that someone has to pay for services. Few would argue that direct service provided to them and to their family should be paid for by them. There is seldom an argument about whether or not adopters should pay for their own counseling time, their own psychological testing, and most would extend this same logic to include their assuming their own child's birthparents' counseling fees, medical expenses, and legal fees. But many adopters come to the personal limits of their dignity when asked to carry the financial burden for children not placed for adoption or for placements other than their own. They experience this as one more punishment for their infertility and it becomes yet one more source of unvalidated anger.

Indeed, it is this very issue which drives increasing numbers of prospective adopters of infants out of the system of licensed public and private agencies and into the unchecked world of independent adoption, where flat fees or percentage of income fees are atypical, and are, in fact, often indicative of an unethical practice. In general most adoption activists feel that only direct reimbursement-for-service charges are ethical in independent adoptions, and these fees may be paid to several service suppliers, from physicians and hospitals to social workers/counselors/educators (birthparents' and adopting couple's), to attorneys (birthparents' and adopters').

Perhaps no aspect of the relationship between prospective adopters and the intermediaries with whom they work is more uniformly uncomfortable for everyone involved than is the issue of finances. Caseworkers don't like to talk about it, often to the extent that they gloss over this topic in their presentations to families, resulting in misunderstandings. Families don't like to think about it, as it points out another way in which they are singled out as very different from families formed by birth. Agency directors are almost always people firmly committed to human services, so that they care very much about the negative impact of fees on their clients, but then again, fees are their programs' lifeblood.

Because the issue of fees is so complex and difficult, this is one more area which should be clearly discussed and as well presented in written form. Financial information should be shared with prospective adopters at the very beginning of a potential working relationship with an agency or intermediary.

The issue of fees does not end at placement. Feelings about the process of adoption color our lives into the future. Children eventually ask questions. Consider several examples...

The first appointment that Dave and I were able to get with an agency resulted in a one-on-one interview being scheduled with a social worker at an old and prestigious agency in our community rather quickly after an initial telephone screening. We were thrilled! We had never expected that it might happen so quickly. We arrived carefully scrubbed and coiffed, ready to make the best possible impression. I was far more nervous than Dave was—probably because for me adoption had been a longer leap. Dave knew adoption. He was living it. He had himself been adopted as a baby.

After brief pleasantries and introductions, the interview began. The social worker proceeded to ask us about our educational backgrounds, our incomes, our financial status, our assets (she was impressed with our address and with a statusy sports car we had bought to reward ourselves for the eight years of childlessness we had experienced.) We had come with a list of questions, but it wasn't our turn to ask questions, we soon discovered. The interview ended before there was time, and another was scheduled. As we were ushered out the door, she left us with, "You are such a lovely couple, I'm sure you'll make fine parents. See you soon."

I was excited, but Dave was quiet and moody all the way home. It was later that he blurted it out. "I can't do it! I can't go back to that agency! She doesn't know anything about us except our finances, but she was already ready to approve us. You know, my parents never mentioned fees! I wonder how much I cost?"

and then...

One December when Dave's and my son Joel was eight or nine, he was watching evening news coverage of the Cabbage Patch doll hysteria. These ugly little creatures with adoption papers enclosed were being sold on a black market that Christmas. Dan Rather told

188

us all about the mania—flashing visuals of the classified ads in the *New York Times* where desperate parents and grandparents offered hundreds of dollars for the right doll and showing us pictures of the stacks of black Cabbage Patch dolls which remained unclaimed on Toys R Us shelves. Joel turned to us and pointedly asked, "Is that the way adoption really works, Mom? Do they give the babies to the people with the most money?"

---

and...

Pam and Dan adopted a healthy white baby from a highly respected religiously-based adoption agency. Their fee was a percentage of their combined income for one year, and amounted to $15,000. Two years later they began the adoption process again. Feeling much more self assured about their parenting abilities, they broadened their thinking and began to ask about minority children and children with disabilities and decided that they could handle this. The social worker profiled a baby—a beautiful Hispanic daughter with a minor correctable medical problem—and they were thrilled! But then she added, "And because this baby would be more difficult to place, we are prepared to adjust the fee to $7500." Their answer was yes!

It was months later that they began to feel uncomfortable and indignant. Their much-loved daughter was a bargain basement baby? On sale because of her color and a slight imperfection? What message did this send to her and to her older brother? If asked, how would they explain it? They sent a donation check to the agency for the other $7500.

---

and as well...

Tom and Caroline, an African-American couple, had dealt with infertility for a long time. They wanted to parent, and, in the community in which they were raised, informal adoptions of kids in need of parenting by extended family members or friends is a warmly embraced tradition. But Caroline and Tom, upwardly mobile, middle class, thought that they wanted to do it "right." They would go through a homestudy. They would adopt confidentially. They would have assurances about the birthmother's prenatal care.

They approached a large local agency about adopting through the process. They were shocked to hear about fees at all! For both Tom and Caroline this idea stirred up deeply rooted feelings about people as commodities. They couldn't do it—buy a baby. Several months later, they adopted privately after making a less formal connection through their pastor.

These are the uncomfortable, uncompromising facts. There are few clear answers to the harsh realities of adoption's financial complexities for agencies or for clients. Adoption is a big money business, and prospective adopters need to find a way to deal with this set of realities.

Some changes are in the works. For instance, several large international insurance companies have begun to experiment in the United States with "adoption insurance," which, in exchange for a hefty premium, reimburses expenses lost when a birthparent changes her mind at or shortly after the birth and adoption of her baby. The issue is controversial for a number of reasons: so far it is available only for independent adoptions and then only through insuror-approved intermediaries, the premiums are very high and many intermediaries feel that the risks are too small to merit paying such a premium, critics have suggested that the knowledge that such insurance is available may entice some less than ethical birthparents to pretend to commit to adoption in order to have their medical and living expenses covered during a pregnancy with a child they have every intention of parenting. Adoption insurance may or may not be a boon. We'll see.

Also on the tide of financial change in the U.S., advocacy efforts throughout the country have been aimed at making the maternity benefits paid for by insured prospective adopters who otherwise would not use them available to cover prenatal and delivery expenses of birthparents who transfer parental rights to these families. Arizona was the first state to make progress in this area. While it has not been without significant problems, the system has worked far more economically, fairly, and with fewer problems than insurance lobbyists originally predicted.

Advocates are also watching changes in the subsidies and other forms of assistance available to families who adopt children with special needs. Once these subsidies were based on the adopters' financial status. Increasingly the subsidies are being linked exclusively to the needs of the child, regardless of the adopters' finances. Several recent cases have involved the retroactive payment of subsidies or reimbursement of medical, educational, and/or counseling expenses for children placed as healthy but who subsequently were identified as having pre-adoptive special needs.

Adoptive Families of America and other adoption advocacy groups continue to monitor state-by-state progress in these areas much as RESOLVE has monitored and supported local efforts at changing laws which would produce mandated insurance coverage for infertility treatment. What will ultimately make either of these efforts successful is the willingness of consumers to get involved in these lobbying efforts— either by actively writing or calling or speaking, or, alternatively, by retaining the memberships that give advocacy organizations the clout of numbers and by writing the donation checks that pay for the direct work of others.

Avoiding Judgment—
Independent Placement as an Escape

"I know, we'll adopt independently. No agency, no homestudy!" Huh-uh. It doesn't work quite that way.

In some jurisdictions non-agency placement is completely illegal. In other jurisdictions it is available in a hybrid form called direct adoption, where birthparents and adopters make their own match and then go to an agency for counseling and education which will win them court approval. In many places non-agency adoptions flourish, and indeed in some locales they are more common than agency adoptions. But, in the U.S. at least, all courts require an approval process of some kind.

Yes, it is true that quite regularly the homestudies done in independent placements are done by court order after the fact of the placement and often seem to be just a formality with few scary teeth. On the other hand, in quite a few cities and states courts have decided to

establish local policy—even when the law does not require it—that calls
for the completion of a parent preparation process before a court will grant even temporary custody of a child to be adopted.

An important question to ask yourself is what do you want to avoid? If you resent having to pass muster and prove yourself a fit parent by some impersonal and non-discriminating list of old-fashioned criteria, that's logical, and I'm with you!. An old-style homestudy can be damaging to dignity and self esteem!

But if you're feeling that adoption is just one more way to become parents and thinking that since parents by birth aren't required to prepare, neither should you be; if it is preparation for the differences which are an intrinsic part of adoptive parenting that you are trying to avoid, you're going to get no support from me! Denying the need to understand and prepare for the differences in adoption isn't fair to the family you dream of building. For some people, the avoidance of conventional process is really a way to deny difference—a way to pretend that adoption is just like parenting by birth. While i am willing to say over and over again that I agree that parenting in adoption has more in common with parenting by birth than it has differences, the differences that do exist are important ones. You need to be prepared to face them so that you can help your children do so.

You read what I had to say about the importance of building a sense of entitlement—including acknowledging difference. Here's a place where you may very well need to sublimate your current need for control in the interests of doing what is best for your family over the long haul.

I can say all this and feel that I'm able to do so objectively. Dave and I adopted independently twice, and we believe in the validity and value of independent placement so strongly that we have lobbied in our own state on several occasions when our legislature has proposed striking it as an option here. Well done, well prepared independent adoption works, and it can work for you.

If, for some reason, you are unable to connect with a modern-thinking agency or intermediary, and the agency or intermediary with whom you finally connect is not equipped to provide honest, competent, enlightening and even exciting parent preparation, please seek out adoptive parent preparation in some form elsewhere as an addition! For example, you can read all that you can. Read the books and subscribe to the newsletters and magazines in this book's resource lists. Attend any and all seminars offered by agencies, parent groups, as continuing education courses at colleges and universities, or, in their local absence, listen to the tapes from AFA or NACAC or regional parent group conferences. Look at area hospitals, the Y, the Red Cross, for an infant-care class with an adoption focus and in the absence of one, suggest its creation. By all means involve yourself in one or more local groups for adoptive parents.

Changes in the Wind

The term and the attitude for the '90s and beyond is indeed *parent preparation*, a process by which adoption intermediaries supply the education, the resources, the support whereby people interested in adopting are empowered to make their own well informed choices which will result in family building by adoption with the greatest opportunity for a successful outcome.

Murray Ryburn, a social worker currently a lecturer at Birmingham University in England, spent a number of years in clinical practice in New Zealand and elsewhere. Ryburn's article "The Myth of Assessment" appeared in the British journal *Adoption and Fostering* (Volume 15, number 1:1991). In it he writes, "In my view the whole adoption process is grounded in a spurious belief which social workers have had to assume for reasons of professional status or societal or judicial expectation. It is the belief that it is somehow possible for us to know best, through a process of assessment, the appropriate type of placements for children and young people who are to be adopted, and consequently who will be good enough parents for those children." Ryburn goes on to point out that "the issue most central to the concept of assessment in adoption is whether there is an independent objective reality against which, through a process of enquiry, prospective adopters (or foster carers for that matter), can be measured, and appropriate placements made."

What an incredible burden social workers place upon themselves in attempting to accept the responsibility for being able to make, definitively, such weighty decisions.

Here at the end of the twentieth century social change is spurring professionals of all kinds—medical, mental health, legal, social service, educational, etc.—to reevaluate their role in relationship to their clients. Where once clients accepted a subservient relationship with paternalistic professionals, increasingly consumers are insisting on retaining control of their bodies, their decisions, their lives. The most successful professionals today are those who see themselves as educators, facilitators, mediators who empower clients to make their own decisions. It isn't so much that social service professionals no longer have a gatekeeping responsibility as it is that they have come to understand the difficulty in making truly accurate assessments and as an alternative have learned that in many cases it is possible to help prospective adopters see on their own that adoption is not a wise choice for them.

It isn't that agencies who empower their clients won't have procedures and regulations. It is that these procedures and regulations will follow from logically developed program planning which has the best interests of all clients at heart and that these procedures and regulations will be shared with clients in written, as well as oral, form. They will be programs which are client-centered (admittedly challenging work when there are three clients—child, birthparents, adopters). Such programs do exist already, and for many couples, the way to deal with their concerns about the adoption system is to seek them out.

And so you've made it. You've decided to adopt. You've decided who to adopt. You've decided how to adopt. You've started the process. You've educated yourself and prepared yourself and what's left is to hurry up and wait. Congratulations, Mom and Dad, a child is on the way!

What an exciting life you face! Embrace adoption's differences! Celebrate the way in which your family will be built! In doing so you free yourself to relish adoption's similarities.

Resources

This list of resources is designed to help you in making the decisions and pursuing options discussed in Part Two of this book. As was the list at the end of part one, this list is not meant in any way to be exhaustive or complete. Instead, it is my personal selection of those consumer-oriented resources which I thought were most valuable, helpful and practical as this book went to press. Important printed resources are introduced every year and at the same time valuable tools are taken out of print. You may very well have difficulty locating some of the books mentioned here on shelves in local bookstores. Your public library can help you borrow the books you need—often even those that are out of print—through the interlibrary loan system. Most of these books and many others can be ordered by credit card over the telephone from A.F.A. The best way to keep yourself informed and current on what's new concerning infertility or adoption related subjects is to ask for current information from RESOLVE, IAAC, AFA, ACC, NACAC, NCFA, etc.

Organizations

Adoption Council of Canada, P.O. Box 8442, Station T, Ottawa, Ontario K1G 3H8. Phone 613-235-1566. This network collects and disseminates information about adoption throughout Canada, facilitating communication among groups and individuals interested in adoption and promoting understanding of the benefits and challenges of adoption.

Adoptive Families of America, 3333 Hwy 100 North, Minneapolis, MN 55422. Phone 612-537-0316. An excellent source for purchase of books and tapes and of referral to local parent groups, AFA is the largest organization for adoptive families in the world. AFA publishes *OURS: The Magazine of Adoptive Families* bimonthly and sponsors an annual national conference designed specifically to reach out to those considering adopting and adoption-expanded families. Its Annual Adoption Information and Resources packet lists several hundred agencies nationally and offers consumer advice.

American Academy of Adoption Attorneys, P.O. Box 33053, Washington DC 20033-0053. A national association of attorneys who handle adoption cases or otherwise have distinguished themselves in the field of adoption law. The group's work includes promoting the reform of adoption lawas and disseminating information on ethical adoption practices. The Academy publishes a newsletter and holds annual meetings and continuing education seminars for attorneys.

Infertility Awareness Association of Canada, 523-774 Echo Drive, Ottawa, Ontario K1S 5N8, CANADA, telephone 613-730-1322. A Canadian charitable organization offering assistance, support, and education to those with infertility concerns by issuance of its bilingual publication *Infertility Awareness* five times a year; establishment of chapters to provide grass roots services; a resource centre; information packages; and a network of related services. Services are bilingual (English and French.) A complimentary information kit will be sent to interested Canadians upon request.

National Council for Adoption, 1930 17th St NW, Washington DC 20009, telephone 202-328-1200. An advocacy organization promoting adoption as a positive family building option. Primarily supported by member agencies, it does also encourage individual memberships from those families who share its conservative stance on open-records/ confidentiality and its wary view of open placements. If you have decided to pursue a traditional, confidential, agency adoption, call NCFA for a referral to a member agency.

North American Council on Adoptable Children (NACAC), 970 Raymond Avenue #6, St Paul, MN 55104. Phone 612-644-3036. An advocacy and education resource concerning waiting children, NACAC publishes the periodic newsletter Adoptalk, which reviews new books and tapes, and sponsors each August an enormous, well respected conference on special needs adoption for professionals and parent advocates. This conference rotates through five geographic areas. If you are considering a special needs adoption, call NACAC first for information about local and national resources, parent groups, and adoption exchanges.

RESOLVE, Inc., 1310 Broadway, Somerville, MA 02144. Phone 617-623-0744. RESOLVE and its over 50 local chapters maintain current references on all infertility and adoption issues. In addition to publishing both national and local newsletters which print book reviews, the national office develops and keeps updated fact sheets on a variety of issues of interest to its membership. Several of these deal carefully with adoption subjects. Locally, chapters periodically offer, in addition to monthly meetings, day long seminars on both infertility and adoption issues. Several chapters periodically survey their geographic service area's adoption agencies and publish a resource guide.

von Ende Communications, 3211 St Margaret Dr., Golden Valley, MN 55422. Phone 612-529-4493. This audio service catalogs the sessions from numerous large national and regional adoption and child welfare conferences. An excellent source for up-to-date information from the trainers who have not written consumer books and for narrowly focused subject information for those who do not have the opportunity to attend large conferences.

Books and Articles

General Issues

The Encyclopedia of Adoption by Christine Adamec and William Pierce (New York: Facts on File, 1991). The title tells you exactly what this is— a collections of essays on nearly every adoption related topic you could imagine, arranged in alphabetical order. Includes hundreds of references to books, articles, studies, etc.

The Psychology of Adoption edited by David Brodzinsky and Marshall Schechter (New York: Oxford University Press, 1990). A collection of essays on a variety of adoption issues—many written by trainers who have not written books and up to now have been difficult for consumers to access.

Being Adopted: The Lifelong Search for Self by David Brodzinsky and Marshall Schechter (New York: Doubleday, 1992). Integrating both psychological and educational theory, the authors offer a model of normal development in adoptees.

Chosen Children: New Patterns of Adoptive Relationships by William Feigelman and Arnold R. Silverman (New York: Praeger Publishers, 1983). A report of a large across the spectrum study (traditional and preferential adopters, domestic and international placements, inracial and transracial, infant and older child, etc.) which attempts to draw inferences about what factors predict positive and negative outcomes.

An Adoptor's Advocate by Patricia Irwin Johnston (Indianapolis: Perspectives Press, 1984). This book's precursor.

Shared Fate: A Theory and Method of Adoptive Relationships by H. David Kirk (Brentwood Bay, BC: Ben-Simon Publications, rev 1984). The presentation of the sociological theory that adoption-built families share role handicaps that can become positive tools for establishing strong, trusting family relationships.

Adoption: Charms and Rituals for Healing by Randolph W. Severson (Dallas: House of Tomorrow Productions, 1991). An approach to the emotional aspects of adoption from a family therapist who is a also poet and philosopher.

You're Our Child: The Adoption Experience by Jerome Smith and Franklin I. Miroff (Lanham, MD: Madison Books, rev 1987). An introduction to the idea of building a sense of entitlement between parents and children.

What Type of Child?

Adoption and Disruption: Rates, Risks and Responses by Richard Barth and Marianne Berry (New York: Aldine De Gruyter, 1988). There is a great deal of mythology about what causes disruptions or failures in adoption. This book looks at the factors which contribute to an outcome of disruption and offers valuable suggestions for preventing them.

"Where Do Black Kids Belong? The Politics of Race Matching in Adoption" by Elizabeth Bartholet, *University of Pennsylvania Law Review*, Vol. 139 No. 5, May, 1991, pp. 1163-1256 (order reprints from AFA.) A review of the results of the research which has examined transracial adoptions with a discussion of how politics has influenced the legal practice of adoption.

A Child's Journey through Placement by Vera I. Fahlberg, M.D. (Indianapolis: Perspectives Press, 1991). Pediatrician and therapist Fahlberg helps both parents and professionals understand how the experience of being moved impacts on children. Provides a clear description of the attachment cycle and how to support attachment in children who have left important early caretakers.

Self Awareness, Self-Selection, and Success: A Parent Preparation Guidebook for Special Needs Adoption by Wilfred Hamm, T Morton and L Flynn (Washington: NACAC, 1985). A workbookish series of questionnaires and exercises for people considering special needs adoption. Order from AFA.

Adopting the Older Child by Claudia Jewett (now Jarratt) (Boston: Harvard Common Press, 1978). Though older, this is a classic resource for those considering this option, written in a totally accessible style.

Helping Children Cope with Separation and Loss by Claudia Jewett (now Jarratt) (Boston: Harvard Common Press, 1978). Another valuable resource for those considering an older child.

The Special Child Handbook by Joan and Bernard McNamara (New York: Hawthorne Books, 1977). Offers an introduction to a variety of disabling conditions and resources available for managing them.

Are Those Kids Yours? American Families with Children Adopted from Other Countries by Cheri Register (New York: The Free Press, 1991). A thorough, practical, down to earth discussion about the realities of and guide to parenting a child born outside the U.S.

How-to: Choosing a Style of Adoption

There Are Babies to Adopt by Christine Adamec (Boston: Mills and Sanderson, 1989). An exploration of various options in and routes to adopting an infant.

Adoption: A Handful of Hope by Suzanne Arms (Berkeley, CA: Celestial Arts, 1990). A revised edition of the earlier To Love and Let Go, this book revisits, ten years later, several birthparents and adopting families who have chosen open adoption.

An Open Adoption by Lincoln Caplan (New York: Farrar, Strauss,
Giraux, 1990). After extensive fascinating interviews with professionals on both sides of the controversy surrounding open adoption, journalist Caplan attempts to present objectively the intimate details of one particular open adoption in which both birth and adoptive parents allowed him to follow their progress from before the birth through a year following the placement, including a disturbing conclusion. The result is a book which is fascinating, and which neither pro-open or pro-confidential advocates find satisfying.

The Adoption Resource Book by Lois Gilman (New York: HarperCollins, rev. 1992). This is the most authoritative adoption how-to available and has been updated several times. Journalist and adoptive parent Gilman carefully explores all types and styles of adoption and provides excellent resources for pursuing specific strategies.

Adoption without Fear edited by James. L. Gritter (San Antonio: Corona Publishing, 1989). A series of essays written by birth and adoptive parents who participated in open adoptions through the same Michigan agency.

Winning at Adoption by Sharon Kaplan (now Roszia) (Studio City, CA: The Family Network, 1991). A multimedia approach to making decisions about adoption style, this well put together package includes videotapes, audiotapes and workbooks.

Open Adoption: A Caring Option by Jean Warren Lindsay (Buena Park, CA: Morning Glory Press, 1987). Though more specifically written for pregnant teens, the audience to whom teen-parent educator Lindsay most often reaches out, this book offers interviews with nearly all of the well known professionals who have an opinion on the relatives merits of openness in adoption and as well offers prospective adopters insight into the thinking of prospective birthparents.

Beating the Adoption Game by Cynthia Martin (New York: Harcourt Brace, Jovanovich, 1988). A classic how-to with valuable insights which will help you to weigh alternative styles.

The Private Adoption Handbook by Stanley B. Michelman and Med Schneider (New York: Villard Books, 1989). A guide to independent adoption written by attorney specializing in the field.

Successful Adoption: A Guide to Finding a Child and Raising a Family by Jacqueline Hornor Plumez (New York: Harmony Books, 1982). While this book is in some respects a how-to, its psychologist author offers some valuable insights about both decision making and parenting issues which would be important to those considering adopting.

Cooperative Adoption: A Handbook by Mary Jo Rillera and Sharon Kaplan (now Roszia) (Westminster, CA: Tri-adoption Library, 1985). A practical step-by-step guide for both birth and adoptive parents considering pursuing the trademarked form of open adoption called Cooperative Adoption. Sharon Kaplan is a highly respected leader in this field.

A Letter to Adoptive Parents on Open Adoption by Randolph W. Severson (Dallas, TX: House of Tomorrow Productions, 1991). A warm and encouraging booklet for families considering open adoption.

Dear Birthmother: Thank you for Our Baby by Kathleen Silber and Phylis Speedlin (San Antonio: Corona, 1982). This is the book that started the discussion of openness in adoption. Startlingly controversial when new, the form of open adoption it then promoted was the exchange of anonymous letters through an intermediary!

Children of Open Adoption by Kathleen Silber and Patricia Martinez Dorner (San Antonio: Corona, 1989). Nearly ten years after the practice began, Silber follows up on the growing children of some of the families with whom she began practicing openness in adoption.

Adopt the Baby You Want by Michael R. Sullivan and Susan Shultz. An attorney specializing in independent adoption shows you the ropes. This includes a good set of cautionary guidelines.

III

Adoption through a Lifetime

9

Making a
Child Your Own

In this third section of this book we will be looking at adoption issues throughout the lifespan. This is where we learn how to negotiate the delicate balance between acknowledging difference consistently and overemphasizing adoption as a central issue in our relationships. Adoption is, after all, a process which will be a part of who we are and who our children are throughout our lives. There are certainly ongoing issues in adoption which will make it an issue beyond the obvious fact of difference in how to deal with the "where do babies come from?" questions from preschoolers. Families built by birth can take for granted a variety of issues which may become obstacles for families built by adoption. But Kirk's important information about the role handicaps that parents and children experience in adoption should not be taken so literally as to mean that adoption should be experienced as a disabling condition. It is a fact of our lives, the way in which our children joined our families, but in most ways no more relevant as a life long label than it would be to refer to Missy as Peter's birth-control-failure daughter or to Ahmad as Bonnie's caesarean-section-born son. We are, and we will always be, more like families built by birth than we are unlike them.

━━━━━━━━━━━━━━

Mel and Lois decided that they wanted a baby, but they'd be darned if they'd do that dance with an agency! So they asked some people they knew how they'd done it and then they called several doctors and lawyers whose names had come up frequently and asked to be given a call if anything came up. Then they went right on with their lives and didn't give adoption another thought. They didn't attend any meetings. They didn't read any books or articles or newsletters. They made no changes in the way they were living.

Six months later, when the call came, they'd almost forgotten they'd ever heard of the attorney whose voice was on the other end of the line. Hey, sorry to call on such short notice, but the couple working with this birthmother had sort of flaked out when they adopted from another source, another couple was on vacation, a third had gotten pregnant since he spoke to them last, a fourth claimed not to be "ready"—believe it or not. Meanwhile, this birthmother had gone into labor a little early, and right now there was this real healthy little boy waiting to go home from the hospital tomorrow, for gosh sakes. Did they want him?

Well, gee, how do you say no to an offer like that? Mel and Lois said yes! The next day they each called in to their employers with the shocking news that they wouldn't be in for a day or two, borrowed a car and an infant restraint from a surprised neighbor (both of their cars were two seaters—no place for a car seat), appeared in court for a waiver hearing, rushed to the hospital, brought home a still nameless son, and then called their parents in distant cities.

The next several months were a blur of changes. The baby was colicky. Neither Lois nor Mel had any idea how to change or bathe a baby, and they had no close friends who were parents to help them learn. They moved to a two bedroom apartment after several weeks of tripping over one another and all the baby gear that began to fill their very neat, very adult world. They traded in one car, but in the rush, ended up with a mini van that

they really didn't like much. Lois' employer wasn't at
all happy with her child care problems and she lost her
job, cutting their income in half. The court's designated
social worker for their homestudy was both disapproving
and unhelpful. Their families were shocked and not real
happy about the adoption for what seemed like a long
time.

In Chapter Seven we talked about the concept of a psychological
pregnancy—the process of allowing yourselves to wallow in an
introspective process of change, making the move from unhappily
childless couple to enthusiastic (if nervous) parents through a several
months journey involving fantasizing and dreaming about, planning and
making practical arrangements for a particular child (whether baby or
older child) who will join the family. This is a journey which begins at
approval if you are working with an agency which will make a placement
decision on your behalf, or, in the case of a parent-initiated adoption, at
the time when a set of birthparents indicates that they have selected you
to be parents of their coming child. Sometimes, for couples who don't
allow themselves a readiness stage, it's skipped completely, as it was
for Mel and Lois.

Often infertile adopters are reluctant to allow themselves to fully
experience the joyful anticipation of a psychological pregnancy. Even
when they "know" they'll be getting a baby, because they have been
approved and are waiting patiently in line at a traditional we'll-make-the-
perfect-match agency, some adopters refuse to get their hopes up. It's
darn hard to believe in the reality of parenthood after all those rollercoaster
years of monthly cycles of rocketing hope and crashing despair.

It doesn't really surprise me that so many couples consciously
deny themselves this opportunity. After all, the infertility experience has
taught them not only that they are more inclined to fail in family planning
efforts than to succeed, but that reassuring professionals don't always
deliver. Sometimes it's even hard, given the fact that our bodies were
unable to allow us to do this parenting thing "right," for us to believe in
our own potential competence as parents. Oh, yes, the agency has given
us a Good Housekeeping Seal of Approval. But they don't **really** know
us, after all. We played the game well, hid all of our warts. We can't really
be as perfect as that stamp of approval indicates, and that very concern
sometimes makes the stamp of approval a real burden for parents to carry.

Guess what? You're right. You can't be that perfect. And, come now, did you really think that that social worker expected you to be? Yes, I know that you did think that, but it wasn't true. In reality social workers know that adoptive parents are normal people. They will become normal parents. They will do some things absolutely wonderfully. They will make some mistakes. They will be real, for sure parents ... and so will you. This time really is different. Physicians could go only so far in trying to assist your efforts to conceive. They couldn't guarantee a baby. But adoption intermediaries really **do** have much more power than the doctors did. If you have worked carefully to connect with reputable, caring professionals, then, barring some disastrous and **highly unlikely** possibilities—the agency suddenly and with no warning going out of business, leaving long lists of families approved and waiting; something entirely weird about a couple's resume that makes them unappealing to any birthparents despite the fact that an agency thought they'd make good parents; a strange twist of fate that results in your being contacted by no birthparents at all despite vast networking—couples who have committed themselves to adopting and have taken an active rather than passive role in pursuing adoption opportunities will become parents. Believe it.

Why is it important to believe it? Because in being able to believe in the reality of impending parenthood, you will free yourself to begin the psychological journey to parenthood. Not that you can't become good parents without having had this pre-adoptive preparation time. You can. Many do. Mel and Lois did! But giving yourselves permission to experience this psychological pregnancy begins the process of claiming, bonding, and attaching between parents and child earlier and tends to result in a less anxious transition upon arrival.

An excellent first step is to begin to plan your child's space in your home. Visiting a children's furniture store can feel strange at first, but you will soon begin to get caught up in the excitement generated by the pretty things. Your needs here are the same as are those of parents expecting to give birth. Your baby will need a car seat, a bed, a place to store clothes, feeding and changing equipment. Selecting these things and having them placed in your home claims space for your child there. But of course, for those who simply can't make the leap of faith, the next best thing is to do the shopping and keep a list of where to find everything you want when you really need it.

━━━━━━━━━━━━━━

After we were approved at the agency, we knew in logical way that we would eventually become parents, but, after all the years of disappointments, our hearts refused to believe. On that logical level we accepted that we needed to get ready, but how? Slowly, tentatively, the spare room was emptied of boxes and the carpenter called to install another window. The walls were painted and the carpeting cleaned. For weeks I would open the always closed door and look in, thinking about a nursery, but somehow not confident enough to really make this spotlessly clean white room into one.

The arrival of our best friends' daughter, Erin, via a completely out of the blue private placement, convinced me that adoption was real. Watching her mother, Linda, become her competent and loving parent, reassured me that Dave and I, too, could and would do this. We felt the need to do a little nesting, but it was still so cautious, so tentative. First, the rocker was moved into the empty room. A box of baby linens collected from our parents went into the closet.

One Saturday morning I awoke early. It was time to do more. I spent the day designing and sketching the outline for a mural. A circus train was almost invisibly traced in pencil on the walls. I went out and bought paint—lots of paint, in bright, primary colors—and on Sunday afternoon began the process of filling in my coloring-book-outlined train. Every day for several weeks I'd come home from my teaching job and pick up brushes. Others got into the act. My parents came to help clean up the spilled enamel on the carpet one night. Dave's mother had the perfect idea for a circus tent window treatment. An old dresser was refinished, and its round, wooden drawer pulls painted to resemble clowns' faces.

The nursery became the focal point of our lives. The door was always open, now, and as we passed, we walked in just to look. Visitors got "the tour" whether they wanted it or not, forced to smile and feign appreciation for my amateurish art. Early in the morning and late into the evening one or the other of us often sat in the empty room, rocking and dreaming.

The day after school was out for the summer, Linda called and suggested that we take Erin and go shopping. We stopped at a children's furniture store. In the window stood the perfect bed for the circus nursery. We special ordered it and expected to take delivery in about two weeks—no rush, after all.

That evening, we got "The Call."

Now, while you are waiting, will be a more comfortable time to begin to read and learn about parenting—parenting in general as well as parenting by adoption. You probably will already have read several adoption how-to books, the best of which also include quite a bit of good information on parenting issues, too. You could buy some of the adoptive parenting books now—titles like *Raising Adopted Children* (Melina) or *Parenting Your Adopted Child* (Siegel)—but, having completed an adoptive parent preparation process, you will find it even more satisfying to focus now not on the adoption aspect of your transition to parenthood, but on the normal, everybody-does-it practicalities. If you will be adopting a very young child, look at Dr. Spock, at T. Berry Brazelton's books, Penelope Leach, at the newest books you can find on infant care. If you will be adopting a child beyond infancy, in addition to the special focus books dealing with adoption issues read the John Rosemond titles or Cline and Fay's *Parenting with Love and Logic*.

Do only what makes you comfortable, but do as many of those things as you can. Browse in the baby section at department stores. Look through the baby books and baby announcements at the card store. Allow a friend who wants to do so to give you a shower. If one is available, enroll in a hospital or Red Cross or Y's expectant adopter's class where you can learn practical infant care skills. If these are unavailable, consider whether or not you would be comfortable signing up for a general infant care class. Those who are adopting toddlers or older children may want to consider taking a Parent Effectiveness Training course or some similar parenting issues classes. Take CPR and first aid courses.

Now is the time when you are likely to begin to feel less resistant to other people's children. Including your family and closest friends in your process brings them with you in the same way that watching your sister's belly bloom brought the family along throughout her pregnancy. Some prospective parents like "borrowing" babies for short stretches by babysitting for family or friends for a few hours or by volunteering in their church or synagogue nursery.

One of the most challenging aspects of arrival will be coping with the tumult! After months of being oh-so-ready, arrival can sometimes become mass confusion. The excitement of others often tends to produce too much of a good thing. When parents give birth there are certain expectations related to the physical process of giving birth which produce much needed support for the family. The physical experience of labor and delivery has been a strain, so there is the expectation that Mom will be tired. She is usually given some resting space. Traditionally in many families grandparents arrive to help with housekeeping so that Mother and Baby can have time alone. As times have changed and extended family members more and more likely to have jobs which make their participation difficult, some families have hired doulas (women whose supportive role might be compared to that of a midwife, but who offer their assistance after the birth) for this purpose. Friends bring or send in meals or offer to run errands.

When families adopt—and even more so when they adopt a child who is not newborn—these supportive steps are often left out. They shouldn't be! It is not uncommon for adopting parents to experience a Cinderella syndrome, finding themselves cooking and cleaning for visiting guests who have overlooked or forgotten how much of new parents' exhaustion after a new child's arrival has to do with the lack of sleep and adaptation to massive change as well as with the recovery from having given birth. There are several things you can do in advance to prepare to deal with or prevent this.

1   Prepare and freeze some microwavable meals or set aside budgeted money for extra help with meals or housecleaning during the first weeks after arrival.

2   Speak to your child's prospective grandparents, aunts and uncles about your needs for arrival week, finding ways to include them which will not deplete your energies. Obviously you want your extended family to claim your child as their own, so you may find it awkward to encourage this while at the same time dealing with your nuclear family's needs. If they live nearby, this may be easier to accomplish than if they live in other cities, as you will be able to limit visiting times. If they will be visiting from out of town, discuss before arrival time what arrangements will need to be made. Would you prefer that they stay in a hotel this time? Can they be helpful to you in other ways as you provide your new baby's needs? Would it be better to send overnight snapshots or videotapes for them to view on arrival day and to speak frequently by phone for the first week or so before planning for them to come for a visit?

3   Advise your friends in advance of the placement of your family's need to have quiet, private time together for a few days before opening yourselves to visitors. A practical way to handle this is to let everyone know that you will be holding an open house on a weekend afternoon a week or two after your child's arrival. Suggest to some that arranging for refreshments and/or helping with preparation and cleanup for this open house would be a welcome and much appreciated baby gift.

4   Arrange for your telephone to be answered by machine for a week or more. The message might announce your news and explain

that the chaos of settling in prevents you from taking phone calls or visits for a few days, thank them for their congratulations and good wishes, and promise to return the call as soon as possible.

While you are waiting, be sure to let your employers know that you are expecting. Do they provide for a parenting leave which is not part of the medical benefits plan? If so, it must be available to parents by adoption as well as to parents by birth. If parenting leaves are not possible and another form of leave cannot be arranged, will you at least be able to take your accumulated vacation time on short notice? Are there adoption reimbursement benefits? Increasingly large corporations are adding this type of benefit, which is relatively inexpensive but very public relations positive both internally and externally.

If you will be returning to work shortly after your child's arrival, begin to think about child care long before baby arrives. Many infant care centers have long waiting lists. While it may be impossible for you to predict exactly when your child is "due," some centers will be flexible about trying to provide a space for you if they know about your pending adoption.

Enhancing Attachments

Jaimee and Steve looked at that wonderful little fat face for weeks posted on their refrigerator, their bathroom mirror, the dashboards of their cars. Soh, Min Jung (soon to be Kelsey) was to arrive from Korea via O'Hare International Airport two months after the letter informing them of her assignment to them. They were so ready by the time the day came to pack the camera, the diaper bag, the stroller, and Grandma and Grandpa into their car for the two hour drive, that they thought they might split from excitement!

The gate area was crowded with waiting families from a several state area. There were banners and balloons and laughter and tears. The plane was delayed. But at last the announcement came.

The babies and their escorts would be last off the plane, but all of the other passengers who filed off first had been well aware of them, and many couldn't resist just hanging around to watch the joyful arrival of

these children into their forever families. For Jaimee and
Steve it was the most beautiful chaos that had ever been! Grandpa took the video. Grandma remembered to thank the escort. Steve and Jaimee fumbled with diapers and heavy winter clothes. Kelsey stared in wide-eyed terror.

The business to be begun during this precious early time together is bonding and attaching—scary terms to most prospective adopters because they've been so improperly used and overworked and misunderstood. There is much to be learned about bonding and attachment theory, beginning with the work of John Bowlby, through the research of Klaus and Kennell, and including the ongoing current work of Michael Lamb. Most of us don't need to be experts in attachment theory, however, because most of us will find that our families attach normally. What we do need is to understand the concept of bonding and attachment, so that we are able to recognize some of the symptoms of possible difficulty in this area and if we find ourselves dealing with problems we can identify them and seek out the help we need as early as possible.

Let me start at the end, rather than at the beginning, in order to dispel the greatest fear most adoptive parents have. Despite the mythology which remains out there, today, in 1991, most attachment experts agree with Michael Lamb, Ph.D., chief of the National Institute for Child Health and Development's Section on Social and Emotional Development, who flatly states that there is **no compelling body of evidence** to support the widely held misbelief in a sensitive period immediately after birth when bonding must occur or the opportunity will be lost forever. Even Klaus and Kennell have been working to dispel the misapplication of their early research on this. But there remains a great deal of general misinformation among members of the media, among nurses and teachers, among the public at large. It is possible that you will find dispelling these myths and correcting misinformation among the challenges you face as an adoption-built family.

We understand now that there are many factors which contribute to attachments or lack of them between parents and children. Attachments can, and indeed very often do, begin for mothers and fathers during pregnancy—including during the psychological pregnancies of adoptive parents. The controversial work of Canadian psychiatrist Thomas Verny theorizes that babies are more aware during gestation than had been previously thought, and that their birthmother's psychological state during her pregnancy can influence their personalities at birth. But attachment is not a genetic connection. Normal infants are able to form attachments with any caregiver. Attachments can be, and often are, transferred from one set of caretakers to another. Over a lifespan, attachments between people change, so that the attachment relationship between parent and infant is different than that between parent and toddler or parent and teenager.

What all this means, bottom line, for families built by adoption, is that it is possible for families to build secure attachments to one another at any time, and that it is probable that well supported, well informed families will do just that. That out of the way, let's spend some time learning about attachment.

Falling in love with your spouse was a kind of attachment experience. Remembering that experience can help you to understand many factors in the attachment experience between parents and children. Despite the mythology perpetuated by books and movies, hardly anyone falls in love in the eyes-meeting-across-a-crowded-room fashion of "Some Enchanted Evening" from the musical South Pacific. Oh, yes, sexual attraction can be immediate and powerful, but falling in love? Not likely.

Falling in love is an interactive experience. Certain things about another person attract you to that person until, through a process of intimate interaction which includes your meeting one another's basic needs, you feel a connection of some importance, attach to one another, and make a commitment. The process of being in love is ongoing, but it needs nurturing. The ongoing give and take between lovers changes over time and affects the quality of their attachments to one another. On a much more primal level, this is what happens between parents and children.

Babies are wonderful little creatures. They are warm and soft; they smell nice and feel good. They are vulnerable and totally dependent. They are pretty hard to resist. In fact, they are made that way on purpose! Babies get their basic needs for food and care and love met because they are so irresistible. Their cries alert their caretakers to their need for attention and, given that attention, they respond with smiles and coos. Very early they recognize the shape and configuration of the human face and respond to smiles with smiles. Over time, as parents and babies become familiar with one another's moods, personalities, and behaviors, an interactive relationship develops. They begin to do what many infancy specialists call a kind of dance together—each partner responsible for part of the interaction.

My favorite teacher of attachment issues is pediatrician and therapist Vera Fahlberg, M.D., who has spent her career working with children and their families experiencing attachment problems and training

professionals about how to prevent attachment difficulties and facilitate
transfers of attachment where necessary. In her books *Residential Treatment: A Tapestry of Many Therapies* and *A Child's Journey through Placement* and in her popular trainings, Dr. Fahlberg discusses the reciprocity cycle between parents and children which leads to the baby's development of trust, security and attachment. Babies display displeasure, discomfort or tension and discharge that tension by crying and squirming and getting red-faced. When a caregiver responds to the displeasure and satisfies the need of the infant, the baby quiets again and exhibits contentment.

The Arousal-Relaxation Cycle[1]

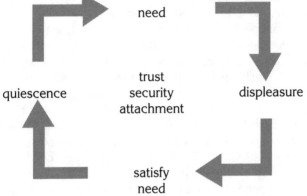

need

trust
security
attachment

quiescence

displeasure

satisfy
need

The parent's role in this cycle is to recognize the displeasure, identify the need, and satisfy it so that the baby can relax. When this cycle is successfully repeated over and over, the child learns to trust and feel secure that his caregiver will meet his needs, and attachment develops. Similarly, as parent and growing child interact with one another a positive interaction cycle develops—parent initiating interaction, child responding favorably—wherein self worth and self esteem are built and attachment enhanced. Without the successful repetition of this arousal-relaxation cycle occurring dozens of times a day, hundreds of times a week, thousands of times in the first year, children do not learn to trust, they do not build successful attachments. When children do not learn to trust at an early age, they experience the world as an unsafe place and they do not develop a conscience. But, when children receive quality care and develop secure attachments to a dependable early caregiver, with competent assistance that attachment can be successfully transferred to another parenting figure.

Everyone who has even a little knowledge about adoption seems to be able to acknowledge that when families adopt older children there is a significant risk for attachment difficulties. Older children are often victims of multiple breaks in attachment or have been attached to people who hurt them in some way and so have great difficulty learning to trust parenting figures. Everybody seems to acknowledge that the process of building transferred attachments with your much older child is complex. It involves your and their being well prepared for a transfer, coming to clearly understand that adoption is an add-on rather than a replacement experience, their being supportively disengaged from earlier attachments and allowed to grieve for them, their being encouraged to open themselves to you, your finding ways to stimulate an arousal-relaxation cycle with them that will encourage their coming to trust you, and your family building attachments to one another. This process is complicated enough that I would not begin to try to deal with it in any definitive way here.

A number of well respected authors and trainers have provided valuable material about attachment problems and solutions for families adopting older children. If you have adopted or are considering adopting a child older than infancy, do not pass Go and collect your child without reading or hearing Vera Fahlberg, Claudia Jewett-Jarratt, Foster Cline, Kay Donley, Barb Tremitiere, Jim Mahoney. Your knowledge about these folks and their expertise will prove irreplaceably valuable to you and the local professionals you work with as you parent your child.

But most of the readers of this book will adopt very young children and little has been written for them about attachment. There is a basic assumption that there is nothing special to discuss. When well prepared parents adopt healthy newborns and take them straight home from the hospital, the odds are very high that their attachment to one another will be relatively uncomplicated. But human babies are not like malleable lumps of Play-Doh® which can be moved about at will for some predictable length of time before exposure to the air results in hardening.

Families adopting internationally and the professionals working with them seemed to acknowledge this earlier than have those working with domestic infant adoption. While relatively little has been written either for clinical professionals or for adoptive parents about the possibility of attachment problems in infant adoptions, an exception, now out of print and providing only a taste at best, was a Holly Van Gulden Wicker booklet for those preparing to adopt babies from India. Holly wrote eloquently about the unusual high-pitched cry common to internationally adopted infants, and about their enormous eyes—seen later to be reflections of the fear of looking up into unfamiliar white faces for the first time. OURS magazine has through the years featured articles on the adjustment difficulties common to children arriving from India, from Asia, from South America. The symptoms discussed were the symptoms of grieving, as these children dealt with the loss of the familiar—familiar caretakers, familiar food, familiar sounds, familiar smells, familiar voices and language, familiar culture—and were forced to make a transitional adaptation. Once again, it has been those adopters who were, by virtue of the obvious in their family, unable to deny difference and forced to acknowledge it, who led the way in dealing with an important adoption-related issue.

Today, however, it remains the exception, rather than the rule, for the parent preparation process of those adopting inracially and in-country to include any specific information about the possibility of awkward attachments in children younger than one year old. This section of this book is an attempt to partially fill that important gap. I acknowledge at the outset that I am not an attachment expert. What I am is an adoption educator and an adoptive parent. What I have learned is not based on academic research with empirical evidence to which I can direct you or even to any journal-reported clinical observation by adoption professionals (most of whom have not observed awkward infant attachment because most parents experiencing it have hidden it from them.) I have learned what I am offering here from two generations of Johnston family personal experiences and from the confirming anecdotal evidence shared with me by literally hundreds of adopters who have seen themselves and their family's experiences reflected in the at first tentatively offered personal anecdotes I have dared to share in the trainings I have been doing throughout the U.S. and Canada these past several years. I have never once done a session on claiming and attaching in which I shared some personal family anecdotes without having had at least one or two parents approach me afterwards to exclaim that they had never before realized what it was that they were dealing with when, riddled with guilt when their babies didn't seem to fit smoothly into their families and their lives, they lived with a grieving infant.

These parents often have not shared their stories with anyone before telling them to me—not with their caseworkers, not with their families, not even with other adopters. Why? Because no one had ever mentioned the possibility of attachment problems with an infant to them before (especially during their parent prep process), so that they had assumed—for over 40 years in two separate cases about which I know—that the only possible reason for their awkward beginnings with their babies had been because they were not good enough parents. Having been given the Good Housekeeping Seal of Approval as perfect prospective parents, they were afraid to go to their adoption workers to ask questions about what they were experiencing, because they feared that in doing so they could risk losing their child by admitting to their caseworker—the most powerful person they had had contact with in their lives—that there were problems.

Some of what follows here will enrage some adoption professionals who don't want to accept responsibility for the poor practices of adoption's past and present. Far too many overworked and underpaid adoption workers and their supervisors presume that they have several months' leeway in which to work at either reunifying a birthfamily or finding just the right adopting parents before jeopardizing a child's ability to attach securely to his forever parents. In too many cases this simply is not true. Very young babies can suffer from attachment difficulties which, if unacknowledged, can affect them over a life time. A variety of factors, including the baby's health, the baby's inborn personality and predisposition to adaptability, the stability and quality of early caregiving, and the attention to detail by social service professionals in transferring between caregivers can be important factors in assuring the development of a relatively uninterrupted cycle of attachment.

Few people are uninformed about how health affects attachment. Babies who are ill or who are in pain are in a constant state of unrelieved tension. This includes babies who are born prematurely, babies who are born drug exposed, babies who tend toward hyperactivity—all of whom are at risk for attachment problems. Since their pleas for help do not result in alleviation of their discomfort, these babies may not learn to trust their caregivers' ability to help them. The problem here is that some of these children are not known to be at risk. Caseworkers do not always realize at placement that a baby is hyperactive or that he has spent his gestational period in an alcohol bath. Even worse, sometimes workers do know these things but don't share them with unsuspecting parents. Why they don't share such knowledge varies. In some cases it is because they really are uneducated in this area and have no idea that it is significant. Sometimes it is because they fear that negative information which they don't understand to be of particular importance may spoil a match or may hinder the new parents' ability to give of themselves unreservedly to their new children. Very occasionally there is a deliberate intent to defraud. But parents have a right to full disclosure and must conscientiously advocate for it.

Adaptability of personality is impossible to measure or, in most cases, to predict. Some people just naturally seem to "go with the flow" while others fight the very suggestion of change. Babies prone to be poor at adapting are at much higher risk for attachment problems than are relaxed and happy-go-lucky children.

Timing is another important factor. It is important to take into account the relative value of time for children. When one is 25, a year is only 4% of a total life, but to a five year old, a year in foster care is 20% of his life. We seem to be able to recognize the likelihood of trauma in that five year old. But a month spent in foster care is written off as inconsequential, despite the fact that when that child is two months old at placement, he will have spent half his life in foster care. Recovering from a change which has entirely disrupted the life a person has known for such a significant portion of it can take time and lots of support. The bottom line is this: traumatized attachments between apparently healthy babies and new parents in adoption are not as rare as adoption workers believe.

Paula and Dennis brought home their third child, Leslie, when she was ten weeks old. Leslie had already been in two foster homes, the first for eight weeks and the second for two. They were immediately aware that something was wrong with this beautiful, healthy baby.

She cried nearly nonstop, in a high pitched, nearly hysterical way that was very different from any of the variety of cries they had learned to interpret in their older two children, both placed straight from the hospital. The daytime crying wore her out so that she easily slept throughout the night. Thank goodness for this! It allowed Paula to recover from the stress and tension of her long days as Leslie's full time caregiver.

Chubby Leslie wanted to suck constantly, but was not only uncomforted by a pacifier or anything other than formula offered from a bottle, she panicked when alternatives were offered. She would be held only in a feeding position, and only when being fed. She craved the warmth of body contact, but not if it involved making eye contact, stiffening her body, arching her back and averting her eyes when held to her mother's shoulder. Unless she was being fed, she found holding comforting only if she sat with her back to her parent's front, facing out.

Suspecting colic or milk allergies, Paula and Dennis had Leslie thoroughly checked by their pediatrician, who pronounced her healthy and overfed. Paula and Dennis were at a loss. They knew something was wrong. They had successfully experienced what they now looked back on as absolutely blissful infancies with their older two children. Thus, confident in their parenting abilities, when Leslie had been with them for two months they anxiously approached their social worker, who promptly pooh-poohed their concerns and suggested that they relax. She offered absolutely no information, referral or support.

Furious, they first contacted the foster parents from whom they had picked up Leslie. This older couple confirmed that the baby had been "fussy" and "difficult" with them as well but offered no solutions. They then contacted the first foster parents, whom they had never met, and from whom they had received no transitional reports. During the course of a lengthy conversation, this foster mom casually dropped in an important piece of information—she had breast fed Leslie, "Oh, not enough to really feed her, since my oldest is three now, but it was enough to give her comfort, and of course there were those immunities I was passing on." Did the agency know? Sure! This foster mom had breast-fed several babies over the last couple of years.

Immunities! Those are passed from mother to infant in the colostrum of her first days of milk production, not for the duration of lactation. Comfort! This baby had been attached to a non-portable pacifier! Leslie had not even been weaned. Since this foster mom knew that Leslie's food was coming from the bottle, not the breast, she had simply stopped nursing abruptly when she handed her over to the second foster mother.

Leslie and her parents were the victims of poor agency practice in several ways:

1   Poorly trained (if well meaning) foster parents who were completely unfamiliar with important attachment issues and even provided inappropriate care (breast-feeding) based on inaccurate information.

2   Too many changes of caregiver. In this case Leslie's birthmother had been ready for adoption and had not wavered at the birth of her child, yet the agency had not preselected parents for the baby by the time she was born. The first foster parents were an unnecessary way station in Leslie's life to begin with, and were

then poorly chosen. They had let the agency know from the beginning that they were going on vacation in eight weeks. The second foster parenting situation could have been avoided completely if the agency had pulled its paperwork together and called Paula and Dennis earlier.

3   Poor transition. Though some gifts and a letter from her birthmother were passed on, no written information about Leslie's schedule or first eight weeks history were passed along either to her second interim caregivers or to Paula and Dennis. It was as if that first eight weeks in a foster home were inconsequential.

Paula and Dennis were lucky. Experienced parents and active in adoption issues, they knew where to turn for help. They made contact with several nationally-known attachment experts as well as LaLeche League, and worked out a routine designed to enhance attachment.

The attachment plan was complex. One parent (in this case Paula) was to do all of the feeding until attachment was more secure. That secure attachment could then be transferred to or shared with Dennis and Leslie's older siblings. A Lact-aid (simulated breast feeder) was attempted, but it was too late for Leslie to remember how to nurse and this just frustrated her further. With the support of their pediatrician, Paula and Dennis carefully measured Leslie's formula and let her eat as often as she wanted, watering it down during the early part of the day and moving to full strength as the day wound down to ensure that she ate enough calories but not too many. Paula "wore" Leslie most of the time in a Snugli™ baby carrier (she resisted at first, but eventually liked it.) For weeks Paula and Leslie went daily to a pool and floated quietly together in the warm water (simulating the amniotic fluid of the womb) while Paula sang and spoke soothing words into the baby's ear. They played floor games, where Leslie lay on her back and her mother knelt over her, singing, laughing, stimulating Leslie to make unwanted eye contact. It took months, but when Leslie was about eight months old, Dennis and

Paula realized that the transition had been made. Leslie was theirs and she responded warmly to their contact with her.

Now seven, Leslie is a bright and secure second grader. Shy and basically a pessimist, though, she is slow to adapt to new situations and reluctant about establishing trust with new people.

How much of who Leslie is is due to Leslie's inborn traits (undoubtedly hers is a relatively inflexible personality) and how much to her unnecessarily negative beginning (having learned early not to trust caregivers, who disappear—two or three times—taking your comfort with them)? We can't know. This is the point. We can never know! Children deserve permanency from the earliest possible moment! Their needs simply have to supersede the needs of either birthparents or of agency administrivia!

As I speak with traditional adopters throughout the country I hear many stories like Leslie's, with one important variant—in most cases these babies are placed with first time parents who have no experience with normal infant adjustment or behavior. Consequentially, most of these parents experience a kind of horror which they are often reluctant to share even with their parenting partner! Since attachment is a reciprocal relationship—baby responding to parent, parenting in turn responding to child, which provokes more response from baby—oftentimes parents of awkwardly attaching babies wonder if indeed they are attaching to their children. The rejecting behavior of a baby like Leslie makes it very difficult for a new mother or father to feel drawn to her. As a result, sometimes parents subconsciously distance themselves to a certain extent from such children, meeting basic needs, but feeling little inclination to force unwanted cuddling or play. This, of course, reinforces the poorly attaching baby's sense that parents aren't for trusting, and a negative vicious cycle is reinforced. Occasionally, parents become so frustrated at being rejected by the baby they have waited so long to love that they are horrified to find themselves on the verge of abuse—tempted to shake the baby into response, to hit a constantly crying child. Such situations promote enormous guilt in the parents, of course, most of whom feel that they cannot possibly share such terrors with spouse or friends or parents or caseworker and simply stuff it down inside to fester over years.

How can readers who are prospective adoptive parents of a very young child work to insure that your child gets the best possible start?

First, educate yourselves and your agency about infant attachment issues. Insist that interim care be used only as a last resort. Consider that this may mean your willingness to accept a child who is still "at risk" in terms of permanent placement because one or the other of his birthparents still has the opportunity to cancel the adoption. If possible, ask to be included in the interim care planning when it comes to making selections about types of bottles or brand of formula or pacifier. Offer to provide sheets, blankets, a music box which will come to you with the baby. If this is not possible, when your child arrives, resolve to remain as flexible as you can in adapting to any already established routines your baby has when he comes to you out of interim care and insist on having access to information about those routines. Even the simplest decisions can make a difference. For example, deciding to use (at least temporarily) the same brand of detergent, fabric softener, body soap, cologne, etc. as the foster parent helps to surround the baby with familiar smells. You have a right to ask for this information and input! Become a part of a parents group and know who to contact and what to do if you suspect any attachment difficulties.

Realistically, however, adopters—especially those involved in an agency adoption—have very little control over the factors that put a baby at risk for claiming and attachment problems. The real power that can bring about change belongs with the professionals who work in adoptions. What can adoption workers who are reading this chapter do to prevent awkward infant attachments? Here are some suggestions.

First, work to insure that your agency's best-interests-of-the-child centered policies consider interim care a step of last resort for infants rather than an administrative convenience. The routine use of interim care is often described as having three benefits: it gives birthparents more time to make their decisions; it protects adoptive parents from the possibility of being disappointed; it give workers more time to make good placement choices. No studies have supported any of these as beneficial in the long run to the primary client in adoption: the child.

I do believe that adoption is not the best plan for all men and women facing an untimely pregnancy. I strongly believe that such parents must be given the most careful and objective of options counseling, and that, where it is needed, enabling emotional and financial support should be given to those experiencing an untimely pregnancy who genuinely feel it best to parent their babies rather than to make an adoption plan. But I also believe that adoption can be and often is a best choice for the child at the center of the decision, and his interests must come first.

The decision to make an adoption plan does not become easier for birthparents over time! It will always be a difficult decision, and even after the decision for or against adoption has been made, most birthparents will experience periods in their lives when they will question the decision. The professional's role is to build on this birthparent client's strengths in helping her to make the best possible decision for herself and for her child, which includes helping her to understand why indecisiveness is not in her child's best interests.

Arbitrarily chosen numbers of days, weeks or months built into certain state and provincial laws which offer birthparents time after the birth to make a final decision about whether or not to make an adoption plan are not in a baby's psychological best interests! Children deserve immediate permanency. Putting a baby in foster care for several days or weeks and then moving him—whether to birthfamily or to adoption—causes him unnecessary trauma.

Administrators who argue that they need this time to find appropriate parents don't convince me. Since agencies and most intermediaries nearly always work with birthparents for at least several weeks before a birth, waiting until after the birth of a child to match prospective parents is an unnecessary delay. Arguing that adopters wish the psychological protection of not having the child until all birthparent rights are terminated or until a child can be "certified" as healthy doesn't convince me, either. Adoptive parents are sometimes more protected than they wish to be. Many of them would prefer to take a legally at-risk placement or to risk the possibility of an unlikely medical condition (pediatricians say that the possibility of a medical condition not obvious at birth appearing within four to six weeks is small) rather than to lose precious time with their children.

I strongly believe that interim care should be avoided if at all possible. Not only can interim care create an attachment risk for the child, but it can be a problem for parents. Expecting adoptive parents to be able to allow themselves to attach unreservedly to their new baby when they know that the placement is in limbo for a period of time invites awkward attachment. As well, adoption professionals should be aware that the very existence of an unnecessary caregiver may confuse the claiming, attachment and entitlement building processes for parents by introducing an additional person for the adopting parents to acknowledge and be grateful to or, even more importantly, by inserting a less threatening and thus easier to dismiss substitute mother for the adopting parents to use in denying the existence of a more emotionally threatening birthmother.

It is not at all uncommon for adopting parents in an insistently confidential adoption to maintain close contact with even the most transitory foster caregivers of their babies for years. These caregivers represent no threat to them or to their children since they have no real claim on the child. They thus alleviate any guilt adopters may feel about trying to forget about or deny the existence of their child's birthparents.

When interim care is unavoidable, establish adoptive-parent-friendly policies. For example, if at risk placement with the adopting couple as foster parents is either impossible or impractical, work to insure that the adopting family is at least identified and encouraged to visit with and interact with the baby in his foster home. Understand that even the smallest decisions about caregiving and routine are usually in the purview of parents and are made in response to their own lifestyle and their own values. Asking adopters to adapt to decisions already made by interim caregivers limits the ways in which they can early on claim their child. Forcing them to adapt to someone else's parenting practices and preferences reinforces any remaining feelings that the child isn't really theirs, anyway, which may cause resentments to develop, delaying the attachment or entitlement building processes.

A major component of change here is the need to train interim caregivers in a new way. Interim care givers must want to empower the prospective adopters of a child who must be in interim care by allowing the adopters to make as many life-style choices which are a part of their claiming as possible. Interim care givers must clearly see that central to their role is its temporary nature. Their job is to facilitate this baby's move to permanency. For example, ask foster care givers to use bottles or nipples selected by the prospective parents and their pediatrician. Allow the adopters to provide crib sheets and blankets and toys which can then be moved with the baby to his new home. Find something portable—a pacifier, a blanket, etc.—and courage the child to attach to that transferrable object as a part of his self-comfort cycle. Encourage foster parents and adopters to promote smoother transitions by together establishing routines which will remain the same after the move—bedtimes, bath times, use of a particular music box.

Finally, as a professional working with artificially formed families, you need to learn as much as you can about attachment and bonding and pass as much of this as possible on to the interim caregivers and the adopting families with whom you come in contact. The trainings and writings of the attachment professionals mentioned earlier (Fahlberg, Jewett-Jarratt, Donley, Cline, etc.) are a good place to start. Martha Welch's book *Holding Time* shows parents ways to recreate the attachment cycle at different ages. Marshall Schechter and David Brodzinsky's book *Being Adopted: The Lifelong Search for Self* was due out just as this book was going to press, and therefore was unavailable for preview, but, given these men's vast experience and expertise in the field I feel certain that this will be a valuable addition to the field. During the parent preparation process acknowledge the possibility of troubled attachments in young children, thus making yourself accessible without threat to families who do experience difficulties in this area.

For many, claiming a child begins with choosing his name. Naming a child is a parent's job, and it is a highly personal process which takes into account cultural and religious factors, family traditions, experiences of the past which have colored our reactions to certain names.

Families adopting older children must carefully consider the impact of changing a child's name. Most attachment experts believe that it is a bad idea to change a child's name once he has reached an age where he responds to that name. The message children can receive from such an arbitrary change is that the child who bore the original name was not a good child, so that the renamed child must pretend to be this new and better person. Of course children will take on their new family's surname, and for many families this will be enough of a claiming factor. For families who feel really invested in giving the child a particular name, experts suggest that a compromise with older children might be to add a new middle name.

Of course there are some instances where there are good arguments for changing an older child's name—when another child in the family already carries that name (consider altering both slightly), when the name coupled with the new surname results in a sound or a set of initials which would open the child to ridicule, etc. But the issue of changing the name of an older child should not be taken casually.

When adopting a newborn, selecting a name may seem straightforward and uncomplicated. It usually is. But the movement toward open adoption has indeed complicated this process somewhat, as birthparents sometimes feel that they should be included in the naming process. This can in many cases become a wonderfully cooperative experience for birth and adoptive parents. But this can also become one of those awkward situations which critics of openness point to as one of the things which inhibit the new parents' ability to feel a sense of entitlement to their child. The awkwardness can be prevented if the professionals are doing their jobs well, so that the counseling process of the birthparents helps them to understand the value for their child and his parents in allowing them to choose the name of the child who will be their own. If this does not occur, parents will need to do their own adapting, compromising with the birthparents only to the extent that will not compromise their relationship with their child.

Professionals often encourage families adopting internationally to think about names carefully. While carrying an unusual or "foreign sounding" name can be awkward for a school age child, it can be equally awkward for a child of an obviously Asian or East Indian or South American

culture to carry a distinctly nonmatching ethnic-sounding name. The
compromises may include choosing a first name which is as broadly
"American" as possible and embracing your child's heritage by including
a name from that culture or country as part of the child's longer formal
name or choosing an ethnic or culturally reflective name from which an
Americanized nickname can be drawn.

It is important to consider that for a child who becomes a Junior
or a III this may be either a positive or a negative. Some children and their
families experience this as a way to embrace one another. Other adoptees
have expressed the discomfort of being so awkwardly and so obviously
different from the person for who they have been named.

Bringing Your Family Aboard

Carol gave birth to two blue eyed sons after the
adoption of brown eyed William. Everybody loved
William, he was one of the gang of cousins who frolicked
in Bubbie and Zeydie's yard at holidays. But at one family
gathering Carol was shocked by her mother's casual
remark to an aunt. "Yes, all of my grandchildren have
blue eyes," she remarked.

"Not William!" chimed in Carol.

"Oh, you know what I meant, Carol," her mother
responded. But Carol wasn't quite sure that she did
know, and it hurt.

As we earlier mentioned, often your extended family is slightly
behind you in accepting and embracing adoption. But the arrival of a
wonderful little person is hard to resist. Extended family can become
involved in the claiming process through the selecting of names.
Choosing a name which honors an ancestor or a willing grandparent, aunt
or uncle can publicly proclaim a child as a member of your clan.

Try to be patient with the laggers-behind, but through the years
look for ways for them to claim your children. Encourage your parents to
spend as much time as possible with these grandchildren. Educate them
about some of the ways in which adoption is not like connections by birth
(for example, in some states, unless adopted grandchildren are either

228   specifically named or the inclusive terms "by birth or by adoption" is added
to a will, adopted children will not automatically inherit from their parents'
parents.) Allow them the silly comparisons which have no basis in fact
("Why, he looks just like Uncle Ralph!")

━━━━━━━━━━━━━━━━

    Pam and Dick were able to laugh about it all
much later, but when their biracial baby Larry first
arrived, and Dick's parents exhibited some uncomfortable reluctance to introduce their new grandchild to
their friends, it hurt. Pam and Dick knew that the problem
was their fear of their friends' racial intolerance.

    They tried to be patient, and so, to encourage
their parents to come to love Larry for who he was, they
made the eight hour round trip to their parents' city every
weekend for several months. It worked. Who could resist
such a beautiful, smiling, bouncing, loving boy?

    One weekend many months after Larry's arrival
Dick's father rushed eagerly to the car upon their arrival
to grab his grandson from the carseat. "You know," he
observed as he covered Larry's face with his kisses, "I
think he's looking a little lighter." The next morning, at
Grandpa's suggestions, the family went to church
together for the first time.

    Now, Dick could have been offended on his
son's behalf by his father's bias. In reality, Larry's skin
was darkening and his hair becoming coarser and curlier
as he matured. But Dick was wise. He recognized that
his father was still playing catch up. He was working to
claim this boy in the ways he knew how. Eventually he
would make it. And he did, leaving behind most of the
bigotry that he had learned growing up along the way.

━━━━━━━━━━━━━━━━

    Your family will need help in fielding the unwelcome or insensitive
comments and questions from their peers. They will need to learn to use
positive adoption language (see Chapter 12). If you arrange an open
adoption, your family may find your open arrangement threatening at
first. They will want to learn, and they will, with your help.

    Perhaps some members of your family would enjoy their own
subscription to *OURS: The Magazine of Adoptive Families*. Pat Holmes'

booklet *Supporting an Adoption* (Our Child Press) was designed   229
specifically for the family and friends of adoption-expanded families, as
was Linda Bothun's *When Friends Ask about Adoption*. Some caring
others may want to read some of the longer books you read. Others will
not. Ask your sister or your dad to attend a local conference with you. If
you can, encourage them to contribute their own thoughts and
experiences about adoption by writing for a local newsletter or being part
of a conference panel.

Claiming is something members of families do over and over in
both subtle and obvious ways whether the children were born to or adopted
by the family. Having our children claimed by their grandparents, aunts,
uncles and cousins is important for them, but sometimes we don't
consciously recognize that it is important for us, too. When we claim the
children of our family's new generation, we reaffirm our own connections
to the current and prior generations. When this claiming doesn't happen,
those old feelings of inadequacy can be stirred again. The more important
the loss of our genetic continuity was in our infertility experience, the more
likely it is that you will find it especially important for your family to claim
your children.

It is not unusual for adopting parents who find certain family
members or friends unwilling to consider their child one of the family to
feel strong resentments which may result in rifts. You will want to do all
you can to openly discuss your concerns and your hurt feelings with this
relative. While no one wants to perpetuate family rifts, the decision to
distance oneself from a stubbornly unsupportive relative is a sign of a
strong need to protect one's child and indicates the development of a
healthy sense of entitlement between parents and child. So for several
reasons, how our families feel about our children who have been adopted
is important to us, as well as to the children, and it is worth our
concentrated efforts to facilitate those attachments.

My son, Joel, is the oldest of the cousins in his
generation of my family. When he was 16 his Uncle Bud,
my brother, casually announced that he had a summer
job for him if he wanted it—on the tent crew for our over
100 year old family business. "Yep, it's your turn, Joel.
Most of the guys in this family have been on the tent crew
when they were old enough to drive and that's how we
worked our way through college. Your great grandfather,
your grandpa, your uncles and second cousins. You'll
be the first of the fourth generation. So, when do you
start?"

The thrill was mine as well as Joel's. Joel heard only the affirmation of himself as a young adult—big, strong enough to swing a sledge hammer, responsible enough to have a real job. I heard something else—everyone in our family does this—including those not born into it. I was affirmed as well as my son.

Now, for my brother, there was no conscious effort or analytical thinking involved here. Had I pointed out to him how grateful I was about this he would have thought I was overreacting. Joel is Joel. He is one of us. What's the big deal? You know, Bud is right.

———————————

=10=

Your Growing Family

I am a person who has worn several occupational hats—some of them at the same time. I have been a teacher, a librarian, an audio-visual specialist, a sales manager, a writer and editor and publisher, an infertility and adoption educator. Once I was even a professional popcorn popper! The hardest job I have ever had is also the one that has given me the most pleasure and the one that was the hardest for me to get—becoming a parent after long and painful infertility.

One of the things that made the job seem hard is that I expected it to come so easily—as a simple by-product of making love to a man I loved very much and found extremely attractive. Of course it didn't. I also expected it to come naturally—kind of by instinct. And of course after I became a parent I wondered along the way if it was harder for me because the "instinct" hadn't been triggered by that mystical experience of "bonding" that all the movies and magazines seem to imply comes magically with the pregnancy and birth experience and creates a kind of super glue that holds families together.

The process of being a parent has been an incredible learning experience. I've done a lot of reading, a lot of questioning, a lot of listening, a lot of conferencing, a lot of thinking, and at this point a lot of parenting—to three kids, now 17, 11, and 8. Are my kids gorgeous? Of course they are—because they're mine! And one of the great things about that is that I feel no embarrassment about telling you that they are good looking, smart, and savvy people. They look nothing like me and nothing like Dave! They don't have my weight problem or my couch-potato attitude toward athletics. They don't have my family's hereditary lazy eye or their dad's nearsightedness and lousy teeth! We can take credit for imparting our values, but none for imparting our genes.

Now, twenty years ago you'd never have convinced me that I'd ever feel that it was great to have kids who were unlike me. Nor could I have imagined that I could look at my two sisters' five children who do resemble me somewhat and then at these three children genetically unrelated to their parents or to one another and feel so total a sense of claiming and overwhelming love of these three, and such a "they're nice kids, but I'm sure glad they're going home with their mothers" attitude about those five who are biologically related to me. But I do.

The fact is that I know now that child rearing is a difficult task for all parents. All parents make mistakes, and you will, too. All parents have issues that make them feel uncomfortable because they don't feel "expert" enough to teach their children about them. One of yours may be adoption. Parents in adoption have some different issues to deal with than do parents by birth. (And it's also true that as adoptive parents there are some uncomfortable issues related to genetic connection that we are relieved of!) How difficult the differences are to deal with depends on several factors, among which are how far the parents have come in the process of building that sense of entitlement to their children that we spoke about many chapters ago, and how far their children have come in building their own senses of entitlement to their parents!

Simplistically put, entitlement is a by-product of secure bonding and attachment between parents and child, child and parents. Or maybe it's the other way around! The important point is that entitlement and attachment are interwoven and interdependent. That three step process that occurs over time rather than all in one rush deserves to be outlined again here, as we talk about children as they grow in adoption-built families. Entitlement involves

1   Recognizing that adoptive families are different from biologically related families in several significant and unavoidable ways. And, as David Kirk, author of Shared Fate, has written, acknowledging those differences consistently rather than trying to reject those differences and pretend that adoption is "just like" what many call "having a child of your own" is the best way to develop communication lines between parent and child. But, at the same time, David Brodzinsky has helped us to see that insistence of difference, making adoption a central issue, is going too far. Families built by adoption have much more in common with families built by birth than they have differences. So this acknowledgement of difference involves walking a kind of tightrope and maintaining balance.

2   All of the members of a family built by adoption work on building a sense of entitlement by learning to deal with the questions and comments from others which so obviously reflect the societal feeling that adoption is second best for all involved. The comments like "Aren't you people wonderful." and "Poor child, how could anyone ever give away their own flesh and blood" or "Do you know anything about his **real** parents?" or "Now that you've adopted you'll probably have one of your own." This is where learning to use positive adoption language will become important.

3   The third step for parents in building a sense of entitlement is to begin to understand and acknowledge your own feelings about your motivations for adoption. They were mostly selfish reasons, but that can be OK. For infertile people this means acknowledging that your infertility has brought you a loss of control, a loss of your individual genetic continuity, a loss of a jointly conceived child, the loss of the physical and psychological gratifications of the pregnancy and birth experiences and dealing with these losses and their impact on you effectively. You adopted because you wanted to be a parent and this was the way! You adopted for yourself, and that's OK! For those who adopted for reasons other than infertility, this step involves acknowledging the selfishness of and putting aside your fantasies about saving someone less fortunate than yourself or doing the world a favor by taking in the homeless, etc.

For your children, a third step in building a sense of entitlement is coming to understand why their birthparents planned adoption for them and dealing with the losses this brings to them. A major loss that most of them feel at some level sometime during middle childhood or after—one that is reinforced by the misunderstanding about adoption of society in general—is that they have been rejected by a significant someone, that their birthparents have "given them away." Kids need to understand that they are loveable, wonderful people deserving of a family and completely blameless for their birthparents' decisions; that through the losses they made many gains, too; and that they deserve the families who love them just because they are who they are!

This is the substance of what we will talk about in this chapter.

How Children Learn

Understanding how it is that children learn and at what ages they are intellectually able to understand information given to them is an important asset when dealing with sensitive issues in parenting—issues like sex education, adoption, morality. The fact is that nearly all "problem" issues in parenting—dealing with sexuality, dealing with divorce, dealing with death, and more—are to a large extent developmental issues. How children accept them and incorporate them into their senses of self is colored by their developmental maturity and by their caregivers' sensitivity to their developmental status.

If parents, in their role as their children's long term teachers, can learn to consider just how relatively sophisticated or unsophisticated their children are before trying to answer questions or deciding how to share certain information, their children will learn with far greater likelihood of misunderstanding.

Let's begin with a highly simplified introduction to a very complex process—cognitive development in children, or how children learn any and all of the things they learn. The remarkable Swiss psychiatrist Jean Piaget, who began observing children during the 1920s and continued to refine what he learned for well over fifty years, changed forever the idea that children are more or less miniature adults.

Piaget discovered that the minds of babies and children are different from those of adults. Since a child views the world from a limited perspective, it is only after he has had many and varied experiences with the things he sees and hears and feels and tastes and tries and experiences in his environment that he is able to think in the very logical way that adults take entirely for granted.

Piaget discovered that kids grow intellectually in five orderly and progressive stages. While children may move at differing rates because of individual and cultural variations, each child moves progressively forward in pyramidal form from one stage to another. More than that, Piaget noted that intellectual development is also tied to physical development. So that even the academically gifted child will need to wait for his physical development to catch up before his cognitive growth can move on.

In moving from stage to stage, children use three processes in their learning. First they *assimilate* (taking in information about something new), then they *accommodate* (putting out information or ideas to be tested) and finally they *equilibriate* (balancing what they've learned and absorbing it for later application.) This is true of all learning, so that learning about math, about riding a bike, about sexuality, about family roles and relationships, about morality, about rights and obligations, about interpersonal motives, and about the functioning of societal institutions is all learned slowly and progressively through the process of assimilating, accommodating, equilibriating. Anna Freud is one of the psychiatrists who has added significantly to Piaget's work. My simplification of her refinements of Piaget's stages of intellectual development follow.

During the *Sensory/Motor Stage* of intellectual development (from birth to about two years of age) a child's major tasks are learning to use and control his body and learning to distinguish himself from others. You will remember that when we spoke about the development of attachment, it was pointed out that child and parent engage in a dance— the child expresses needs, the parent meets those needs, and the result of doing this over and over is that the child comes to trust that a consistent caring someone other than himself, a person to whom he becomes firmly attached, will always be there to meet his needs. At about 18 months, a child, having "mastered" his body to an amazing extent in so short a period, begins to move seriously to mental activity. For example, he can begin to understanding that hidden things still do exist and enjoy peek-a-boo games.

Since children are exploring the world and learning to move away from parents during this time, experimenting with whether or not parent will be there when child returns, this stage brings with it for adoptive parents' a first test of their sense of entitlement! Each parent needs to be able to enjoy and adjust to the child's moving away from and moving back, giving the child his first sense of permission to separate and to trust both his competent self and his parents.

In the *Preconceptual Stage* (from about age 2 to 4) children think very egocentrically, assuming that they are somehow magically omnipotent—personally responsible for all that occurs in their world. All things are alive and feel because, after all, he is and he does. The child assumes that the world is as it appears to him, and he cannot conceive of another point of view.

This stage is followed between ages 4 and 7 by the *Pre-logical/ Intuitive Stage*. Now begins some pre-logical thinking, but only with one concept at a time. For example, a child in this stage is still likely to feel that half a cup of milk which fills a small glass seems more than half a cup of milk which doesn't fill a large glass. He might have trouble labeling blocks as both blue blocks and plastic blocks at the same time.

During this time the child begins to relate differently to his parents than he did before. Prior to this time, parents were largely seen as need-fulfilling persons. Now, increasingly the roles of mom and dad are differentiated, with boys beginning to feel competitive with Dad and girls competing with Mom. The child's huge strides in his cognitive development means that he becomes curious about the surrounding world and will begin to ask some very important questions—where babies are from, for example. He is more active socially. This is the stage at which he is first likely to have some beginning awareness about basic adoption issues.

Commonly called middle childhood, the *Concrete Operations Stage* (ages 7 to 11 or even older) begins in about first or second grade. Children this age can begin to think logically about things they have personally experienced and to make deductions about them. They remain limited, however, by their experiences and they are unable to think abstractly. By this time children are able to think backwards and forwards in time (so now can understand that the half a cup is half a cup whether in a small or large glass). Because this stage is so long and children grow so rapidly during this time, many psychologists have pointed out that middle childhood sometimes seems to have two distinct halves, 6 or 7 to 9 or so, and 8 or 9 to 11. This is a stage rich in all kinds of fantasies. It is also a stage during which children test, and test, and test!

The fifth and final stage of cognitive development is called the *Formal Operations Stage*, and it occurs sometime after the age of twelve (though in some people, not at all!) Children who become logical thinkers understand the theoretic and think abstractly. They are able to form hypotheses, to deduce and induce—even about things that they have not themselves experienced. Sometimes we assume that because a child of twelve or older is physically mature they must be cognitively mature as well.

As a former teacher of junior high aged children I learned on the job how incorrect this is. The movement from concrete thinking to abstract thinking is a difficult transition that can take many years. When I was a teacher of ninth grade English one of the things I learned in the field rather than as a part of my teacher education trainings was that ninth graders asked to provide concrete information in essay form on a literature test can nearly always do very well, but that an often unpredictable proportion (if assumptions are based on physical maturity) will be able to abstractly analyze the material in a novel or an essay. One year not long ago I taught freshman English part time in a very academically oriented and well respected private prep school. These students were all talented, self directed, and parent-supported. Peer pressure mandated academic success in this environment, and most kids were expecting to go to very selective and prestigious colleges. But many of these ninth graders were having a difficult time in their first year in high school, not because the material itself was too hard, but because the assumption of all of their teachers and of the curriculum itself was that all of these students were already abstract thinkers. They weren't! Some were still operating cognitively as concrete thinkers.

While giving children information that is too sophisticated for their level of cognitive development surely can't hurt them, it doesn't help them either. In essence, they simply don't learn it—to use the familiar cliche, it goes in one ear and right out the other. The sad reality of this is that most of the time parents don't even realize that this has happened, and they go blithely along their ways, feeling self congratulatory about having "done their duty" in sharing what they know about whatever imposing subject they've just rambled on about—sex education, adoption, etc. It seems almost a cliche to share that old tired joke again, but it does ram home the point about what happens when we try to teach children about things which they are simply unable to process.

———

Jimmy came in from play one day with an important question for Mom, "Where did I come from?"

Ah, here it was, that dreaded question Mom had feared answering poorly. She'd practiced her response over and over in her mind, making certain that she remained calm, that her terminology was accurate. So she began, "A man and a woman feel a certain way about each other...and the penis...and the vagina...and the egg...and the sperm..."

After what seemed like a long time to Jimmy she finally concluded, "...and usually in about nine months, a baby is born. Does that answer your question, Jimmy?"

"I guess," came the reply. "Did you know that Johnny came from Cleveland?"

———

If you are one of those parents who would enjoy learning more about how children learn, I recommend that you seek out through a good children's bookseller a book which presents Piaget for parents. I have personally found helpful Mary Ann Spencer Pulaski's *Your Baby's Mind and How It Grows: Piaget's Theory for Parents* (Harper, 1978, though now out of print.)

It frustrated and in some ways angered Dave that his sister Mary Jane claimed that she did not know that they had been adopted until she was 10 or 11 years old. Dave, after all, felt that he had always known they had been adopted, and in fact one of the things he appreciated most about his parents' style of parenting had been their complete openness about adoption issues. They had used library books, had dinner table conversations, and answered every question he had asked entirely to his satisfaction. He figured that his sister was not telling the truth, and he couldn't understand why she would lie about something like this, which he felt would hurt their parents feelings. It was not until we began learning about what kids understand about adoption when that it dawned on Dave and me what likely had happened here.

Dave is older than his sister by slightly over two years. Additionally, she had a learning disability, which made learning more difficult for her than for Dave. Though they were chronologically just two years apart, her cognitive development was probably more than three behind his during their early and middle childhood years. As Dave's parents shared books appropriate for children his age and age-appropriately answered the questions of their curious older son, his sister, though sitting there, too, was not paying a whole lot of attention! By the time she was old enough and intellectually mature enough to process this information, Dave had entered that very introspective time when kids are doing a lot of fantasizing but not much talking. Their parents assumed that both kids were doing just fine.

It was really true that Mary Jane hadn't known she was adopted until later. Despite the fact that adoption talk had been going on around her for several years, it ended by the time she was ready to listen to it. It wasn't until her own questions came up at age 10 or so that the conversation started again, and when it did, the fact of her adoption came as a big surprise!

In a landmark study of what children understand about adoption and when they learn it which was conducted at Rutgers University, Dr. David Brodzinsky and a research team that included his wife, Anne Braff Brodzinsky, discovered that both adopted and nonadopted children tend to be able to logically understand the concepts of adoption at the same time, though children who were themselves adopted do learn the jargon of adoption faster than do their non-adopted peers.[1] Few six year olds in the Brodzinsky study, for example, could differentiate between birth and adoption. They thought that people were either born *or* adopted. These six year olds were unable to understand the motives that underlie adoption. The children in this study progressed, though, until adolescents were able to define adoption with sophistication as "a sociological form of substitute care that is based on the principle of protecting the rights and welfare of children."

The stages this study defines parallel closely the stages of cognitive development identified by Piaget and Freud. By about ages 3 to 5, the Brodzinsky study showed, children may know the words and can effectively parrot their own arrival story, but they don't understand the concepts involved. For example, many children don't know the difference between birth and adoption and so equate the two ("Well, John was born, but I was adopted.") They need to be helped to understand that they were indeed born and then adopted. (More on this in a later section on sex education.)

By about age six kids know that birth and adoption are different but have trouble with how adoption works and can't quite grasp its permanency. During this stage, which is colored by rich fantasies and a great deal of magical thinking for all children, adoptees are likely to have some fears about being abandoned by their adoptive parents. After all, they may reason poorly, I was bad enough that my birthparents, who supposedly loved me, let me go. This knowledge has some important ramifications for parents who are considering how best to impart their children's adoption stories. Many adoptive parents who are committed to transferring a clear message that their children's birthparents are good people worthy of great respect and affection tell their children that their birthparents loved them very much and so chose adoption for them. To a child unable to reason and think abstractly, this story doesn't wash! Thinking concretely, children told this story are likely to make a progression which says that if their birthparents loved them and so chose to let them go when things were hard, then since their adoptive parents love them, too, if things get hard (and they are very likely to somewhere along life's way!) that they, too, will find new parents for them.

Educators have noted that when children of this age are given more information than they are comfortable with, they may actually feel that curiosity in general is potentially painful, so that they try to suppress their curiosity, and this can lead to some school problems, as they become quite inhibited. A few adoption educators, including Steven Nickman, have actually suggested that the likelihood of conflicted thinking about such weighty issues as adoption in the very young is a good reason for not sharing the fact of adoption with a child until he is seven or eight. Those who disagree with this position and continue to advocate early telling do so primarily because they fear that the presence of "secrets" in a family can be lethal to relationships and they have not been able to develop a compromise model that takes all of these factors into account.

Somewhere during that middle childhood span of ages 7 to 11 children begin to understand adoption's permanence, even though they are often still unable to understand the function of the intermediary. Since all children of this age do lots of fantasizing with friends, envisioning what it would be like to have idyllic, permissive parents, children who were adopted experience a conflict. For them, there really are another set of parents out there, so for adopted children—especially those in confidential adoptions—the typical fantasies of middle childhood are also possibilities.

We have noted earlier the six losses felt by adults in the infertility experience—loss of control, loss of genetic continuity, loss of a jointly conceived child, loss of the physical and emotional satisfactions accompanying pregnancy or the ability to impregnate, and, if they do not adopt, loss of the opportunity to parent. In his book *The Psychology of Adoption* (Oxford University Press, 1989) Dr. Brodzinsky includes an essay called "The Stress and Coping Model of Adoption Adjustment" in which he writes about the losses which children experience in adoption. He draws our attention to the work of many researchers—Nickman, Sants, Brinich, Kirk—who have noted various individual losses experienced by adoptees, and Dr. Brodzinsky gathers them here for us to consider: the loss of their biological parents, the loss of a genetic connection and genetic continuity, a loss of status associated with being different, a loss of confidence about who they are, and, as a result, to some extent the loss of a feeling of stability in their relationship with their adoptive family.[2]

These are enormous losses for one so young to handle, far beyond the kinds of progressively more difficult losses which normally teach us how to deal with loss! It is not at all atypical for adopted children to begin to exhibit signs of grieving and loss during these middle childhood years— the denial, the anger, the bargaining, and so forth. All too frequently these changes in behavior go unrecognized by child, by parents, by professionals, as being related to the feelings of loss about adoption which these children are simply too cognitively immature to put words to without help.

Middle childhood aged children can either be very verbal or very
quiet, and they be more or less talkative than they were before. Because
so much fantasizing is going on in the normal child now, adoption issues
must be kept in the open during this time, and parents must take great
care to send positive messages about adoption being a good thing to
wonder about and inquire about. Claudia Jewett-Jarrett points out in her
seminars that this is a time when a great deal of confused thinking goes
on, despite parents' best efforts at adoption education.

████████████████████

I went to a Claudia Jewett seminar one fall when
my son was eight or nine. *Helping Children Cope with
Separation and Loss* was new at the time, and it formed
the basis for her training that day. I remember feeling
smug and satisfied when she mentioned how common
it was for middle graders—especially boys, who tended
to begin to have negative feelings about themselves at
this time—to begin to let their tendency toward magical
thinking confuse what they had already been told about
their adoptions. "No, not my son, I thought. We've told
him the story and he knows it. His birthparents were very
young and they weren't finished growing up themselves
yet, and not ready to be parents to any baby, so they
planned adoption for him because they wanted him to
have a mom and a dad who were ready to be parents."

Still, one day the next week as we sat and folded
socks and sorted laundry when he began to talk about a
friend who was pregnant, I used the entree. "Joel, do you
ever wonder why your birthmother chose Daddy and me
to be your parents instead of being your mom herself?"

"Oh, I know why she gave me away," he replied
(the negative adoption language which he'd never heard
from us sent chills up my spine!) "It's because I was
ugly."

Reality check, Mom! Try that story one more
time!

████████████████████

Somewhere beyond the age of nine, as they move toward
adolescence, adoptees begin to understand the permanence of adoption

and as well the active role of the intermediary. They can begin to understand that a transfer of parental rights occurred and that this has had a legal impact. During these years children begin to have many questions, but they are often driven underground. During middle school or junior high years is the perfect time to introduce Susan Gabel's *Filling in the Blanks: A Guided Look at Growing Up Adopted*. This workbook is designed to be used by a child with the assistance of an adult—parent, counselor, social worker, therapist—and has been carefully crafted to take into account children of all backgrounds, colors and abilities being raised by families of all configurations formed by all styles of adoption. This is a particularly good book for parents to own and read *before* their children arrive, so that they can begin to understand how children of this age will be thinking several years down the road and begin to gather the data and information that will be needed to fill in the book at that time.

Since a major task during the adolescent years for all kids is separation, adoptees often struggle with identity issues. Conformity is an important part of being a teen, and adoptees often feel "different." Envy is a common emotion during adolescence, and adoptees often envy the genetic connections of their peers' families. Most teens and their parents spend a good deal of their time being angry at one another, but for teens who were adopted, the complication of that anger can include an unexpressed fear of being abandoned again. They may feel a need either to over identify with their adoptive parents and reject their birthfamily or vice versa. For many adolescents whose birthparents were themselves young and still in school, the new ability to reason brings their birthparents' dilemma clearly in focus. They begin to empathize with their birthparents, even to the point where normal teen rebellion against "systems" becomes focused on an angry perception (true in some cases) that their birthparents were cheated by "the system."

The struggle to avoid losing control is powerful. Sometimes, this can frighten adoptive parents who have a shaky sense of entitlement. What if she's "just like her birthmother" and gets pregnant? What if he embarrasses us by defying our values? As our children begin the final stage of learning to be independent, the one we know will result in their really leaving us and our home to be independent young adults, families can find this testing overwhelming.

Constance's younger daughter Lauralie rebelled thoroughly as a teen. Her older sister, also adopted but psychologically more "like" Constance, had seemed to be perfect. Lauralie refused to compete with her sister. Her choice of friends was from the group her mother considered "losers." She experimented with dangerous substances, dangerous activities, dangerous relationships. Very bright, her grades suffered.

Constance found her infertility before her again. Not only did she resent being so completely out of control of her situation, but she also harbored a terrible, unspeakable belief. A child born to her wouldn't have been like this.

What Constance had forgotten—or perhaps never recognized at all—was that there are no guarantees in parenting. While Laurelie's behavior might have been adoption-related, many teens who are born to the parents who are raising them test in the same fashion. Constance, however, in her disappointment, needed a scapegoat. Adoption was it.

Finally, having reached the age of abstract thinking, kids can begin to understand the evaluative role of an intermediary in adoption who functions to protect a child's best interests. Now as well, they can begin to understand the motivations of both birth and adoptive parents. During these years when all teens are most prone to be uncommunicative with their parents, adoptees receive an important message from their peers: what you are thinking may hurt your parents' feelings, so don't talk about this adoption stuff with them. Adoptive parents need to work hard to make it clear that this is not true. Keeping communication open is the key to it all. Kids need to feel that it is okay to talk about anything with their parents.

Even more importantly, in order to consistently reinforce the sense of trust that comes with firm attachment, from their earliest questions, children must be able to trust that their parents will tell them the absolute truth. Whether adopting an older child or an infant, parents must be committed to helping their children do what Kay Donley has called "making friends with the ghosts of the past"—fully accepting the importance of their placement history.

Opening the Lines of Communication

My six year old son and I had spent the summer afternoon at Rosi's. He had played in the backyard and fussed over Rosi's baby, John-David, while Rosi and

Cindy and I folded and stuffed RESOLVE newsletters. Cindy was still waiting for her first child, and I felt a little guilty as the conversation turned to the any-time-now excitement simmering at our house about the possibility of another adoption. But it was hard—and really unnecessary with these good friends who were all in the same place—to suppress the anticipatory nervousness. Despite the fact that for two years the nursery had been sitting completely ready—sheets on the bed, Pampers in the changing table, hand made quilt awaiting only the embroidered birthdate carefully folded over the rocker— I had more or less steeled myself for another possible disappointment. She might, after all, change her mind.

Several years later, when all of us had our children and got them together, we sometimes reminisced about that afternoon when we'd all been part of a real for sure arrival. I had returned home to a ringing phone, had picked up to hear my friend Mary's voice, "Where were you all afternoon! Congratulations! You have a daughter!"

She had arrived. At long last Erica Brooke was here.

Families who adopt have arrival stories which they and their children love to hear in the same way that families formed by birth love to recite the tales of racing through rush hour traffic to get to the hospital on time. "The call" or "the letter" become part of family lore, along with how Mom and Dad got engaged, Grandpa's brush with death on the ice at the village pond when he was seven, the time Johnny got lost on vacation. Repeating these stories over and over and over is a part of the way that families claim one another as "us" as opposed to the "them" that is the rest of the world.

These stories are the first ways that we begin to talk about adoption with our children. For the youngest of children adoption information is both offered and received as an experience of gain. But as children approach middle childhood, they are likely to become increasingly aware that in order for the gain to occur, they and their birthparents had to experience an enormous loss. If they haven't felt that loss themselves, as they enter school they will soon be exposed to the negative societal reactions to adoption.

When children are very young they accept adoption so matter-of-factly that they are likely to bring up adoption quite frequently on their own. It will be several years before children become uncomfortable enough about adoption's differences to feel that it is not something to share freely.

———

When Joel was in second grade he brought a friend home from school to spend the night. The boys were followed everywhere by Erica, then about 18 months old, who adored her big brother. She was not talking much, but engaging in long conversational sentences of babble and baby talk.

At dinner she began an animated monologue directed at Joel's friend, Danny. She was so obviously trying to communicate something specific, that Danny turned to Joel at the end of the speech and asked, "What did she say?"

Joel casually replied, "I dunno. I think her birthmother might have been Chinese."

———

But through the years, talking about adoption becomes more complicated, because what children are worrying or wondering about and what we want them to know become more complex. As children enter the later stages of middle childhood and move into adolescence, they may be particularly unlikely to initiate discussion about adoption on their own. It becomes a challenge for parents to look for news stories and other ways to "casually" open the door to discussion for their children.

———

As usual, the holiday season brought a spate of human interest stories in the news which included a reunion between adopted-away siblings. One T.V. station was especially entranced by the story of the children of a dying birthmother who were attempting to find their older half sibling, who had been adopted at birth in a confidential placement. With so much visibility focused on the story, the adoptee was soon found, and the T.V. station filmed an emotional reunion (no mention at all of the of adopting parents, of course) in a hospital room.

Evan, who was 15, watched intently. He turned to his parents and said, "Why would she do that, after all her parents have done for her? That woman isn't her real mother."

His mother, Kathleen, remained casual and calm. "I don't know about that, Evan. I think that if I'd been adopted I'd think sometimes about my birth family and be interested in meeting them. I think sometimes about your birthmother and your birthfather, who were pretty close to the age you are now when you were born. I wonder sometimes about which one you look like and I wonder how they are doing now. Don't you?"

A long discussion ensued. (Just testing, Mom. What's okay to ask? What's okay to feel?)

For many families the car becomes the place where lots of significant talking takes place. Most parents quickly learn to play the cards they are dealt and to use every opportunity they can find for education.

"Tell me again, Daddy, about when you and Chad and Mommy came to meet me at the airport when I came home from India."

"My birthfather, Darryl, was mean to me sometimes, but not always. I remember once, when..."

"Do you 'member that time, Aunt Candy, when we all went to the hospital to try to see Sam in the nursery before he came home?"

"I remember when my foster mom, Mrs. B., made a big cake for my fifth birthday and invited my kindergarten class to walk to our house to see the new puppies and have some cake."

On the other hand, it's important for new parents to realize that children learn quickly which buttons when pushed get the most interesting reactions from their parents, and for many adoptive parents, adoption produces an interesting reaction. Middle childhood youngsters are particularly adept at "using" adoption. At bedtime, for example, many children who know that their conscientious parents who stand for no delays will drop everything to deal with an adoption related issue, will stall lights out with an adoption-related question.

By the time their children reach adolescence few adopters have not been hit squarely between the eyes with an angry child's bullet, "You're not my *real* mom. My *real* mom wouldn't treat me like this!" Most of the time such comments are not really adoption related! They are diversionary tactics designed to throw parents off balance enough that the child can win the battle.

―――――――

"Hurry up, Dad, I'm gonna miss the opening tip off if we don't leave now."

"Brian, we can't leave until you finish the list of jobs I asked you to accomplish this weekend. I sure would hate to see you miss that basketball game," said Dad.

"But I'll do it tomorrow, Dad. I have to leave now," came the reply.

"Sorry, but that's not the way it works. I'll be happy to drive you to the fieldhouse as soon as the jobs are completed."

"I hate you!" screamed Brian." You can't tell me what to do! You're not my real father!"

Dad remained cool. "Well, you know, Brian, I understand that you aren't very happy with me right now, and I can understand that you might have some concerns about your adoption that you'd like to talk about, too. I'll be happy to talk about those things with you as soon as that list of jobs is completed."

―――――――

Using Books to Talk about Adoption

Many families find books a good way to open conversation. Books do provide a good start, but they can't become the only source for stimulating adoption discussions. Using books to open conversation must never become a crutch to dealing positively and specifically and personally with your own and your child's personal issues. I offer here some brief guidelines for incorporating books into the way you teach your children about themselves and their family.

From the beginning understand that even though a book does not describe a family just like your own it may provide some valuable discussion points for you and your children. Just because you adopted inracially, for example, doesn't mean that a book about transracial adoption, one like *Real for Sure Sister* by Ann Angel or *Is that Your Sister?* by Sherry Bunnin would not be just right for your nine year old. Just because you adopted transracially doesn't mean that Valentina Wasson's classic *The Chosen Baby* (bad title, good book!) wouldn't interest and help your child. Because your family was not built by both birth and adoption does not mean that your children wouldn't find value in Jane Schnitter's *William is My Brother* or Stephanie Stein's *Lucy's Feet.* Just because you are fertile rather than infertile doesn't make books which portray families built entirely by adoption inappropriate.

Every child's favorite book, of course, is his own. Most families purchase a traditional baby book for their children, but families built by adoption have in the past been reluctant to participate in this tradition. At issue has been that baby books are traditionally oriented to begin with pregnancy and birth, so that often adoptive parents felt awkward and uncomfortable about the missing blanks in their children's books. On the other hand, often in the past the selection of baby books for adopted children was poor and the quality simply not up to par with the books for children born to their families. Some adoption educators of the past who were concerned that children would feel different without a baby book advocated that parents use a regular baby book anyway. Today's adoption-expanded families have more choices if only they will take the time to look. Two particularly beautiful baby books for the family built by adoption include Hallmark's *Welcome Home* and the adoption version of the most widely used babybook of all—the Chicago Lying-In Hospital's *Our Baby's First Seven Years*, which is distributed by Gibson Card Company. If not carried on store shelves, these two books may be ordered through retailers who carry Hallmark or Gibson products. Additionally, A.F.A. and several other catalogs now feature independently created adoptive baby books such as *My Story* from Cygnet and *Baby Face.*

Adoptees placed beyond infancy each own (when their cases have been managed by really good caseworkers at highly professional agencies) a Lifebook, which, in essence, is a combination baby book, photo album, scrap book, etc. which has been designed to pull together the significant paperwork, photographs, mementoes and anecdotes that record a child's life. In reality, every child, including those born to the families in which they live, but most especially including children adopted at any age from birth on up, should have a Lifebook.

These and the family photo albums or photo boxes will provide the most consistent opportunity to talk about adoption. But other books—books about adoption, books about families, books about cultures, books about differences, books which carry subtle messages about permanence and continuity—can provide a comfortable way either to introduce information or to open the door to communication.

My background in both library and literature means that our house is filled to the top with books. When I was teaching school, the idea of using books to help children deal with difficult issues—a speciality called bibliotherapy—was a new and innovative idea that is very mainstream now. Because my job is as an infertility and adoption educator, and one of the most popular training sessions I do for both parents and professionals is on books, books, books, my office is overflowing with children's books—both good ones and bad ones—about adoption.

Not my kids' shelves, though. They each have a few adoption titles on their personal shelves—their personalized copies of *Our Baby: A Birth and Adoption Story*, by Janice Koch, for example. Our family's copy of *The Mulberry Bird* by Anne Braff Brodzinsky, is a favorite. It started out in Joel's room, moved to Erica's and now lives in Lindsey's room. As they watched the progress in my office last winter on *Lucy's Feet* by Stephanie Stein, my girls—just the right age for this one—were determined to own their own copies, autographed, of course.

Additionally, whenever they are in my office and see something they find interesting, I willingly take that book home to be read. Of course we've read and enjoyed all of the Perspectives Press titles not already mentioned (*Where the Sun Kisses the Sea* is so beautiful both to look at and to listen to that we "borrow" a copy regularly.) In addition Erica asked for a copy of *Don't Call Me Marda* by Sheila Kelly Welch, and its publisher, our friend, Carol Hallenbeck, sent her a copy. *A Family for Jaime* and *The Day We Met You* made one time hits with my youngest. *Oliver* has been fun on more than one occasion. But filling the family shelves with every adoption book on the market overemphasizes the impact of adoption, creating a situation bordering on insistence of adoption (ID Behavior.)

Besides, more than the stories that are specifically about adoption, I find that adoption education works even better when the stories aren't about adoption at all. Every child personally touched by his own or a friend's or relative's adoption should own the most beautifully illustrated version of Margery Williams' *The Velveteen Rabbit* that his parents can find. Here we can begin the discussions of "realness" as a part of relationships.

"What is real?" asked the rabbit. "Does it mean having things that buzz inside you and a stick-out handle?"

Real isn't how you are made," said the skin horse. "It's a thing that happens to you. When a child loves you for a long, long, time, not just to play with, but REALLY loves you, then you become real."

"Does it hurt?" asked the rabbit.

"Sometimes," said the skin horse, for he was always truthful. "When you are real you don't mind being hurt."

"Does it happen all at once, like being wound up," he asked, "or bit by bit?"

"It doesn't happen all at once," said the skin horse. "You become. It takes a long time. That's why it doesn't often happen to people who break easily or have sharp edges or who have to be carefully kept. Generally, by the time you are real, most of your hair has been loved off, and your eyes drop out and you get loose in the joints and very shabby. But those things don't matter at all, because once you are REAL, you can't be ugly, except to people who don't understand."

Robert Munche's funny (yet so sentimental that it always makes me cry) story *Love You Forever* sends a wonderful message about permanence and continuity to children in adoption-expanded families, as does the classic by Margaret Wise Brown *The Runaway Bunny*. Many people would add Shel Silverstein's *The Giving Tree* to this list of non-adoption books for adoption-expanded families.

In choosing books you also need to be careful. For example, the Dr. Seuss book *Horton Hatches an Egg* carries positive messages about what makes a real parent, but it paints the birthparent, Maizie, in a terribly negative light. My collection of books not to use includes the P.D. Eastman title *Are You my Mother?* Even some adoption-specific books need to be avoided because of their negative adoption language (though creative parents have always known that there's a lot to be said for changing the script of a read aloud book when necessary!)

If you are a book lover and a book buyer, consider that it isn't just your own children who need to learn about adoption. Your child's friends and cousins and schoolmates need this education, too. Consider giving copies of some of your family's favorite adoption-positive titles as gifts at birthday parties. Most particularly make it a practice to donate copies of books on adoption to your school's and your place of worship's libraries.

Embracing Diversity

As adoptive families, we are—even those of us who are Caucasian and have adopted white children—minority families. And thus we have been given a rare opportunity to help our children become part of a less biased and bigoted future. Our challenge is to help our families celebrate diversity and multiculturalism without moving beyond A.D. (acceptance of difference) behavior to I.D. (insistence on difference) behavior. It is an exciting opportunity.

Once again, books are a good way to begin. In addition to the wonderfully inclusive books whose very purpose is to embrace diversity (like *Free to be a Family* by Marlo Thomas and friends and *People* by Peter Spier) some of the best books to use in trying to help your child learn to celebrate differences rather than to be intimidated by them are those that are general interest stories featuring ethnically-inclusive illustrations (anything illustrated by Jerry Pinckney, John Steptoe or Alan Say are good bets.) Vera Williams' Caldecott Honor Book *More, More, More! Said the Baby* embraces a wide variety of cultures and combinations of cultures without mentioning that fact at all! Robert Munche's hilarious story *Something Good* features a pair of Caucasian parents with two daughters of color, doesn't mention adoption, and tells a wonderful tale of the relative value of children!

Families who have adopted transculturally or transracially need to find books which will help their children learn about their cultures of origin so that they can build aspects of this birth heritage into their positive senses of self. On the other hand, it is equally important that children who have been adopted have many books which embrace the cultures of the families into which they have been adopted. Families who celebrate their Irish or Italian or Jewish or Latvian or whatever heritage through the way they worship, the way they eat, the way they observe holidays, the mixture of languages they use claim their children by bringing them into the fold. Your own family's culture is the one you will share sociologically with your child, and it may be quite different from the genetic heritage he shares with his birthparents.

One of the things kids dislike most is being different from their peers. Oh, right, they don't want to be much like Mom and Dad, but they want to be just like everybody else. Finding himself the only one he knows who has been adopted can make a kid feel pretty weird, geeky, nerdy, different. It's enough to make a person just hide, forget about it, try not to call attention to oneself!

Just as every child deserves to be wanted for who he is, every kid deserves to know somebody something like himself—someone with whom he can identify, and hopefully, in whom he can confide. Since adoptees represent only about 2% of the population of children, parents need to find ways to insure that their children know other adoptees. Parent groups are the easiest place to begin.

There are interesting patterns observed by the volunteer leaders of adoptive parent support groups across the world. Traditional (infertile) adopters of healthy, same race infants are the least likely of adopters to belong to a parent group from their child's earliest days (denial of difference at work), while it is this same group of parents who are most likely to make contact with a group looking for help with problems when their children reach adolescence. Also observed is the fact that even international adopters and the adopters of special needs children tend to belong to the group during their children's preschool years and move away from the group during middle childhood, often coming back again as their children reach pre-adolescence.

Middle childhood is a busy time in family life. It is during these years that families become caught up in an overwhelming schedule of school, lessons, teams, clubs, and so on. Often the adoptive parent support group is the easiest thing to let slide. Yet children who know other children who joined their families by adoption tend to feel less different, more entitled, as members of adoption-built families. Additionally, adoptive parents groups are your best source for referral to an adoption-sensitized and adoption-informed professional should you at any time need help along the way.

But what if a formal support group is not for you? Some adopters fear that joining a group would lead to I.D. behavior. There are many other reasons for not joining a group. What if there isn't one near? What if the nearby one focuses on a particularly style of adoption and you don't feel a fit? What if you just aren't a joiner, much less one who would feel comfortable with the possibility that someone might expect you to do something as a volunteer for the group? Informal support can be equally valuable! Making an effort to make and nurture social relationships with other adoption-expanded families you meet through your agency, through a parent group or infertility support group, through your house of worship, through your children's school, can be a comfortable way to accomplish this goal. **But**, if you choose this route, I encourage you to remain connected to the more formal world of adoption support and education by maintaining at least one subscription/membership to a national level adoption support group. I highly recommend that that one group be Adoptive Families of America, which will bring with it a subscription to *OURS: The Magazine of Adoptive Families.*

Continuing Education

Whether you choose to maintain your local adoption connections formally or informally, resolve from the beginning to continue your adoption education. In many communities half day or day-long conferences on adoption-related issues are an annual or biennial event. In Indiana, for example, a biennial Adoption Forum on adoption how-to issues, parenting issues, search and support issues, has been cosponsored by a consortium of groups and agencies throughout the state and is attended by 400 or so people. The New England Open Door Society, Adoptive Parents Committee of New York, OURS of Northeastern Wisconsin, Concerned Persons for Adoption in New Jersey, Families Adopting Children from Everywhere in Maryland and dozens more groups throughout the country sponsor significantly-sized regular conferences aimed at ongoing adoption education. Stay in touch with your agency or with A.F.A. or N.A.C.A.C. and their affiliated groups in order to remain well informed about these opportunities.

While subscribing to *OURS* and/or the newsletter or magazine of a local or regional parent group you may also wish to investigate other well prepared adoption-related newsletters and magazines prepared specifically for adoptive parents but not serving as the periodical of a group. Lois Melina's *Adopted Child* focuses on one adoption issue in the four to six pages of each of its six annual issues. Cynthia Peck's *Roots and Wings* is in a magazine format. *Adoptnet* addresses issues in openness and more.

Just as you would include a parenting handbook like Dr. Spock's on your family's bookshelf, use your local library to help you select at least one of the several excellent handbooks for adoptive parents. Lois Melina's *Raising Adopted Children* (HarperCollins, 1986) is the most encyclopedic in nature. Other fine choices as I go to press are Stephanie Siegel's *Parenting Your Adopted Child: A Complete and Loving Guide* (Prentice Hall Press, 1989) and Judith Schaeffer and Christine Lindstrom's *How to Raise an Adopted Child* (Crown Publishers, 1989). If you are looking for help specifically in talking to children about adoption you may find helpful Miriam Komar's *Communicating with the Adopted Child* (Walker, 1990) or Melina's *Making Sense of Adoption* (Harper-Collins, 1989). New titles are being introduced every year, however, and remaining in touch with a local parent group or with A.F.A., A.C.C., N.A.C.A.C. and/or N.C.F.A. can help you to learn what up-to-date resources are best.

═ 11 ═

Special Issues Along the Way

Growing up in an adoption-expanded family brings different, but not necessarily more difficult, challenges for children, just as parenting in adoption presents different, but not necessarily worse, challenges for parents. In this chapter we will explore a variety of issues which may arise as your adopted family matures.

Cultural Issues in Claiming Your Child

My Daughter's Dowry[1]
by Arthur Dobrin

This you inherit:
The gold of Africa's sun
Bathing a boma of straw;
Gospel singing to close the sores.
And your other part
Chosen to keep the Word
In two thousand years of wandering.
This is yours,
You who came to us
The color of fawn,
African girl,
Daughter of Jerusalem

Who is your child? What is his or her cultural heritage? In reality all of us are a blend of nature and nurture, heredity and environment. Some of us were born to and raised in families with a strong ethnic, religious, or national identification and others come from what my own family has called a "Heinz 57 varieties" family. Some of us marry partners from cultural backgrounds similar to our own and others do not. Who our children are is a blend of all that we are as well as all that their birthparents were.

Genes you and I can do nothing about. We will not influence how tall, how fair or dark, how intelligent or athletic our children brought to us through adoption become. But much of who are children become we will help them become.

One of the ways in which families claim their own is by sharing their cultural heritage with one another. We are the psychological and sociological children of the parents who raised us—whether those parents were our birthparents, our step parents, our grandparents, our foster parents, our adoptive parents. Your religious beliefs, your ethnical values, your holiday customs, your family rituals are the ones which your children will live. In healthy families, adolescents tend to work very hard to reject much of that, but as adults, most people from functional families see themselves as culturally bound by and extended from the families in which they were raised.

You and your extended family will be your child's family. You must take ownership of this responsibility. Recently I realized that some families who are trying hard to follow David Kirk's advice about consistently acknowledging difference in adoption may have in fact been pushed over the edge toward an unhealthy insistence of difference because they have misunderstood what adoption educators are saying about cultural education.

———

Maddie and Erv had adopted Anjulie from India when she was only three months old. Practicing Jews, they had taken Anjulie through a formal conversion, giving her the Hebrew name Elizabeth as her middle name, retaining her Indian name, Anjulie, as her first. The Cohens made a conscientious effort to make Anjulie aware and appreciative of her Indian heritage, including ethnic foods in their menus, reading colorful tales of Indian heritage, ordering wonderful costumes and toys from their Heritage Key catalog. Alongside that, they were raising Anjulie as a proud Jew, taking her to Tot

Shabbat on Friday evenings and religious education on Sunday mornings. Their family was thrilled! Everyone was already planning for this 4 year old's Bat Mitzvah to occur in nine years.

Maddie and Erv thought they were doing a good job until they went to "the conference" sponsored by their adoptive parents' group. At the adoption conference they attended a session on embracing your child's cultural heritage. A panel of parents went on and on about their successes with culture camp, their efforts to bring families of their child's culture into their circle of acquaintances, their dependence on the adoption group to provide playmates of similar cultural background for their children.

Maddie was nodding in agreement right up to the point when the discussion turned to religion. The Korean adopters pointed out that in their very large city they had a Korean Methodist church, and that they had started worshipping there. Two once-Presbyterian adopters had immersed themselves and their three children—two biracial and one Caucasian—in a Baptist church in the inner city, and were "learning to be comfortable." Maddie knew that she couldn't go this far. Their reform synagogue was as inclusive as any in their city. There were people of Ashkenazi and Sephardic origin. There were a handful of families of Ethiopian heritage. But there were no Indians. There would be no Indians. Maddie and Erv were angry. They dropped out of the group. They had missed the point. Or was it that the parent group had?

This is one of those tightrope issues. When a child who has been adopted "matches" his family racially—all of European extraction, all of African background, all Asian—families face this conflict relatively simply. Their children become the religion and absorb the cultural heritage of their parents with no questions. Had Anjulie been of European heritage, Maddie and Erv would have experienced no conflict.

But when a European-American family adopts cross culturally, their challenge becomes to help their child embrace the culture of their adoptive families—becoming Catholic or Jewish or Assemblies of God, learning to love Italian or Irish or Lithuanian food, celebrating holidays with special traditions—and to consider themselves and their children entitled to this heritage, while at the same time helping their children become interested in, learn about, and feel comfortable with and proud of their racially or ethnically different genetic background.

The purpose of this is not to emphasize as more important or to preserve intact the heritage different from the one in which they will be raised. This would be impossible, as we discussed in an earlier section on considering transethnic adoptions. The purpose is to prepare these children to move in a world which will automatically identify them, label them, make assumptions about them based on the way they look. Other Asian or African or Hispanic people will be attracted to your children as they grow, will expect them to identify with them, will be confused and perhaps judgmental and intolerant if these children are isolated from and ignorant about or rejecting of their Korean-ness, their African-ness, their Chicano-ness, their Pakistani-ness. The point is to instill a sense of pride in our child about all of who they are.

Yes, as a transcultural adopter, your family becomes a family of color. But you are not expected to reject your own heritage so much as you are expected to expand it and to help your child do the same! Hopefully you have always been comfortable with and interested in cultures other than your own. If so you will eagerly explore the diversity of your child's birth heritage and other diverse cultures as well—embracing difference! Kay Donley has referred to adoption as an "add on" rather than a "substitution" experience for both children and adults. Here is one of the clearest examples of how that is true.

Your Child at School

From at least the age of six the center of family life tends to shift from home and house of worship to the controlling factors of school. Everything begins to revolve around the school day, the winter/spring/summer vacation schedules, homework, playmates who are classmates, etc. Music lessons, scouts, athletic teams, all seem to be influenced in some way by school. Even for children who have been in large day care centers each day during their preschool years, the onset of school takes on special significance and colors family life in a new and unique way.

At school, for the first time, parents will forfeit an important measure of protective control over their child's environment. They will not necessarily know all of the parents of their child's classmates. They will not have an opportunity to assess their child's teachers' adoption sensitivity. To complicate things even more, soon after children enter school they also make an important intellectual shift. Having reached a new cognitive level of development they will be primed to view adoption in an entirely new way.

Early-elementary-aged children are often more competitive with peers than they were before ("My dad is taller than your dad" ... "Well my dad is smarter!") and have learned to look for the special chinks in the armor of their peers that will allow them to sling just the right insults ("Fatty Patty two by four, couldn't get through the kitchen door!" ... "Who set your hair on fire?" ... "I know why you look different than your brother. You're adopted. Nobody wanted you!")

It is nearly always at school that children will be for the first time, suddenly and forever, made aware of the important fact that adoption isn't just gain ("Mommy and I were sooooo happy when the lady called and told us you were born, and so were Grandpa and Grandma and Auntie Tess and cousin Sudie...") but that it also means some rather profound losses ("Well, what was the matter with your real mother that she couldn't keep you?" ... "Gosh, I wouldn't want to be adopted. Then I wouldn't have my daddy!")

Perhaps the most important thing for parents to realize about the experience of their children at school is that they won't necessarily know what goes on there. Many hurtful things can be said out of earshot of protective or mediating adults on the playground, in the restroom, on the school bus, in the hall. Ambiguous comments may come out of the mouths of caring but uninformed or downright insensitive teachers. Some kids tell their parents *everything*. Most do not. Conscientious parents, then, spend significant time checking in, checking it out with their kids—using quiet time before bed, the breakfast table, transportation time in the car to carefully explore (while at the same time not prying into a new found need for privacy) and, more than anything, sending the message that they are available, accessible, ready to talk about anything and everything.

Somewhere in second or third grade or so the family tree assignment will come home. For many parents, this is a real tough one, and often it isn't because the child is uncomfortable so much as it is a painful reminder to parents of their infertility and their lack of genetic connection to a child they have come to see as so profoundly their own.

First, keep in mind that this first one is not a genogram. The point of this one is not to learn which of our relatives were brown eyed and which blue eyed and what recessive traits we are likely to carry. That one comes later—at about eighth or ninth grade—as a part of a science biology project. It's going to be a bummer! But let's deal with the first grade family tree first.

This first assignment of a family tree is part of a social studies project. The class is most likely to be discussing what countries everybody immigrated from or how long they have been citizens of this country. For this kind of project it is important for both you and your child—as a claiming mechanism for you both to remember that socially, your child is your own. Your values and your cultural background are your child's, too. The fact that your great-grandmother was a missionary in China or that your great-grandfather died in a concentration camp or that someone in your family experienced the internment of Japanese-Americans during World War II is a part of who your child is as well. This is not to suggest that one can ignore the fact that genetically your child has a different background. He does—and it may bring with it racial difference as well. Parents definitely need to keep these differences in mind. But this first family tree experience is a good time to explore family lore. When placing Greatgrandma Rohrer's name on the right line we can talk about the fact that it is her recipe for raisin-filled cookies that we make for Daddy every Christmas because it is a family tradition. It might be a good time to take Great-great-grandfather Selby's Civil War hat out of the closet and hang in on Kareem's wall (he is, after all, the oldest son in this generation!)

As the years go by, there will be time nearly every year to add to this discussion of the nature and the nurture that is a part of who we are. And there are several ways to approach it.

Adoption educator and therapist Joyce Maguire Pavao, who was herself adopted as a child, has suggested that we no longer really have family trees. With so many children growing up in families which include birthparents, stepparents, adoptive parents, foster parents, more and more of us have something more akin to a family orchard!

In a past issue of *FACE Facts* (the excellent magazine of the progressive and innovative regional parent group Families Adopting Children from Everywhere, based in Baltimore, Maryland) adoptive parent Pat Hall described her approach to the family tree project. Pat drew and cut out a pair of family trees and explained that sometimes trees get sick or for some reason can't be saved and that horticulturalists (she called them "tree doctors") will remove healthy branches from one tree and graft them onto another tree in order to keep the first tree's fruit available. Healthy trees that have room for more branches and a good space in which to grow and flourish are the family trees to which these baby branches are grafted. Pat's daughter had an interesting twist to her show-and-tell the next day. She wanted to take in her lifebook and explain the grafting process.

This brings us to another issue about the school and adoption. Should the school know? Sometimes, of course, it will be clear: if the child is racially different than his parents or siblings, if the child arrives at an older age in mid school year. But for many traditional adopters who have adopted inracially, whether or not to tell the school is a subject of debate.

The concern is that in unnecessarily identifying one's child's difference 261
publicly one unnecessarily exposes the child to the stereotypes of
adoption-ignorant or adoption-insensitive or adoption-prejudiced people.

This is a legitimate concern. Quite frankly, I can clearly
understand why parents refuse to automatically check unnecessary
boxes that ask about adoption on registration forms. I have myself
approached a preschool or elementary school or two and asked them to
tell me why they felt they needed this information. In most cases, the
administrators don't know! If that is the case, there is no reason to supply
the information, and in fact there is reason to request of the school system
that the block be dropped from the form. (Does this remind you of our
discussion of what information it is appropriate for adoption agencies to
request? It should!)

But there is another, perhaps more important, factor to consider
here. Even if you don't tell, your children probably will—especially at a
very young age when they still consider adoption an exciting source of
specialness and thus feel pride about it, before peers have burst their
bubbles. Certainly it is unhealthy to suggest that adoption be a family
secret. This implies that there is something wrong with it. What you can
do instead is help your children understand that this is very personal
information, that it is theirs to share selectively with people who care about
them and with whom they want to share it, but that because it is very
personal and private, they need to feel that they are themselves in control
of sharing it.

By middle school adoptees will have experienced multiple
exposures to other people's positive and negative reactions to adoption.
They may have taken it "inside" for a time and decided not to share it all
if that can be avoided. On the other hand, adolescence with its attendant
body changes often makes adopted children very curious about their
genetic heritage. Girls may wonder whether their breasts are likely to be
large or small, and without a very detailed history or in the absence of a
communicative adoption, when a young woman can begin to menstruate
is a guessing game. Boys who do not have a genetic parent present against
which to gage themselves may wonder if they will ever be tall, if they will
be muscular, if they will have athletic abilities in any sport. Encouraging
and supporting these natural curiosities is an important part of allowing
your child to begin to separate. Many middle school aged children will
enjoy the experience of working through adoption-related interests in a
new light by using Susan Gabel's *Filling in the Blanks: A Guided Look at
Growing Up Adopted* with their parents or another adult. Others may balk
completely at this idea and consider it intrusive. As we discussed earlier,
the most important adoption-related parenting task of middle school
through high school aged children is to keep the doors of communication
open.

Statistically, children who were adopted tend to have a higher incidence of learning disabilities and attention deficit problems than do children raised in their families of birth. We cannot be certain why this is true, but there are some obvious risk factors common to some (though certainly not all) people who make adoption plans which are known to influence learning problems. First, children who were adopted were very often born to very young mothers. As a group these young mothers not only have had poor or very limited prenatal care, but sometimes they have denied their pregnancies for a long time and have had poor nutrition. Their pregnancies are complicated by the fact that they are themselves still growing. Sometimes birthparents have used dangerous chemical substances (drugs, alcohol) which produce dangerous amniotic baths for their children to spend nine months in. Additionally, one of the primary causes of unplanned pregnancies is impulsivity and poor judgment, traits which are often related to ADHD and several learning disabilities and which have a strong genetic component.

It is nearly always impossible to predict and thus to avoid adopting a child with a learning disability, but this is probably not the issue anyway.

―――――――

P.W. was an apparently healthy baby when placed into Ann and George's eager arms. Always active and curious, it was when he entered pre-school that more serious questions arose about P.W.'s distractibility and inability to follow directions. At age three P.W. went through speech and hearing screening, through psychological testing and observation, and more. Nothing specific was identified. Ann and George felt intensely guilty. Maybe they were just inconsistent in their discipline? Maybe they hadn't read to him enough? Were they just bad parents?

It was when P.W. was in third grade that persistent Ann finally made the professional connection that led to her family's getting the help for P.W. that he needed. Despite requests from an adoption-sensitive and internationally respected psychiatrist, the agency which had arranged P.W.'s adoption refused to release delivery records or the data they held about this boy's birthfamilies. The doctor, determined to find this young man the help that he needed, was furious, but referred the family to extensive and expensive testing sources. It turned out that P.W. had a severe and complex form of dyslexia (more than likely hereditary), as well as an attention deficit, hyperactivity disorder (ADHD—also most likely hereditary.) P.W. now receives helpful medication and his parents are spending thousands of dollars a year on private tutoring for his dyslexia.

They both say that it has never occurred to them that they wouldn't have accepted P.W.'s placement had they had full knowledge, but they are resentful of the many years of butting up again brick walls, the significant wasted money, the enormous family stress, and the wasted time that it took them in order to identify P.W.'s problems and obtain the help they needed.

It behooves prospective parents to be alert to early symptoms of learning problems and to be prepared to deal with them. Adoption professionals, on the other hand, must responsibly advocate for disclosure of anything that may help families built by adoption parent their children effectively.

Sex Education and the Child Who Was Adopted

It's universal. Sex education makes nearly all parents anxious. The anxiety felt by adoptive parents, then, is not necessarily related to the fact of adoption, though adoption does, of course, color how we present certain elements of the sex education of our children—for example our ethnical or religious values about the rightness or wrongness of premarital or extramarital intercourse; our definition of responsible, safe sex; our attitude about various family planning options. Sex education is another case of clear difference.

Anne Bernstein is a child psychologist, who, for her doctoral dissertation in psychology, worked on a study of what children understand about reproduction from their earliest ability to verbalize through their intellectual maturation as abstract thinkers. Her study formed the basis of a great guide for parents to use in sex education called *Flight of the Stork* (first published by Delacourte in 1978 and updated, expanded and republished by Perspectives Press in 1994).

What Bernstein's study discovered was that children's understanding of adoption followed their intellectual development in a pattern that followed Piaget right from the beginning. Bernstein summarized several levels and attached colorful labels to each stage:

1   **The Geographer** (ages 3-7). At this level of understanding, kids think that babies have always existed, either in mothers' bodies or in some *place* like heaven and that all grownups are mommies and daddies.

2   **The Manufacturer** (ages 4-8). These children have come to believe that babies are built like houses or dolls, but how? They can only imagine based on their own experience and knowledge. Maybe babies were made outside the body and then swallowed, coming out like a bowel movement? If they come from eggs, am I eating a baby for breakfast?

3   **In Between** (ages 5-10). Early reasoning has begun, but the child limits herself to what is technically possible from personal experience and has trouble letting go of old beliefs, so there's still quite a bit of magical thinking.

4   **The Reporter** (ages 6-12). These children know the jargon of reproduction but don't understand why the egg and sperm have to unite to start the process.

5   **The Theoretician** (ages 10-13). These children still struggle to understand why the ova and sperm have to get together (couldn't there be a complete baby in just the sperm or in just the egg?). Unlike the Reporters they generate elaborate speculations just as scientists have done through the ages.

6   **The Abstract Thinker** (11+). Finally able to reason like an adult, children at this level can put it all together. Finally the young person understands that two different entities—sperm and ovum—can combine to form an entirely new entity. Children who have achieved this level of sophistication can distinguish between moral, social and biological factors in reproduction.

Dr. Bernstein's 1994 version of *Flight of the Stork* incorporates Dr. Brodzinsky's adoption research to offer valuable advice for families built by birth or adoption.

    Just as it is with all other education, the challenge of sharing just enough to be helpful and satisfying but not too much to become boring, demands that parents try hard to be aware of their children's developmental maturity level. Many parents find Janice Koch's book *Our Baby: A Birth and Adoption Story* a good place to begin. This is a sex education book designed for children no younger than a mature two up to about the age of seven. It provides the opportunity to share the concept of conception and birth along with a personalized arrival story. It does, however, use specific and correct language (penis, vagina, etc.) and a few parents of young children are uncomfortable with such specificity. Do remember that all sex educators suggest that in order to lay the foundation for good communication later, it is important to avoid euphemistic labels for body parts and body functions.

As adolescents separate, sexuality can become a central issue for those who were adopted. Can you remember when it first occurred to you that your parents actually had sex together and how ludicrous that seemed? Adopted children have two sets of parents about which to fantasize. One set—the birthparents—may be (for children in the majority of today's adoptions, which are confidential) perpetually young and vibrantly sexual. In fantasy they may be frozen in time at the ages when the adoptee's conception and birth occurred—an age which may be very close to the adoptee's current age. The other set of parents—his social and psychological parents—are, to an adolescent, old, not with it, behind in the times, and definitely more conservative than everybody-else's-parents. On top of this, this child probably knows that his parents are infertile, and this may color his fantasies about them. Do they make love at all? Are they sexual if they are not fertile?

Fears about sexuality are common among teens. Most are homophobic and may go out of their way to establish themselves as proudly and publicly heterosexual (even if they are not). Some may find their parents' infertility threatening. They may feel a need to distance themselves from this frightening specter by refusing to identify with their infertile parents or even finding ways to remind them of both their infertility and their status as "not real" parents.

At the same time, though, adoptive parents are fantasizing as well. Those same forever young birthparents in a confidential adoption linger for them as well. Will their children work so hard at detaching themselves from their social parents that they will need to identify so strongly with their genetic parents to recreate the situation of an early conception and birth. Will these separating teens ever talk to us again?

Adolescence is not much fun for parents. But then, you may remember that it wasn't much fun being an adolescent kid, either. It gets better.

Later Contact with Families of Origin— The Search

Can you imagine, really, looking at your face in the mirror every day, watching your body develop, noticing the interests and tastes that seem so "foreign" to other members of your family and not even *wondering*? I didn't think so. It is normal and natural for children who were adopted to fantasize liberally about their birthfamilies and to wonder how like or unlike them they are. Marshall Schechter says that every adoptee searches in some way, though that search may not be a concrete one that results in information about or contact with a family of origin.

The sealed record controversy rages on, but, frankly, more and more adoption professionals—even those who continue to feel that promises about confidentiality already made must be kept, even those who argue most vehemently against open adoptions through the childhood years—are coming to feel that for the future records and contact should be accessible to consenting adults.

Interestingly, while now, in the early 1990s, the majority of adoptive parents continue to prefer a confidential adoption, and while a large percentage of prospective adopters and adoptive parents of very young children are quite threatened by the existence of their children's birthparents, large numbers of these same parents change their view over the years. This seems natural, too.

Having claimed their children, built healthy senses of entitlement and attachments between them, having allowed their children to test the moving away from and coming back cycle throughout their childhoods, most adoptive parents do become confident in the realness and the permanence of their relationship with their children. They also become nearly as curious as their children. Where did that crooked smile come from? What kind of stomach can tolerate all that pepper sauce on scrambled eggs? What genes created the scrappy athlete who is this tiny girl? This intellectual dreamer planted in a family of active outdoorspeople—who shares that philosophical bent?

Most professionals in the field of adoption, though not all, believe that adolescence is not a good time to open an adoption that has been confidential to that point. Adolescence is a time of such overwhelming change, so many factors pulling at the need to detach from the security of family or to rush back to its shelter, that most adolescents are not prepared for such a jolting new connection. While adolescents may cope quite well with an adoption that has been open from birth or at least for several years, adolescence—despite the fact that this is the time when adoptees may begin to become insistent about it—is not a good time for making a first time connection with birthfamilies. A suggested alternative

is that this is a time to reach out for more detailed information from the
agency or the intermediary. With the visible and vocal support of their adoptive parents in this quest, young adoptees can be reassured that when they have reached adulthood, they may count on their parents to support their needs.

While it is true that statistically it would still appear that the majority of adult adoptees do not make use of open records in places where they already exist, the numbers are increasing. We don't know why these changes are taking place. Is it because adoptees are feeling less guilty about their interest, less constrained? Is it because they are being pressured by a society when they aren't really interested at all? Could it be that they search in order to take control—to protect themselves from a surprise contact from a birthparent? The why is not so important as is the fact. More and more adoptees are reaching a place in their lives when they search.

Not all comings together between birth relatives and the children for whom adoption plans were made are successful. Often expectations are unrealistic. Birthparents for whom adoptees have remained frozen as infants may find that they don't like the adults their children have become. They may hope for a parental connection and find instead arms-length resistance. Adoptees who have felt "different" from their adoptive families may find that the birthparent with whom they first connect is not like them either! They may be surprised by the differences in values and interests that may well have come as a result of their taking on more of their adopters' cultural heritage than they realized. New relationships are always awkward. The genetic connection between social strangers often results in ambivalence. Eventually most "reunions" result in a pleasant, though not intense, ongoing relationship.

We do know this: that in spite of the horror stories that circulate and feed fantasy, in the overwhelming majority of cases once a birthfamily and an adoptee have made contact the adoptee does not abandon his psychological and cultural family. Once curiosity has been satisfied, most adoptees find that indeed their closest connections are not with the people who look like them and share their genes, but with the people who raised them and provided the secure base from which they move out into the world—their parents. For most adoptive parents, then, there is nothing to fear in the search that may come. In fact, there is much to be said for supporting your children's possible interest in searching so openly that you will be automatically included in the process.

Social worker and adoption educator Sharon Kaplan Roszia (*Winning at Adoption* and *Cooperative Adoption*) offers important advice. The decision to search can only be the child's. It is tempting for parents who consider themselves liberated and progressive to consider doing a search on their own and presenting the information tied in a large bow as a gift to their children on some significant birthday or other special event. Don't, advises Roszia. Adoptees are the people least in control in an adoption situation. If adoptive parents thought they were out of control, if birthparents believed that they weren't given supported choices, adoptees had no say in the matter at all! It is important, then, that young adult adoptees be given the opportunity to make their own decisions about whether or not to make a contact with birthfamily and when. Your role, Mom and Dad, is to be supportive of that decision.

Does Adoption Slay the Dragon?— Infertility's Aftershocks

After all the frustration of infertility, it would be wonderful if just by adopting, one could wipe out the negative memories and experiences and the pain of infertility. It cannot work that way. An infertility experience significant enough to result in the decision to adopt has taken a physical, emotional, financial toll on us and resulted in a great deal of time gone by. One would hope that at the same time the infertility experience has offered us the opportunity to learn to communicate more effectively with our partners, to more carefully analyze our motivations for parenthood, and has made us stronger people.

Adoption is an alternative path to parenthood, but, as we discussed in Part One, it cannot prevent infertile people from feeling the full brunt of infertility's other losses—the loss of control, the loss of personal genetic continuity, the loss of a jointly conceived child, the losses of the physical and emotional gratifications of making/becoming pregnant and giving birth. These losses are likely to be heard from again, often arising unexpectedly to cause twinges of discomfort, occasionally evoking powerful aftershocks.

There are a variety of triggers. Some are tied directly to parenting... Finding oneself at a playground or a Swim and Gym class or a play group or a birthday party in a group of mothers of babies or toddlers who suddenly begin to share their pregnancy and labor war stories. Forcing oneself to be a superparent (after all, you were Good Housekeeping Seal approved!) and refusing to allow yourself to humanly resent moments of parenting. Hearing your frustrated child cry "Mommy, I wish I grew in your tummy!" Or flinching as the angry teenager rails, "My real dad wouldn't be so mean!" Watching a child with an artistic or athletic talent you can't even relate to blossom to stardom and wondering where that came from. Receiving an unexpected letter from a birthparent in what was before a confidential adoption. Observing your child move

to sexual maturity. Letting go, and feeling a twinge of fear that the
connection isn't tight enough and that they won't come back. (They will.)

A few triggers are entirely personal. Watching your daughter or daughter-in-law go through a pregnancy and feeling sadness that you can't relate as a part of "the sisterhood." Becoming a grandparent as your child gives birth. Or, perhaps worse, hearing your child say those dreaded words, "We're having a little problem getting pregnant, but, we've probably just gotten our timing wrong." Finding yourself at menopause—the final closing door.

None of these reactions is abnormal. None indicates that you have not resolved your infertility. It was a profound loss. Those losses are usually revisited.

On the other hand, there are some subtle indicators that entitlement may not be developing well and that there may be work yet to be done... An obsessive drive to prove oneself a super parent. An unwillingness to accept the uniqueness of your child and a tendency to try to mold him in your own shape. A tendency to be outrageously overprotective. Or, oppositely, an inclination toward overpermissiveness or inconsistency in disciplining borne of a feeling that you have no right to be firm or a fear that your child won't love you if you are. An overpowering fear of your child's birthfamily, which drives you to send clear messages that you don't consider curiosity (and never a search!) acceptable.

If you begin to experience these last symptoms, reach out to a support group or to a counselor familiar with infertility and adoption issues. They can be worked through. It is never too late.

████████████████████

Claudia is a strong, successful business woman. She thrives on being in control of her life, and she refused to let a complication like a fertility impairment get in the way of her decision to become a mother. She moved straight from the doctor's office to the lawyer's office and quickly adopted independently. There was no reading, no support group, no seminar, no parent preparation.

When her child was in middle school, (doing beautifully, by the way) Claudia agreed to accompany a nervous friend who was thinking about adopting to an adoption symposium. She slipped quietly into the back of a class entitled "Bringing Home Baby" expecting to bask in the pleasant deja vu memories that her child's arrival evoked.

Instead, the presenter was talking about the need to prepare. She was going through something about losses in infertility. She was recommending books to read. Suddenly, and without warning, a fact that Claudia had refused to acknowledge hit her squarely between the eyes. Her daughter had another mother as well as herself— a birthmother. She had not given birth to her daughter.

It wasn't the words or the presenter or the symposium that really burst the dam for Claudia. The time had simply come when she could no longer deny the truth that there was indeed "an elephant in the living room." It was a painful day that led to painful weeks. She entered therapy and dealt with all those issues which had been buried for so long.

Her relationship with her daughter improved. Her relationship with her husband improved. Her relationship with herself improved.

Parenting is a challenging responsibility. Those of us who have chosen to adopt have more than likely reaffirmed our interest in assuming this responsibility several times before reaching our goal. In fact, we've probably reaffirmed that goal far more often than do most parents by birth. Perhaps that is why we as adoptive parents tend to feel so guilty when we experience those perfectly normal days that every parent has when we wonder why we ever got ourselves into this. Sometimes, in the very middle of parenting, it can look as if we'll never have privacy again, never have another night of full sleep, never have "extra" money.

But far more frequent and important are those days when you realize how fast time is flying and you wish for it all back—when that big guy who wouldn't be caught dead in your lap any longer snuggles up for a back rub when nobody else is around, when you go through some old things and pull out a baby dress that you can't even imagine she ever fit and she grabs you from behind smelling all summery and sunny, when you attend a concert at school and actually find beautiful the music of the sixth grade band. It is these moments, common to all parents, that reaffirm that being parents is more important than becoming parents and cause the differences in adoptive parenting to recede to insignificance.

=12=

Adoption Advocacy—
You and Me
against the World

People touched by adoption almost daily experience the mixed messages of a larger society which finds adoption strange, somewhat threatening to the integrity of their own families and senses of connection, and most assuredly second best as an alternative for all involved. On the one hand parents hear the "Aren't you people wonderful" messages and on the other they are told "Too bad you don't have any kids of your own." Birthparents hear that they are bad or irresponsible for having practiced unsafe sex and that children raised in single parent homes are at great risk for all kinds of awful things, but on the other hand they also hear "How could anyone ever give up their own flesh and blood?" Adoptees are told that they are "lucky" that someone as good as their adopters took them in when those birthparents "who loved you very much" made the choice to "give you away." They are urged to feel "grateful and loyal" to their adopting parents, while at the same time they see the overwhelming curiosity that society has about the "real" genetic relatives who meet one another—often for the first time—in media spotlighted "reunions."

Those of us who are adults could make the indignant and idealistic claim that the reason we want to change this view is "for our children." This is true. Child advocates could claim that they wish to change the view of adoption as second best in order to assure that the birthparents of children born at risk to families which perhaps should not be "preserved" have the option of adoption open to them. This is true, too. But the reality is that we as adoptive parents want and need to change this view for ourselves as well. It hurts to be thought of as out of sync, unusual, or incomplete. It's painful to know that many of the people who interact with us on a daily basis view our relationships as somewhat less than real and to a certain extent feel sorry for both us and for our children.

How people develop negative views is a complicated stew of blending many years' worth of truth and misunderstanding, fact and fiction. Personal experience, media exposure, word choices, advertising gimmicks are all seasonings added to the pot. In this chapter we will look at that stew and examine ways to "adjust the seasoning" to make adoption a tastier dish for the world at large.

The Language of Adoption[1]

Those who are native speakers of English sometimes are not aware of how unusually colorful and diverse our language is when compared to others. Through centuries of borrowing liberally from the languages of the people who have conquered and been conquered by English-speakers, our vocabulary has been remarkably expanded. No other language has as many synonyms as does English. Why we have entire books, called thesauruses, which focus on nothing but synonymity! Thus in no other language does word choice result in such subtle nuances of difference.

English speakers use this variety to remarkable advantage, understanding clearly how word choice affects marketing, friendships, politics. Poorly chosen words can lose sales, incite debate and even start wars! People who work with the public at large understand this. That's why Chrysler sells New Yorkers rather than Podunkers and Ford offers Mustangs rather than Tortoises.

Language choice also enhances stereotypical thinking. This is why authors create naive and innocent characters who always come from Iowa or Indiana and name their not-too-bright characters Bubba and place them in the South. During the second half of the twentieth century we have come to clearly understand that choices in words can effect bias and discrimination. Beginning with the civil rights movement of the 50s and 60s and moving right through the women's movement, the sexual revolution and the gay rights movement, minority groups have used language as a battle ground for promoting understanding of their unique issues. The pressure to use these more politically correct (P.C.) terms, has produced, over time, subtle changes in understanding, as well.

As one who has made a career in the field of words—as an English teacher, then as a writer and public speaker and publisher—I am fascinated with the nuances of language. It was exciting for me to use Rosemary Maggio's *The Dictionary of Bias-Free Usage: A Guide to Non*

Discriminatory Language (Oryx Press, 1991) in writing this book. I'm quite sure that if you look carefully, you'll catch me in a number of errors in political correctness, but I'm trying! The time has come to insist on a P.C. language of adoption as well.

The concept of Positive Adoption Language (PAL) was first introduced in the 1970s by Marietta Spencer, a social worker with the Children's Home Society of Minnesota who has also been a pioneer in the push for post-adoption services. During the 1980s several adoption activists and advocates—myself included—became missionaries for the use of PAL.

Positive Adoption Language is a vocabulary chosen to assign maximum respect, dignity, responsibility and objectivity to the decisions made by birthparents and adoptive parents concerning their family planning. By using PAL we hope to eliminate the emotional overcharging that perpetuates societally held myths about adoption. The use of this vocabulary shows those involved in adoptions to be thoughtful and responsible people, reassigns them authority and responsibility for their actions, and, by eliminating the emotion-laden words which sometimes led in the past to a subconscious feeling of conflict or competition, helps to promote understanding among members of what has come to be called the adoption circle (as opposed to the adoption triangle, which seemed to imply "sides.")

In learning to use PAL, one begins with a modern way of looking at the concept of family. In our society, historically people have been considered to be members of the same family when one or more of four conditions are met: they are linked by blood (as are birthfather and son), they are linked by law (for example husband and wife), they are linked by social customs (as would be a woman and her husband's sister), or they are linked by love. But as the concept of family has changed somewhat in western society, we have also come to believe that any two people who choose to spend their lives committed to one another are indeed a family. A couple who has chosen a childfree lifestyle, a homosexual partnership, and a single parent with children are understood to be just as much a family as are a married couple who have conceived and birthed six children together.

We don't blink at the concept of two non-genetically related people who share one or more of these connections being members of the same family...except in adoptions. Though in adoption parent and child are linked by love and by law, the fact that they are not connected by blood has often meant that some people are unwilling to acknowledge their relationship as genuine and permanent.

It is not at all uncommon for people who do not understand the permanence of adoption and then bondedness of adoption-connected people to ask questions such as "Do you have any children of your own?" or "Are they natural brother and sister?" or "Have you ever met your real mother?" and to assume that adoptions are tentative ("Will the agency take him back now that you know he's 'handicapped'?" or "What if his real mother wants him back?")

Perhaps we could let comments like these go if they were made only to reasoning adults who could pretend, at least, to "know what I mean." But the stereotype of adoption as not genuine is so deeply ingrained that many adults think nothing of making such comments within earshot of our precious concrete-thinking children. We must effect change!

Yes PAL can sometimes result in longer than usual sentence constructions and demands that we change very old habits. With practice, we can do it, though. You'll make mistakes, and sometimes, for the sake of clarity it will necessary to use the qualifiers you have worked so hard to eliminate, but the effort is worth it!

Adoption is a method of joining a family, just as is birth. It is also a method of family planning, as are birth control pills, condoms, and abortion. Though the impact of adoption must be acknowledged consistently by those who are working to help one who has been adopted or one who has made an adoption plan successfully assimilate this fact into their senses of self esteem, adoption should not be thought of as a "condition." In the limited instances when it is appropriate to refer to the fact of adoption at all, correct PAL suggests that you say "Kathy was adopted" (referring to the way in which she arrived in her family) rather than phrasing it in the present tense ("Kathy is adopted"), which implies that adoption is a disability with which to cope. In an article or situation not centering on adoption (for example during an introduction, in an obituary or news or feature story about a business person or celebrity) it is usually inappropriate to refer to the adoption at all.

Everyone has a set of *birthparents*—a *birthmother* and *birthfather* who conceived us and gave us birth—though not all of us live with our birthparents. Children who were adopted (sparingly referred to when necessary as *adoptees* or *adopted people*, but preferably referred to only as human beings) will always have two sets of parents. Their birthparents gave them birth, and the people who adopted them—who become their social, legal, psychological, cultural parents—are simply their parents: *mother, father, mom, dad.*

It is best to avoid terms such as *real parent* or *real family*, *natural mother* and *natural father*, since these terms imply that adoptive relationships are artificial, tentative, less than whole and less enduring than genetically-linked relationships. Using a term such as *children of your own* furthers old style thinking of children as chattel. The poet Kalil

Gibran, writing "On Children" in his collection *The Prophet* summarized best the relationship between parents and their children, no matter how the connection began.

On Children[2]
And a woman who held a babe against her bosom said,
    speak to us of children.
And he said:

Your children are not your children.
They are the sons and daughters of life's longing for itself.
They come through you but not from you.
And though they are with you they belong not to you.

You may give them your love, but not your thoughts.
For they have their own thoughts.
You may house their bodies, but not their souls,
For their souls dwell in the house of tomorrow, which
    you cannot visit, not even in your dreams.
You may strive to be like them, but seek not to make
    them like you.
For life goes not backward nor tarries with yesterday.

You are the bows from which your children as living
    arrows are sent forth.
The Archer sees the mark upon the path of the infinite and He
    bends you with His might that His arrows might
    go swift and far.
Let your bending in the Archer's hands be for gladness,
For even as He loves the arrow that flies, so He loves
    also the bow that is stable.

Though it was once true that birthparents were given few choices in dealing with an untimely pregnancy, and that in years past they may well have *surrendered* or *relinquished* or *given up* their children to adoption, today's birthparents have a different experience. Empowered to make the best choices possible in a difficult situation, these men and women truly make adoption plans for their children. PAL speakers would encourage you to keep this in mind as well in speaking about women who do not choose adoption. These women *choose to parent* their children rather than to have an abortion or to make an adoption plan, they do not *keep their babies*.

Unlike in the era of the orphan trains of the 1800s, children are not *put up for adoption* on the station platforms of towns along the way. Their parents or court systems *plan adoption* or *make adoptive placements* for them. Should these children spend time in care between their birthparents and the home of their adopters, PAL speakers prefer that we refer to that care as interim care by *interim caregivers*, since the older terms *foster parents* and *foster care* have become so confused and their deliberate impermanence so misunderstood that most people use them nearly interchangeably and synonymously with adoption.

Parents once submitted to *homestudies* so that inappropriate prospects could be weeded out, but today's prospective adoptive parents participate in a *parent preparation process*. In choosing a style of adoption, some couples do not adopt in their country of citizenship, but instead arrange an *intercountry* or *international adoption*. We no longer use the term foreign adoption because the word *foreign* carries such negative connotations in the English language. Similarly, parents who chose to be in direct contact with their child's family of origin can arrange *open adoptions*, but those who prefer privacy may instead choose a *confidential adoption* (as opposed to the more negative label closed adoption.) When parents choose to parent children facing the challenges of *disabilities* and other *special needs*, we don't label these children *handicapped* or *hard to place*.

Perhaps the most difficult situation to find a P.C. PAL term for describes the situation wherein adopted people meet members of their birthfamilies. This is often referred to as a *reunion*—particularly by a sensationalizing media. Many adoptive parents and nonsearching adoptees find this offensive, since it seems to imply a re-meeting and carries with it the image of people who share a common store of memories or experiences getting together to reminisce. In fact, most adoptees join their cultural families as babies and have no such memories in common with their families of origin. Some therapists have suggested that the use of such an emotionally overpowering word has been responsible for setting up unrealistic expectations of either birthparents or adoptees who have initiated a contact with the other. A suggested alternative has been the simple term meeting, though some searching birthparents and adult adoptees find the fact that this term is so emotionless disconcerting. We continue to look for just the right term here.

You get the idea, I'm sure. Learning to use positive adoption language, and encouraging members of our friends and families, our clergypeople, our children's teachers to do so, will help over the years to exert a subtle shift that will have a positive effect on adoption in general.

Adoption has an image problem. From the musical *Annie* (which spun off of the cartoon series "Little Orphan Annie", which in itself was a spin off of a popular 1800s poem by the colloquial Hoosier poet James Whitcomb Riley) to sitcoms and soap operas, pulp fiction and serious literary fiction, adoption has often been misrepresented and misunderstood. Even worse, adoption gets a bum rap in the non-fiction world of journalism as well, as far too many journalists (with a few notable exceptions where a publisher's stylesheet does not allow it) adoption is noted inappropriately in news stories, obituaries, and more. This results in an almost obsessive need to attach inappropriate qualifiers ("This is Bull's adopted son, Mark") in situations where one would not dream of doing so in a non-adoptive family. When, for example, have you heard an introduction such as "I'd like you to meet Bill's birth control failure son" or "Allow me to introduce Mary's caesarean section daughter, Jill"? When reporting the murder of a parent by his child, have you ever seen a sentence like "Humboldt, 33, confessed that in a fit of rage he killed the mother to whom he was prematurely born"? Yet I know that you could list a number of famous criminal adoptees—David Berkowitz (Son of Sam), the Hillside stranglers, and more.

Society at large holds some widespread negative assumptions about adoption, and this widespread mythology produces a number of significant negatives. Not only do such negatives compromise our own attempts to build positive self esteem in our children and to encourage our personal families and friends to see our relationships as authentic, but they overflow into the much broader public policy arena. Dorothy DeBolt has referred to what she calls "A worship of the womb" which she believes results in too many social workers and judges placing children at further risk by refusing to terminate the parental rights of absent, abusive, or incompetent parents by birth. Counselors have noted for years that pressure from peers leads many young parents not ready or able to parent competently to refuse to consider the adoption option in dealing with an untimely pregnancy. In fact it is the most cognitively mature birthparents and often the oldest ones who do make adoption plans. The result is that a significant number of children born to very young mothers are at significant statistical risk for abuse, neglect, failure to thrive, educational impoverishment, living at or below poverty level, and many of these children find their way into the adoption system years later, no longer healthy infants easily placed but older children with very special needs.

Adoption is entirely exploitable...

As soon as I picked up the urgently ringing phone the voice on the other end cried, "I've had it!"

"First it was those crazy Cabbage Patch dolls. When they were so popular that a black market developed, **everybody** got on the cutesy adopt-a-reject bandwagon. The state wanted me to adopt-a-highway and the city a park, my local zoo has an "adopt-a-wild-child" campaign, the International Wildlife Coalition wants me to adopt a humpback whale, the Save-The-Redwoods League recruits adoptive parents for trees. All of them come with adoption certificates. All of them make me a parent to the object I'm sponsoring. Meanwhile, I've had to deal with the aftermath of that horrible movie Problem Child.

"I've tried to be patient, really I have, but yesterday when I walked into the video store and saw a stack of dusty used videotapes piled under a sign that read "Adopt-a-video" I reached my saturation point!"

People who are involved with adoption issues on a daily basis are becoming increasingly concerned about the negative adoption imagery besieging our families today. Of special note because they seem to be spreading so rapidly, are programs taking an adopt-a theme which have proliferated since the Cabbage Patch doll craze of the early 1980s. These programs range from those mentioned by my friend Susan in the anecdote above to silly not-for-profit fundraising ideas (such as Adopt-A-Rubber-Duck river races sponsored by a local radio station to benefit a food bank,) city adopt-a-park and adopt-a-pothole programs, commercial adopt-a-product promotions, ecological and wildlife education programs (U.S. Air's in flight magazine ran a three page article supporting them in October, 1991), to Humane Society animal placement programs.

Granted, the English language is a complex and varied one, and the words adopt/adoption have more than one meaning. In addition to the primary definition ("To follow a legal and social process permanently transferring parental rights from a set of birthparents to a set of adoptive parents,") the second and third definitions of the verb form ("To take and follow by choice or assent" or "To take up and use as one's own") have non-family-related meanings, describing the processes by which schools adopt textbooks, campaigns adopt themes, etc.

The adopt-a projects, though, trade not on the secondary definitions, but on the family building definition of adoption, conjuring up a quick and clear picture which then produces a marketing advantage. Every marketing person I've ever spoken to about my concern about this admits that it is the immediately recognizable image of sheltering an otherwise unwanted "orphan" that makes such a theme attractive and successful. That's why these exploitive, tug-at-the-heartstrings programs *always* include an adoption certificate naming the sponsor as "parent" as a premium.

Those of us who are parents by adoption and adoption activists, however, believe that such programs trivialize a very serious topic and that they further myths and misconceptions about this family planning method to yet another generation of children. Unfortunately, they turn upon a kind of "save the rejects" image that may seem cute and harmless to grownups, but which confuses concrete-thinking children—be they adopted or not.

Those who are skeptical about the very existence of adopt-a confusion argue that it is up to adoptive parents to work with our kids to explain the realities of adoption. They are absolutely right, of course. And as adoptive parents we *do* work with our children (and with the children of friends and relatives) to help them sort through the differences between adoption of people and adoption of animals or adoption promotions. But because children are not abstract thinkers, this is not an easy task. Besides, we can only reach the children closest to us, not the children who use their own and their parents' misinformation to throw playground barbs at our kids. We wonder, then, why we adoptive parents should have to spend all this time explaining a confusion, when, by just sensitizing good people responsible for developing marketing programs we could instead eliminate this particular confusion entirely!

Adoption is difficult enough an issue for young children without adding to the confusion through commercial projects. Research by David Brodzinsky at Rutgers University has shown that children who were adopted are really no quicker to understand the complex social issues which underlie adoption than are their non-adopted peers, though children who were adopted do learn to parrot the terminology much earlier.

Perhaps you have not experienced adopt-a confusion in your own family (or at least you may not be aware that such a confusion is at work,) but such misconceptions are widespread among pre-school and elementary-aged youngsters. Three examples of adopt-a confusion among children under 10 (who are almost universally intellectually too immature to reason logically) typify those I hear about as occurring regularly in cities across the continent...

A five year old friend (adoptee) was "given" a giraffe by her grandparents through their much-loved zoo's Adopt-An-Animal program. Over the course of several months the child was very upset to learn that not only could she not take "her" animal home or care for it directly, but she also could not consider it "hers" after the year had passed, when a different animal was substituted for "her" giraffe in the next year's campaign. In another city, another child learned that an acquaintance had been assigned the same specific animal as had he! A third child was told by a non-adopted friend who had participated in such a program that if his parents wanted to, they could trade him for a "better" child next year, as his family had in "upgrading" their zoo adoption. Children waiting in foster care for permanency have been teased by peers with taunts such as, "We adopted a giraffe. Nobody wants you!"

Each of these children has become very confused and concerned about his own situation. In each case parents had had no idea before this experience that they were participating in a program which would lead to such stress for their kids or others' children. That's because all of the adults involved—zoo administrators, parents, etc. could think abstractly and thus were able to see clearly the difference between adoption of people and sponsorship of animals sold as adoption. These adults simply forgot that children are incapable of following a line of reasoning this complex to a clear conclusion and that they take everything very personally.

My son, who was eight at the time of the first round of Cabbage-Patch-mania, watched an evening news feature story on the black market developing in these ugly little creatures who spring from the dirt accompanied by adoption papers and turned to ask,

Similarly, school-aged children who look at the lists offered in programs such as most zoos', offering different "prices" for different varieties of "wild children" are often led to ask their parents how much they themselves cost and whether a brother or sister was more or less expensive and why! The issue of money and adoption is certainly a part of our helping our children understand the process, but not at eight! No amount of explanation about how adoption fees work and how they are disbursed can be absorbed by a non-reasoning small child.

I've heard from several families who have "adopted" an animal from Humane Societies. In contrast to other "adoption" projects, on the surface these seem "like" human adoption, in that there actually is an investigation and approval process, the animal is the family's to take home and nurture, the Societies stress the permanence of the relationship, and thus participation in the program seems a good "lesson" for children in what adoption is about.

Because of their more direct connection to human family adoption, I find these animal companion programs far less objectionable than adopt-a-wilderness-river programs. (And please note Humane Society of the U.S., that I am using your preferred term *animal companion* instead of the more familiar term *pets* in an attempt to follow your line of P.C. reasoning!) But despite good intentions, these, too, can be confusing. In several cases problems have started when animals brought home turned out to be serious problems—biting, failing obedience training, etc.—and the family have come to the realization that they would have to find the animal another home or return him to the Society. Soon after, their children began to experience nightmares or other acting out behavior. Upon investigation it has been discovered that these kids were afraid that if they were "bad" they, too, would be "returned"—or even "put to sleep."

The way to prevent these confusions is really quite simple. Adoption is a process by which families are planned and formed. To trivialize it in a commercial way insults the birthparents, adoptive parents, and adoptees who have been personally touched by this process. We no longer find it acceptable to trivialize other minority groups in this society. The proliferation of adopt-a-promotions has become about as humorous to many of those personally touched by adoption as are shuffle-footed pickaninny humor or Pollack jokes to the minority groups they deride.

For the sake of children waiting for adoption and those who have already found their permanent families in adoption, we adults must insist that adoption be treated in a dignified manner.

How to proceed becomes the challenge. My own year long experience with the Indianapolis Zoo and some national reactions to it serve as an interesting example of what works and what doesn't. The Indianapolis Zoo has, as of January 1, 1992, become the first zoo in the country to change the name of their animal adoption program, publicly announcing that the change is out of sensitivity to concerns raised by adoption-touched people. The new program, Animal Amigos, may not be transferable to your zoo, because it was chosen to allow the Indy zoo to take advantage of their relationship with a licensed cartoon character (a parrot named Amigo who had been the official mascot of the Pan American Games held in Indianapolis a few summers ago), but there are alternatives for your zoo, your highway department, your local merchant to consider.

I've been an anti-Cabbage Patch campaigner for years. I had carefully penned indignant letters, made articulate but annoyed phone calls to people in high places, and had some but few successes. People either got so defensive that they dug in and refused to admit they were wrong, wrong, wrong, or they got it but didn't care what "the crazy adoption woman" thought.

Sometimes I was even embarrassed by the response I got. For example, once I wrote an indignant letter to the editor of a small newspaper in response to a "humorous" article on environmental adopt-a programs as alternative gift ideas for infertile people tempted to spend money on unproductive high technology. I put on my very official sounding title as then chairman of RESOLVE's national board of directors and waxed on about how tough infertility was, how offensive this joking was, and then shared the examples of adopt-a confusion cited above. My letter was printed all right—along with a direct response from the editor, who pointed out that he thought I was some kind of a nut who couldn't take a joke. The lessons learned? There were two: 1. The editor had felt defensive about being attacked and had thus dug in, and 2. Since adults are supposed to be tough and to be able to take a joke, leaving out the insult to adults and focusing only on confusion to children might have been more productive (though in this case the article was really an adults-only piece.)

In approaching the zoo I decided to work differently. I dropped my indignation and annoyance and began with compliments about everything there was to like and admire about the zoo. This was easy to do, because there is *lots* to like about our zoo—we have a gorgeous, brand new facility here, and we'd love to have you visit it and our beautiful city! My approach presumed that the zoo staff were good folks who had likely

made an honest mistake in that they simply didn't know that anyone
might be confused or offended by their program.

I centered my information about confusion in children. It really doesn't matter what adults think if children are confused by it. For an institution for whom children are a major audience, how children react to a program is very important. This may mean that you are likely to be more successful effecting change in adopt-a programs which are child or family focused (and most are!)

I kept in mind at all times that I was dealing here with marketing and development people. What would make sense to them was how their mistake might be affecting their pocketbook. In the case of this family-sensitive institution, I could point out that adoptive parents, who tend to be slightly more affluent on average than families in general are also very motivated as parents to provide educational and cultural experiences for their children and thus probably belong to libraries, zoos, museums, etc. in proportionately high numbers. As an educational program, animal sponsorship might be attractive, but when this highly visible program was marketed as adoption, it provided enough offense or danger of confusion to make these families decide to avoid it—and in some cases zoo membership as well—and that sometimes they took their extended families with them. I offered my help not just in brainstorming about possible alternatives, but in publicizing and fundraising for the new program.

In general, I made certain that I was a positive, non-threatening, cooperative person with whom to work (I really am anyway most of the time!) In response, I found that the Zoo staff were equally pleasant and positive. They never needed to find themselves on the defensive. Contrary to one very well meaning but unfortunately worded article written in a midwestern newspaper during Adoption Awareness Month, the Indianapolis Zoo and I did not do battle! We didn't need to! We worked together to bring about change that would work for our mutual benefit.

The result of this effort has been amazing. The Indianapolis Zoo is getting well deserved attention from the media and the community at large. Local memberships have increased. Several national organizations have written letters of support and/or are considering honoring this zoo in some visible way. From throughout the country people touched by adoption are sending checks of from $5.00 to $100.00 to show their appreciation.

All of this will undoubtedly have a domino effect. Other zoos have already made inquiries about the new program, and our zoo's staff is keeping close track of how the change affects memberships and sponsorships. If this program is successful (and you can and should help to make it so by sending your own tax deductible donation of any size to

John Reynolds, Indianapolis Zoo, 1200 West Washington St, Indianapolis, IN 46222) other zoos and then other programs will undoubtedly follow suit. I encourage you to hold up this program as a successful model when making your own efforts in your community!

Eliminating adopt-a confusion and using positive adoption language and imagery are important goals for adoption advocates. Because we care about adoption, about waiting children and most of all about our own kids, most of us understand that at times we will feel called upon to become advocates of adoption sensitivity. Some of us are letter writers, some of us are public speakers, some of us are lobbyists or sales people, some of us are one-on-one conversationalists. Still others of us find it uncomfortable to take a personal public stand, but we want to support those who are willing to speak out on our behalf, so we become members of organizations and donors to campaigns that such organizations, with their strength in numbers can make successful. Each of these types of advocates is an important link in the advocacy chain— and one of these links is you.

During the summer of 1990 the release of the movie *Problem Child* sent shivers through the adoption community. The movie's story and script were incredibly offensive to adoption agencies, to waiting children, to infertile couples, and more. To top it off, the movie, with its slapstick humor and PG rating was aimed at a primary audience of concrete-thinking children! Parent groups throughout the country, assisted by A.F.A. and N.C.F.A. (whose director, Bill Pierce, even appeared on "Entertainment Tonight") led a campaign for change. They were at least partially successful. Though the movie itself stayed on the screens, advocates convinced many local video rental stores to remove the movie from their shelves and, perhaps most significantly, when the movie made it to network T.V. the most offensive scenes had been dropped and several lines of dialogue dubbed over to make them less insulting to those touched by adoption. It might not have been a complete victory, but it was progress!

Those Caring Others

Sometimes its the people who touch us most directly who need our attention first—the grandparents who feel a need to introduce their much-loved grandchildren with qualifiers ("Judy and Tyrone adopted Tawanda, you know"), clergypeople who forget that in speaking to one family in a post service reception line they are speaking to those all around, teachers who mean well, but just can't get it right.

Erica came home from school today (really, the very day I was writing this!) with a beautiful report card. On the bottom of it, her teacher, who absolutely adores her and makes no bones about it, had written "Erica, always know that I'd take you as my own, any time, any day. You are a peach. Love, Mrs. H."

Now, I know very well that Mrs.H. meant this as the highest compliment to my daughter and to us, her parents. What she has forgotten is that Erica joined our family by adoption. For many children Erica's age (fifth grade) such a message could be very confusing. Just like all other fifth graders, she is experiencing days when she'd like to trade her parents in for any other convenient set. But for children who were adopted, as was Erica, the fact is that the normal fantasizing about having a better set of parents is complicated by the fact that she very likely could have had a totally different set. It could set her up for conflictual grieving. In fact, it did. Last year when this same teacher made similar comments in class, Erica had several bad days which finally produced a long discussion between us of why birthparents make adoption plans and how hard it is sometimes to be adopted.

I'll have to talk to Mrs. H. about this again. As a former teacher I am well aware of the mixed perceptions of adoption among teachers in general. Some teachers single these children out as "special" and especially admire their "wonderful, selfless parents." Other teachers believe that children who were adopted are at risk for problems, and, if they know of the fact of adoption seem to wait for the proverbial shoe to drop. In reality, teachers are very normal people, with the same mix of fact and fiction to deal with as has the rest of the world. But with teachers, parents can find an advantage. These are people who truly care about kids, who understand how kids learn and care about educating them, who are themselves usually omnivorous learners. Teachers and school counselors will soak up information you are willing to provide them. Make certain they have copies of fact sheets and booklets you have found helpful, and engage them as your allies, in helping your children deal with their adoptive status.

"It's too bad that there have been no children of your own, but it's wonderful of you to have taken her in," commented the smiling clergyperson as she patted the head of the brown toddler who clung to the skirt of the blond, blue-eyed woman she addressed. "Do you know anything at all about her real parents? How could anyone give up such a beautiful child?"

In the line behind them I cringed as I heard her words. The pastor was well meaning, of course, but I knew that her words stung the family for whom they were meant. No children of their own? Real parents? Did the years they had spent working to build a family, the weeks they had spent consoling a terrified grieving baby, who, for the first time in her short life looked up into white face and blue eyes, the nights they had walked the floor with a baby wracked with the pain of a parasite that had accompanied her from the land of her birth count for nothing? Wonderful people who had rescued a waif? Did she not know of the thousands of others who waited for babies, could she not realize how lucky they felt themselves to have been given the privilege of parenting this beautiful child? And their daughter, tired and cranky and ready to go home, yet listening to the words of the adults over her head. What did she take in from this exchange? What message about herself and her family was added to her internal tape?

Between me and the adoption-built family waited another family—mom, dad and daughter. The dawdler was fourteen, a freshman in high school, bright and popular, and—unknown to the pastor—pregnant. They too heard her words. What did they think I wondered. How did this caring professional's subtle prejudices weigh upon their minds and contribute to their thinking as they worked so hard to sort through a maze of options—parenting, abortion, adoption?

Can you let instances like these go? I think not! Each of us must find ways that will allow us to become adoption educators at the level we find most comfortable. Perhaps it is a private telephone conversation or a note. Of course you can pass along the brochure describing an adoption educational event you think might help. Perhaps you are braver than that. Can you volunteer to do a brief in-service training for staff at the schools, doctor's offices, scout leader training, or houses of worship which touch your family's lives?

The Politics of Adoption

Cynthia Martin created a stir several years ago when she authored a how-to book on adoption which she titled *Beating the Adoption Game*. The title certainly caught the attention of many—prospective parents who immediately sensed that here was a book that was written by someone who understood where they were coming from, as well as outraged traditional practitioners who felt that such an image trivializes a dignified service to children and families.

The image—adoption as a game to be played—may not be a pretty picture, but many touched by this process would say that the analogy certainly works. Over the last decade it's been used more and more frequently, and we'll use it again here to talk about the key organizations which impact society's view of adoption—the players in the game.

The world of adoption is a rapidly changing one. Today, in the early 1990s, adoption, once thought of as a family building option only for white, middle class, infertile couples looking for a healthy baby is—in principle—amazingly diverse.

I emphasize the phrase "in principle" because the fact is that minority families continue to be both poorly recruited and insensitively treated by far too many agencies who have placement responsibilities for large numbers of children of color, couples who have more than one child by birth and single prospective parents are rarely seen as "families of choice" except in the placement of children with special needs, and working class and poor families often find themselves challenged in their quest to build families by adoption. Young women facing an unplanned pregnancy find it extraordinarily difficult to get the truly objective counseling that will allow them to make unpressured choices about options, so that, on the one hand, far too many children for whom adoption might be an appropriate option remain with abusive or neglectful birthfamilies while at the same time far too many women feel that they have been pressured to choose adoption.

As we discussed in earlier chapters, the menu of options for building a family by adoption ranges from public and private agency adoption and adoptions arranged by the more traditional non-agency sources (doctors, lawyers, clergy) to entrepreneurial independent services which offer consultations on self-marketing, provide education, and refer to counseling as requested. Birthparents and prospective adopters of both infants and older children can put all the control into the hands of professionals or may choose to retain personal control over all decisions in finding and choosing a family. Adoptions vary on a spectrum ranging from the traditional confidential form in which no identifying information (and sometimes little non-identifying information) is shared, to those which involve close ongoing communication and/or visitation between birth and adoptive families in a kind of extended family form. International adoption continues to occur, though the countries from which children arrive seem to change almost monthly, with each country establishing its own procedures and requirements. Agencies abandon the practice of adoption and new agencies form every year. Consumer groups begin and old ones die. Legislation is introduced and passed or defeated.

The game is confusing, and the rules constantly changing, and, no matter how idealistic we are in talking about recent positive changes in adoption, healthy babies—no matter what their racial status—are more often than not adopted (after payment of large fees) by white, middle class families; far too many children linger in foster care rather than finding permanent families in adoption; and birthparents feel improperly served. These continuing inequities have resulted in strongly negative reactions to adoption "as practiced" from groups as diverse as the National Association of Black Social Workers and Concerned United Birthparents and the American Adoption Congress to the National Committee for Adoption. And everybody seems to have an answer to how to "fix" adoption's problems.

Becoming informed and staying informed is not an easy task. But doing so is worth it. A recurring theme throughout this book has been David Kirk's premise that it is families who fairly consistently acknowledge the differences in adoption (rather than denying them) who are best able to build the kind of empathic communication with their children (acknowledging that each of them has experienced both significant losses and significant gains in adoption) which fosters healthy attachments between parents and children. To practice this kind of acceptance of difference is possible in adoption only when we keep ourselves in touch and informed—when we know the players on the field. What follows is a brief introduction to the most significant of those other "players."

The consumers of adoption-related services are birthparents, adoptive parents, and adoptees, for many years referred to as the adoption triad or triangle, but increasingly termed the adoption circle, as this term seems to imply a less "sided" and therefore "divided" attitude. Let me introduce you to the national players representing the Consumer Team, which in most cases serve as umbrella organizations for dozens of regional and local groups in the adoption consumer movement.

Adoptive Families of America, the publishers of *OURS: The Magazine of Adoptive Families*, reaches out to support, educate and advocate on behalf of all kinds of adoption-built families—families who are built by both birth and adoption and those adopting after infertility, two parent and single parent families, adopters of infants and older children, uni-racial or multi-racial families, families formed in the U.S. or through international adoption, etc. AFA's membership includes in excess of 15,000 families and over 250 group-members (parent support groups providing services within local or regional communities.) A.F.A. has, during the last several years, begun to work harder and harder on legislative issues of import to adoptive families, lobbying on the national and international levels as well as monitoring events and issues in the individual states and providing a clearinghouse function that puts lobbyists in one state in touch with those working on similar issues in others. A.F.A. national membership does not include automatic membership in a local affiliate, but you will want to become a member of a local parent group! You will find that some local A.F.A. member-groups focus on a specific approach to adoption (adoption from a specific country, special needs, etc.) and others are more broadly focused. You will also find that not all local parent groups are AFA members (some who are not can be located through NACAC, below.) (Membership $24. AFA, 3333 Hwy 100 N, Minneapolis, MN 55422)

RESOLVE, Inc. is the national network of 54 chapters providing services in over 70 cities to 15,000+ couples dealing with a fertility impairment and the professionals who work with them. Adoption information, education, referral, and support are an integral part of RESOLVE chapter services. Membership ($35 to $55 annually) covers both local and national services, including both newsletters, access to fact sheets, monthly meetings, symposia, etc. On a state by state basis RESOLVE is working with professionals such as the American Fertility Society to achieve reproductive parity for infertile couples through mandatory coverage of infertility treatments under insurance plans. (RESOLVE, Inc., 1310 Broadway, Somerville, MA 02144.)

Infertility Awareness Association of Canada (IAAC) is a networked Canadian charitable organization offering assistance, support, and education to tose with infertility concerns by issuance of its publication *Infertility Awareness* five times a year; establishment of chapters to provide grass roots services; a resource centre; information packages; and a network of related services. Membership is $30 Canadian annually. (IAAC, 523-774 Echo Drive, Ottawa, Ontario K1S 5N8, CANADA, telephone 613-730-1322.)

North American Council on Adoptable Children (membership= 5,000 groups, agencies, and individuals) focuses on the needs of waiting children. Through legislative advocacy efforts and networking, research and policy analysis, the quarterly newsletter Adoptalk, grants for the development of replicable local training and support services, and most prominently through its wonderful annual August training conference (one of the world's largest adoption conferences) which rotates throughout five regions in the U.S. and Canada, NACAC deals with parent group issues and professional practice concerns that impact upon special needs adoption, children in interim care and all children in need of permanency. NACAC can refer you to a network of 500 local parent groups throughout North America. (Membership: $25 individual or parent group, $100 to agencies and organizations. NACAC, 970 Raymond Avenue #6, St. Paul, MN 55104.)

Concerned United Birthparents advocates for adoption reform based on the experiences of its 5,000+ members, most of whom feel that adoption was not a good choice for them. Lobbying for open adoption records and espousing the philosophy that adoption should only be seen as a last option when there is no possible way to preserve a family by birth, CUB produces a bimonthly newsletter, offers search assistance, produces fact sheets and pamphlets concerning many adoption-related issues (a recent one deals with child abuse in adoption,) and offers meetings in a number of local branches across the country. Admittedly, many adoptive parents will find CUB's philosophy and tone abrasive and threatening. They, speak, however, for a significant constituency, some of whom are the birthparents of our children, more of whom are the birthparents of our peers and their younger siblings. As adoption-built families there is much we can learn from CUB. (Membership: $35. CUB, 2000 Walker, Des Moines IA 50317.)

American Adoption Congress is an umbrella organization for several hundred local search and support organizations across the United States. The majority of AAC's membership is comprised of searching adult adoptees and birthparents, however, a significant number of their members are adoptive parents (many of whom also belong to the smaller affiliate organization Adoptive Parents for Open Records.) A newsletter is published sporadically, but the bulk of services are provided through well organized annual regional and national conferences which deal with adoption aftermath issues for all triad members and offer training sessions for those who wish to lobby effectively for opening adoption records. (Membership: $40. AAC, PO Box 44040, L'Enfant Plaza Station, Washington DC 20026)

Committee for Single Adoptive Parents provides information for U.S. and Canadian singles interested in adoption opportunities. (CSAP, P.O. Box 15084, Chevy Chase, MD 20815)

Adoptive Parents for Open Records advocates for the opening of previously confidential records to allow easy access between birthparents and siblings and children who have been adopted. There is no membership fee. Activities are supported by donations. (APFOR, c/o Carol Gustavson, 9 Marjorie Dr., Hackettstown, NJ 07840)

Professional Associations

The players include not just consumers of services, but service providers as well. Their influence is broad, because it is accompanied by the credibility of professional credentials. In the U.S. national league professionals in the adoption game include these key and emerging players:

American Academy of Adoption Attorneys a fairly young (just over two years old) organization comprised of attorneys who make independent adoption a part of their legal practice. The organization's goals include networking, striving to standardize practice, etc. (P.O. Box 33053, Washington DC 20033)

Child Welfare League of America is the oldest professional organization for individuals and agencies practicing in the field of child welfare social service. This well respected organization sees adoption as only one aspect of the many issues in its field. It publishes a professional journal and several newsletters, studies and makes suggestions concerning practice standards, publishes professional books, etc. (440 First St NW, Ste 310, Washington DC 20001)

National Association of Black Social Workers serves as a social service advocate for the African-American community. Among its adoption-related concerns are that children of color are best served when parented by adults of color and that transracial adoption can be seen as a form of cultural genocide. ABSW advocates the establishment of strong state-by-state and even federal guidelines (similar to those in the Indiana Child Welfare Act) which would ensure that African-American children are raised by Black parents. (15231 W. McNichols, Detroit MI 48235).

National Committee for Adoption an advocacy organization promoting adoption as a positive family building option, this membership organization is in some ways a hybrid. Primarily supported by member agencies, it does also encourage individual memberships from those families who share its positive view of adoption (NCFA has produced an award winning PSA campaign featuring famous adopted people,) its conservative stance on open-records/confidentiality and its wary view of open placements. NCFA was instrumental in forming the Congressional Coalition on Adoption, and has attempted to fill an important statistical gap left by the government in gathering state-by-state data concerning adoption in its Adoption Factbook II. (Individual membership $50. NCFA, 1930 17th St NW, Washington DC 20009).

National Federation for Open Adoption is another fairly new organization for agencies and practitioners focusing on the emerging field of open adoption. NFOA sponsors professional training conferences and publishes a quarterly newsletter. (c/o Independent Adoption Center, 391 Taylor Blvd Ste 100, Pleasant Hill, CA 94523).

National Providers of Direct Services

And, finally, there are a number of not-for-profit organizations which are direct service providers rather than membership organizations and which actively participate in the political world of adoption.

The CAP Book (700 Exchange St., Rochester NY 14806) publishes a national photolisting book of U.S. children who wait for adoption and can be placed across state lines.

Joint Council on International Children's Services from North America (c/o Susan Cox, P.O. Box 2880, Eugene OR 97402) is a coalition of adoption agencies and parent groups interested in intercountry adoption. Its activities include a quarterly newsletter and an annual conference.

National Adoption Center (1218 Chestnut St., Philadelphia PA 19107) offers general information on adoption and computer matching of waiting children and waiting families.

National Adoption Information Clearinghouse (Ste 600, 1400 Eye St., NW Washington DC 20005) through a government grant provides the public with information about all aspects of adoption. Services, many of which are free, include publications, database searches, referrals, and copies of state adoption laws.

National Resource Center for Special Needs Adoption (P.O. Box 337, Chelsea MI 48118) is dedicated to improving the availability of adoption and post-adoption services of special needs children and their families.

Perhaps you have assumed that, as adoptive parents, the only services you would need would be those designed for adoptive parents. Wrong! Understanding the concerns and needs of birthparents and adult adoptees is an important part of your education. It will help you to develop your own well-informed opinions about issues and will prepare you to better meet your own family's current and future needs. I would encourage you to make the commitment to your family's education that subscribing to some of the newsletters and attending some of the conferences of the organizations listed here will provide. You will not always agree with what you read and hear, but you are likely to find that there is more common ground here than there is disagreement. Listening to one another, working together, those of us touched in any way by adoption bear the responsibility for adoption as it evolves for the 21st century.

Resources

As with the earlier sections of this book, the following resources are not an exhaustive list, but a selected collection of the in-print materials which I felt were most helpful as this book went to press. Contact RESOLVE, Infertility Awareness Association of Canada, Adoptive Families of America, and Adoption Council of Canada for the most up-to-date resources.

Unlike the earlier sections, however, I've included some materials which some adopters may find less useful for one of two reasons: either because they are too academic in tone or because they are offensive because of their negativity. These materials have been marked with an asterisk (*), and I consider them must reading for clinical professionals. Somewhere, later down the road after placement, some parents will find them of interest as well.

Understanding and Enhancing
Adoptive Family Relationships

* *The Psychology of Adoption* edited by David M. Brodzinsky and Marshall Schechter. (New York: Oxford University Press, 1990). A collection of essays on a variety of adoption issues—many written by trainers who have not written books and up to now have been difficult for consumers to access.

Adoption: The Lifelong Search for Self by David M. Brodzinsky and Marshall Schechter and Robin Marantz Henig. (New York: Doubleday, 1992). Integrating both psychological and educational theory, the authors offer a model of normal development in adoptees.

A Child's Journey through Placement by Vera I. Fahlberg, M.D. (Indianapolis: Perspectives Press, 1991). A careful look at how transfering a child from a known environment to any long term new placement—hospitalization, interim care, etc.—affects attachment, with specific suggestions for avoiding unnecessary moves and facilitating those which are unavoidable.

*Residential Treatment: A Tapestry of Many Therapies by Vera I. Fahlberg, M.D. (Indianapolis: Perspectives Press, 1990). An explanation of how the process of mileu therapy works with troubled children.

Our Child: Preparation for Parenting in Adoption—Instructor's Guide by Carol A. Hallenbeck. (Wayne, PA: Our Child Press, rev 1989). A fully scripted curriculum guide for offering a "Lamaze" course for prospective adopters.

Helping Children Cope with Separation and Loss by Claudia Jewett (Boston: Harvard Common Press, 1978). The classic consumer-directed look at how children experiences losses of all kinds—death, divorce, adoption, etc.

Perspectives on a Grafted Tree: Thoughts for Those Touched by Adoption edited by Patricia Irwin Johnston (Indianapolis: Perspectives Press, 1983). A collection of poems written by birthparents, adoptive parents, adoptees, and professionals in the field in an effort to demonstrate the gain and loss, happiness and pain that are part of the adoption experience for all involved.

*Shared Fate: A Theory and Method of Adoptive Relationships by H. David Kirk (Brentwood Bay, BC: Ben Simon Publications, rev. 1984). See discussion in Chapter Four.

*Exploring Adoptive Family Life: The Collected Papers of H.D.K. by H. David Kirk (Brentwood Bay, BC: Ben Simon Publications, 1988)

You're Our Child: The Adoption Experience by Jerome Smith and Franklin Miroff (Lanham, MD: Madison Books, rev 1987). See discussion in Chapter Four.

Holding Time by Martha G. Welch (New York: Simon & Shuster, 1989)
An aid for parents dealing with attachment problems.

Helping Children Learn

Flight of the Stork by Anne C. Bernstein (Indianapolis: Perspectives Press, 1994). How children learn about and come to understand sexuality and reproduction.

The Long Awaited Stork: A Guide to Parenting after Infertility by Ellen Sarasohn Glazer (Lexington, MA: Lexington Books, 1990). One writer's view of how infertility issues may rise again for couples who pursue quasi or tradition adoption or give birth after struggling with infertility.

Communicating with the Adopted Child by Miriam Komar (New York: Walker Publishing Co., 1991). Advice on how to talk with kids about adoption.

Making Sense of Adoption: A Parents Guide by Lois Ruskai Melina (New York: Harper & Row, 1989). Advice on how to talk with kids about adoption.

Raising Adopted Children: A Manual for Adoptive Parents by Lois Ruskai Melina (New York: Harper & Row, 1986). A somewhat "Dr. Spockish," encyclopedic handbook on adoption issues.

Your Baby's Mind and How it Grows: Piaget's Theory for Parents by Maryann Spencer Pulaski (New York: Harper & Row, 1978). Developmental psychology of children

How to Raise an Adopted Child by Judith Schaffer and Christine Lindstrom (New York: Crown, 1989). Advice on how to deal with ongoing adoption issues and how to talk with kids about adoption.

Parenting Your Adopted Child: A Complete and Loving Guide by Stephanie E. Siegel (New York: Prentice Hall Press, 1989). Advice on how to deal with ongoing adoption issues and how to talk with kids about adoption.

*American Adoption Congress (P.O. Box 44040, L'Enfant Plaza Station, Washington D.C. 20026) is a national umbrella organization for the myriad of small local organizations nationwide which offer support to searching birthparents and adult adoptees and which actively lobby for change in the adoption system.

*Concerned United Birthparents (2000 Walker St, Des Moines, IA 50317) is a national support and advocacy organization for birthparents who have found adoption to be a negative force in their lives. Their newsletter and a variety of fact sheets on issues of coping and search can be highly informative for adoptive parents and professionals.

* *The Psychology of Adoption* edited by David M.Brodzinsky and Marshall Schechter (New York: Oxford University Press, 1990). (see above)

Adoption: The Lifelong Search for Self by David M.Brodzinsky and Marshall Schechter (New York: Doubleday, 1992). (see above)

Perspectives on a Grafted Tree: Thoughts for Those Touched by Adoption edited by Patricia Irwin Johnston (Indianapolis: Perspectives Press, 1983). (see above)

Lost and Found: The Adoption Experience by Betty Jean Lifton (New York: Harper & Row, rev 1988). An adult adoptee describes the impact of her confidential adoption on the formation of her identity.

An Adopted Woman by Katrina Maxtone-Graham (New York: Remi Books, 1983). A fascinating look at one woman's search for her family of origin.

* *The Dark Side of Adoption* by Marsha Riben (Detroit: Harlo, 1988). A scathing indictment of adoption by a woman who believes that adoption nearly always represents unnecessary family separation.

Dear Birthfather by Randolph W. Severson (Dallas: House of Tomorrow Productions, 1991). A warm and loving booklet.

* *The Adoption Triangle: The Effects of the Sealed Record on Adoptees, Birth Parents and Adoptive Parents* by Arthur D.Sorosky, Annette Baran and Reuben Pannor (San Antonio: Corona Publishers, rev 1990). A classic report calling for a revolutionary change to totally open adoption prepared by three long term adoption professionals.

Because subscription rates are subject to change, I have not provided current rates. Please write for current information, and consider enclosing a stamped, self addressed envelope for a response.

Adoptalk is the newsletter of North American Council on Adoptable Children (address above).

Adopted Child is a monthly 4 page newsletter which is written and published by journalist/author and adoptive parent Lois Melina, who features a single topic covered in depth in each issue (P.O. Box 9362, Moscow ID 83843).

Adoption Helper is a quarterly Canadian newsletter offering practical assistance for Canadians seeking a placement. (189 Springdale Blvd., Toronto, Ont. M4C 1Z6 CANADA).

Adoptnet a bimonthly magazine focusing on new issues in adoption— particularly openness. (P.O. Box 50514, Palo Alto, CA 94303).

* *CUB Reporter* the newsletter of Concerned United Birthparents. (address above).

* *National Adoption Reports* is the quarterly newsletter of National Committee for Adoption. (address above).

OURS: The Magazine of Adoptive Families from Adoptive Families of America (address above). The world's largest circulation adoptive parenting periodical. (address above).

* *The Roundtable* from National Resource Center for Special Needs Adoption at Spaulding for Children offers special focus information targeted primarily for professionals in the field. (NRCSN, 17390 W Eight Mile Rd., Southfield, MI 48075).

Roots & Wings a bimonthly mulit-focus magazine published by adoptive parent Cynthia Peck. (15 Nancy Terrace, Hackettstown NJ 07840).

Many local and regional adoption support groups publish excellent newsletters, such as *FACE Facts* from Families Adopting Children from Everywhere in Maryland, *News* from FAIR from Families Adopting in Response in California and many more!

When Friends Ask about Adoption: Question and Answer Guide for Non-Adoptive Parents and Other Caring Adults by Linda Bothun (Chevy Chase, MD: Swan Publications, 1987). A booklet designed to be given to those whose lives may touch our families.

Supporting an Adoption by Patricia Holmes (Wayne, PA: Our Child Press, 1984). A booklet for families, teachers, clergy, doctors, and others who may come in contact with adoption-built families.

Adoption Awareness: A Guide for Teachers, Counselors, Nurses and Caring Others by Jeanne Warren Lindsay and Catherine Monserrat (Buena Park, CA: Morning Glory Press, 1989). A complete, careful and supportive discussion of numerous issues related to adoption as an positive option for people dealing with an untimely pregnancy.

Finding Books for Children

Adoption Literature for Children and Young Adults: An Annotated Bibliography by Susan G. Miles (Westport, CT: Greenwood Press, 1991). An extensive bibliography of children's books with an adoption focus designed to be used by caring adults in selecting appropriate materials.

The best source for an up-to-date list of the best in children's books on adoption and culturally sensitive materials for families adopting across racial or national lines is *Adoptive Families of America's Parent Resources* catalog, which is included in each issue of *OURS: The Magazine of Adoptive Families* and is also distributed separately.

Also be certain that you are on the mailing list of Perspectives Press, the infertility and adoption publisher, P.O. Box 90318, Indianapolis, IN 46290.

Advocacy

For a thorough discussion of the organizations who serve as advocates for the adoption community, see Chapter 12.

Epilogue
Infertility Revisited

That summer was a season of milestones. My high school class had its 25-year reunion, and I discovered that many of my classmates were grandparents. Meanwhile, our oldest child became a teenager during the same month that we gave away the remaining diapers and the changing table in our youngest child's room.

My mother began to think about retiring from her job and spending her 60s and 70s traveling and enjoying her grandchildren. On the other side of the family, my father-in-law (already retired for almost twenty years) fell asleep while watching a baseball game and never awoke. His partner of over sixty years, my husband's mother, who had been disabled by a series of small strokes that had clouded her memories, frustrated her always cheerful tongue, and robbed her of her ability to care for herself, came to live in a skilled-care facility five minutes from our home.

We had, in our 40s, become members of the "sandwich generation," caring for a very dependent parent and very young children all at the same time.

No series of life events had before demonstrated to us so clearly the long ranging impact of infertility. My husband and I are an infertile couple. So were his parents. The senior Johnstons' experience with infertility began during the 1930s and continued into the 1940s as they experienced multiple miscarriages and premature birth, and ultimately built their family by adoption. Our own infertility experience began in 1970 and we actively pursued family building options until the 1984 adoption of our third child completed our family.

Infertility has colored many aspects of the Johnston family's life through three generations now. Two generations of children have been parented by older than average parents. Two generations of career and transferability decisions were influenced by available medical care, insurance coverage, and by the timing of where expectant adopters were on an agency waiting list.

My in-laws were empathic to our family building issues. Yet because of the extraordinary changes in infertility testing, treatment, and options, their experiences were dramatically different from ours. And what infertile couples today must deal with is dramatically different from my husband's and my experiences in the 1970s and '80s.

We've come a long way from the time in the 1940s when testing and treatment was so unrefined that little help was available. Far fewer than 30% of couples who sought treatment could expect to become pregnant then. Medical options were few for these couples. Diagnosis of infertility produced cloudy answers, limited surgical help was available, and very little drug therapy was prescribed.

The options for infertile couples in the 1940s consisted primarily of donor insemination and adoption. Back then, adoption was a fairly easy process due to the large numbers of available infants. Older children or children with health problems were considered virtually unadoptable then, and many spent their childhood in orphanages.

Progress was slow until the research began to increase in the 1960s and 1970s. For my own peers, much had changed. Ovulation-inducing drugs and other hormonal therapies provided answers to many infertility problems. Microsurgical techniques were developed, offering much better odds for correcting structural abnormalities of the reproductive system. On the other hand, the so-called sexual revolution of the '60s had resulted in an increase of infertility caused by sexually-transmitted diseases, and even some birth control devices were found to lead to permanent infertility.

With the sexual revolution and the advent of wide-spread birth control, also came a decline in adoptions. More and more single mothers were opting to raise their children themselves.

The 1960s also brought an awareness of the serious side effects of chemicals on human reproduction. Environmental pollutants were identified as reproductively dangerous. The wonder drug of the 1950s, DES, which had been thought to successfully treat the miscarriage problem that had prevented my mother-in-law from giving birth to a living child, was found to produce drastic problems in the children it helped birth.

In the late '70s a miracle was born—Louise Brown, the first baby born through in vitro fertilization—and this astonishing new hope for infertile couples precipitated an avalanche of new research that quickly changed what we can do about hormonal balances, control of ovulation, laser and micro-surgery, manipulations of sperm and ovum, and more.

As an infertility and adoption educator, much of the work I do centers around helping couples make good decisions for themselves during their infertility experience. The decisions these couples are making today are quite different from those that Dave and I confronted a dozen years ago. While we were still in treatment infertility was still so non-technical that our group insurance company never balked once at covering any of the many years of low-tech treatments and surgery that we underwent. In vitro fertilization was so very experimental and unsuccessful an option only eight years ago that it wasn't an option we thought twice about in planning our third child.

On the other hand, when we were in the process of adopting for the first time, no one ever suggested a special needs child as an option, and no one ever discussed open adoption as a possibility. Yet our third child was defined by our agency a having special needs, and her adoption is an open one.

As I move around the country doing workshops, I constantly encounter changes in the field of infertility. Options are increasing every day. GIFT, ZIFT, IVF, AIH, DI, GnRh, PROST, HCG, HMG, CVS—those are last year's buzz words. This year, couples deal with such issues as adoptive embryo transfer, frozen embryos, egg donation, zona-drilled sperm, pentoxyfillin, Natural Cycle Ovum Retrieval and Intravaginal Culture Fertilization (IVC) and more—and all with the probability that many of these medical advances will not be covered by insurance.

Adoption decisions today demand knowledge of the Interstate Compact, adoption subsidies, and constantly changing immigration regulations. The adoption issues of the '90s include openness options, AIDS, and drug exposed babies. And the concept of living childfree rather than living childless is getting increasing support as a lifestyle option.

Psychosocially the fields of both infertility and adoption have changed, too. Though the media have paid much attention to infertility during the last decade, much of the coverage has been sensationalized and unsympathetic. The infertile are often portrayed a obsessive, selfish yuppies who would do anything to satisfy their "baby craving."

As for coping, the old Barbara Eck Menning model of infertility as a process of grieving for a child never conceived and never born which lifted me out of depression fourteen years ago doesn't work for today's couples. Today we recognize that infertility is more than a single loss. In this book we've identified and worked with six. And we recognize that today's choices and the resulting regained sense of control demand, rather than allow, that infertile couples be informed consumers as they expend their time, money, emotional energy, and physical capabilities in pursuit of a child.

One thing seems clear to me: it simply makes no sense anymore for couples to even consider going it alone. The advantage of plugging into the resources of one of RESOLVE's 54 chapters in the U.S. or an I.A.A.C. support group in Canada, to Adoptive Families of America when adoption becomes the option of choice include not just support, but even more, access to the most up-to-date information and advocacy on both local and national levels.

Several years ago my father-in-law and I talked about all of these changes of a half century. It was the best of times to be infertile, I opined. Much could be done, and advancing technology meant that almost 70% of couples who seek appropriate medical help can expect to give birth to a child.

This wise man reflected and replied that indeed it might also be the worst of times to be infertile. Options for himself and his wife were few, but they were clear. Infertility could not be dragged out for years as a couple would try just one more new technique or treatment. My in-laws' infertility had indeed ultimately been clear-cut and final, a loss to be mourned and resolved and moved on from. They adopted three children in rapid succession and were asked to make no decisions at all about age or abilities of the child, degree of openness with the birthfamily, or the possibility of a transracial or transethnic placement. Having been raised with a generation of folks who didn't expect to be in control of their reproductive lives, this lack of empowerment was not so uncomfortable. While I'm sure my father-in-law envied the empowerment my husband and I were given by the menu of options open to us, I'm also sure that he did not envy the weightiness of our decisions.

As I talk to couples today, I see his point. When *is* enough enough?

Maybe my father-in-law was right. The infertility roller coaster ride is long, has many twists and turns, catapults us faster and faster, and seems to go on forever. Is this the best of times or the worst of times to be infertile?

The answer to such a question could not be more individual. What's more, I'm not sure that the answer matters so much as does the way we view the journey. What I wish most for you is that you will not become the dragon's victim, that you and your partner will meet this challenge and together find your personal path to victory, to the place which is right for only you two.

As for ourselves, Dave and I embrace our infertility today. Without it we would be different people—who knows whether better or worse. Without it we might have been parents sooner; our youngest would be leaving for college now. Infertility has colored nearly every aspect of our life planning, and we find ourselves in a different place financially, emotionally, physically, temporally than the one we expected to be in when we started our journey to parenthood over twenty years ago.

As were the prince and princess, Dave and I were forced, when we met the dragon, to travel roads unmapped. We were angry and frightened at our loss of control. We railed and fought. But in charging through the thickets to find our way, in deciding together which turns to take, we found something more wonderful than we could have imagined and we've arrived in the place we most want to be.

Of this we are certain: without infertility the three children who light us with the joy of living would not have been ours to parent. Different children might have brightened our lives—children with his crooked teeth, children with my lazy eye, children who sounded or looked like us. But they wouldn't be *our* children—Joel and Erica and Lindsey—the children we were meant to parent, the *treasure* in the dragon's lair.

References

I

Chapter 1

[1] This scenario has been borrowed and then significantly adapted and embellished from 1976 version of *How to Survive the Loss of a Love*, by Melba Cosgrove, Harold Bloomfield, and Peter McWilliams. The 1991 revised version (Bantam Books) no longer contains this clarifying anecdote. Too bad! But the book remains a good resource for those dealing with loss of any kind.

[2] In writing her classic book *Infertility: A Guide for the Childless Couple* (Prentice Hall, 1976; revised in 1988) Barbara Eck Menning was the first to tie the emotional reaction to infertility to the grief pattern (surprise, denial, anger, isolation, bargaining, depression, acceptance) first identified by Elisabeth Kubler-Ross in her book *On Death and Dying*. Ms. Menning wrote that couples experiencing infertility were experiencing a kind of death—the death of a child never conceived or never born. This theory has been helpful to thousands of couples, but it has been my experience that many couples cannot identify with this specific loss. This is why I have found it more helpful to identify for couples a broader spectrum of loss, from which they can then identify the losses most meaningful to themselves.

[3] Mason, Mary Martin. *The Miracle Seekers: An Anthology of Infertility*, can be ordered for $14.95 from Adoptapes, 4012 Lynn Avenue, Edina, MN 55416.

[1] Tannen, Deborah, Ph.D. *You Just Don't Understand: Women and Men in Conversation* (New York: Ballantine, 1990) p. 73.

[2] Tannen, Deborah, Ph.D. *op. cit.,* p. 26-27.

[3] Carter, Jean W. and Michael. *Sweet Grapes: How to Stop Being Infertile and Start Living Again.* (Indianapolis: Perspectives Press, 1989) p. 132

II

Chapter 4

[1] Brodzinsky, David M. "A Stress and Coping Model of Adoption Adjustment," *The Psychology of Adoption.* New York: Oxford University Press, 1990, p. 20.

Chapter 6

[1] Bartholet, Elizabeth. "Where Do Black Children Belong? The Politics of Race Matching in Adoption," *University of Pennsylvania Law Review* (Volume 139, Number 5: May, 1991) p. 1172-73.

[2] Gross, Gregory. "Banana Splits: A Biracial Family in Paradise." *Interrace,* Volume 3, No. 2. March/April, 1992, pp.19-20.

Chapter 7

[1] While describing children as commodities is entirely offensive, this is the reality of what we are discussing!

[2] Critics prefer to use the more negative term *closed adoption.* Similarly, opponents of open adoption refer to it as *experimental adoption.* In this book in both this instance and elsewhere I have tried myself to use whichever language the proponents of a system prefer. I believe this is the fairest way to promote communication and discussion of an issue. In

the same vein, were I writing about abortion, I would use the terms *pro-life* and *pro-choice* as the terms self-selected by those sharing each of these philosophies, rather than to label groups *anti-abortion* or *anti-choice* or *anti-life*.

[3] McRoy, Ruth and Harold Grotevant. *Openness in Adoption: New Practices, New Issues.* New York: Praeger, 1988.

[4] Berry, Marianne. "The Effects of Open Adoption on Biological and Adoptive Parents and the Children: The Arguments and the Evidence." *Child Welfare*, Vol. LXX, No. 6, Nov./Dec. 1991, pp637-651.

[5] Hallenbeck, Carol. *Our Child Preparation for Parenting in Adoption--Instuctor's Guide.* Wayne, PA: Our Child Press, 1984, p. 24.

III

Chapter 9

[1] Fahlberg, Vera. *A Child's Journey through Placement.* Indianapolis: Perspectives Press, 1991. p. 33.

Chapter 10

[1] Brodzinsky, D.M, Singer, L.M., and Braff, A.M. "Children's Understanding of Adoption." *Child Development*, Volume 55, pp. 869-878.

[2] Brodzinsky, David M. "A Stress and Coping Model of Adoption Adjustment," *The Psychology of Adoption.* New York: Oxford University Press, 1990, p.7

Chapter 11

[1] "My Daughter's Dowry" by Arthur Dobrin first appeared in *Perspectives on a Grafted Tree* (©1982 Patricia Irwin Johnston, Perspectives Press) and its author has graciously extended permission for its use again here.

[1] A copy of the single page fact sheet "Speaking Positively: An Information Sheet about Adoption Language" by Pat Johnston is available free with a stamped, self addressed envelope from Perspectives Press, P.O. Box 90318, Indianapolis, IN 46290 USA, and may be photocopied at will without permission if used in its entirety and properly credited.

[2] From *The Prophet* by Kahlil Gibran. (©1923 by Kahlil Gibran and renewed 1951 by Administrators C.T.A. of Kahlil Gibran Estate and Mary G. Gibran.) Reprinted by permission of Alfred A. Knopf, Inc.

[3] A copy of Pat Johnston's fact sheet "Adopt-A Confusion: How Using Adoption to Catch Attention, Touch Heartstrings, and Raise Big Bucks Exploits Kids Who Were Adopted and Those Waiting for Permanency" is available free with a stamped, self addressed envelope from Perspectives Press, P.O. Box 90318, Indianapolis, IN 46290 USA and may be copied without permission as long as it is properly credited.

Index

About the Author

Patricia Irwin Johnston is an infertility and adoption educator, who, over the course of the last dozen years, has been providing trainings for consumers and professionals throughout the United States and Canada.

Her personal experience in a family which dealt with two generations of infertility and was expanded through three generations by adoption led her to many years of active volunteering with the consumer groups in these fields. She has been a RESOLVE chapter founder, president and regional representative and spent three years chairing RESOLVE's national board of directors. Pat served for three years as a member of the first national advisory committee of Adoptive Families of America and chaired AFA's first two national conference committees. She chaired Indiana's Adoption Forum Coalition for several years and worked on the Indiana Attorney General's Adoption Medical Registry Task Force. The North American Council on Adoptable Children named her one of 1989's Adoption Activists of the Year and the Adoptive Parents Committee of New York named her 1992's Friend of Adoption.

Pat's earlier books, also from Perspectives Press, include - *Perspectives on A Grafted Tree: Thoughts for Those Touched by Adoption*, *Understanding: A Guide to Impaired Fertility for Family and Friends*, and *An Adopter's Advocate*. Her newest book, *Taking Charge of Infertility* (spring 1994), develops and expands upon the decision making material in Part I of *Adopting after Infertility* to structure a format for practical decision making about treatment as well as alternatives for all infertile couples.

The Johnstons and their three children live in Indianapolis.

Let Us Introduce Ourselves

In 1992 Perspectives Press celebrates its tenth anniversary as a publisher focusing exclusively on infertility, adoption, and related reproductive and child welfare issues. Our purpose is to promote understanding of these issues and to educate and sensitize those personally experiencing these life situations, professionals who work in these fields, and the public at large. Perspectives Press titles are never duplicative. We seek out and publish materials that are currently unavailable through traditional publishers.

In addition to *Adopting after Infertility*, the books we have published during our ten year history have included:

For Adults
Perspectives on a Grafted Tree
An Adoptor's Advocate
Understanding: A Guide to Impaired Fertility for Family and Friends
The Miracle Seekers: An Anthology of Infertility (now out of print)
Sweet Grapes: How to Stop Being Infertile and Start Living Again
Residential Treatment: A Tapestry of Many Therapies
A Child's Journey Through Placement

For Children
Our Baby: A Birth and Adoption Story
The Mulberry Bird: Story of an Adoption
Real for Sure Sister
Filling in the Blanks: A Guided Look at Growing Up Adopted
Where the Sun Kisses the Sea
William Is My Brother
Lucy's Feet

Our authors have special credentials: They are people whose personal and professional lives provide an interwoven pattern for what they write. If you are writing about these issues, we invite you to contact us with a query letter and stamped, self addressed envelope so that we can send you our writers guidelines and help you to determine whether your materials might fit into our publishing plans.

Perspectives Press
P.O. Box 90318
Indianapolis, IN 46290

Hm832Tn
74